英语学术风格写作
English Writing of Academic Style

姜来为　编著
李晓文　主审

哈尔滨工业大学出版社

内 容 简 介

本书共六章,包括英语学术写作之特点,撰写科研论文,标点符号的用法,有效引用的方法,如何避免被指控剽窃,项目/基金申请。书后附有附录:表和图的形式,记录原始资料。本书突出的特点是涵盖了学术论文写作的所有要素,从标题的写作到文献参考的写作;而且所有语法方面的论述也都紧紧围绕与学术论文写作相关的核心内容展开。

本书可用作高等院校研究生的英语学术写作课教材,也适用于对英语学术写作感兴趣的读者,还可供专业工程技术人员撰写英文文章时参考。

图书在版编目(CIP)数据

英语学术风格写作/姜来为编著. —哈尔滨:哈尔滨工业大学出版社,2024.2
ISBN 978-7-5767-1266-7

Ⅰ.①英… Ⅱ.①姜… Ⅲ.①英语-论文-写作-研究 Ⅳ.①H315

中国国家版本馆 CIP 数据核字(2024)第 047647 号

策划编辑	王桂芝
责任编辑	陈 洁
出版发行	哈尔滨工业大学出版社
社　　址	哈尔滨市南岗区复华四道街 10 号　邮编 150006
传　　真	0451-86414749
网　　址	http://hitpress.hit.edu.cn
印　　刷	辽宁新华印务有限公司
开　　本	787 mm×1 092 mm　1/16　印张 17.5　字数 415 千字
版　　次	2024 年 2 月第 1 版　2024 年 2 月第 1 次印刷
书　　号	ISBN 978-7-5767-1266-7
定　　价	68.00 元

(如因印装质量问题影响阅读,我社负责调换)

Preface 前言

什么是"学术写作"？

首先，可以把学术写作看作是有组织的研究活动，这种活动是学者以书面形式体现、为其他学者而产生的活动。学术写作是一种主题鲜明的写作，涉及的是某学术领域所关注的科研问题，其目的是在总结前人研究成果的基础上就某一特定主题提出新的观点。

学术写作所涉及的主题和问题都是学术领域所关注的，它使作者得以就某一主题发表具有权威性的观点，因此属于命题性写作，即首先对已有的某一观点进行阐述。例如，首先确定某一主题中的具体问题，然后表明对这一问题已有观点的看法：赞成、不赞成或者是提出进一步完善的观点。

对某一问题的说明和解答，需要作者首先查阅和分析已有的相关资料。作者的文章建立在对已有资料的解释和引证的基础上，然后作者阐明自己的观点如何不同于已有的观点，进而引出作者就同一主题的新观点。作者的新观点要由作者的独立性研究加以佐证。

学术写作是一种基于可靠信息的推论过程，既要对已有资料加以评论，又要用已有资料作为佐证加以推理。新信息的提出，既要经过对已有资料的查询，又要建立在原创性研究的基础上，因此学术文章中的推论和观点必须是客观的，不应带有个人情感，作者的观点应由融入论文结构中的可靠的证据来证实。

在各类纪实性文体中，学者们最感自豪的是能在代表行业发展的最新动态的学术刊物上发表学术论文。学术论文是整个研发以及实验过程完成后的必要环节，在论文中作者给读者提供所需要的信息，例如发现了什么、如何发现的以及其具有的意义等。优秀的学者不但对他们的研究工作感兴趣，同样对学术论文的写作质量也感兴趣。因为他们深知，如果他们不能通过自己的学术论文达到有效地传递信息的目的，那么他们所做的一切科研、技术上的努力就会失去一定的意义。

本书的目的

即使是在同一学术领域内，学术论文的文体也会有所不同。因此，在向某一刊物投稿前，要先熟读该刊物对论文结构及文体（包括对注脚、标题、直观的表和图、段落的长度等的专门要求）等的格式要求，再选读几篇论文。

尽管各刊物的文体风格有所不同，但是大多数的文章在其目的和结构上还是有很明显的相同之处。较成熟的论文都会遵循业已形成的传统约定，即论文结构主要由四部分组成：引言、方法和材料、结果、讨论或结论。这四部分要分别体现不同的目的。

本书的目的就是要向对学术写作感兴趣的读者提供指导性的建议和参照标准，指导其如何在学术环境下构建书面文本，从而提高学术写作能力和自信，使其更有效地参与学术活动。本书也能帮助读者从事一些如摘要、学位论文、国际和国内各类学术期刊上发表论文的写作，包括：

（1）如何写出学术文章，包括从最初的想法到写出能够发表的学术文章。

（2）认清清晰、简洁和准确在学术写作中的重要性。

（3）明确什么是基于证据的写作。

本书最重要的目的就是清楚地表明提出主题或论点，再以充分展开的证据为之辩护的重要性。

本书不同于其他写作教材之处在于本书不仅出自教师的个人经验或参考书，如比较有名望的教科书（市场上可以随处找到这类图书，而且这类图书常常又是很有帮助的），本书的主要特点在于它把国际标准，或者说是国际学术惯例和格式作为基准。

所谓基于证据的写作是指作者能够很好地处理下述问题：了解应具备什么条件才能够写出需要对已有的证据进行分析的论文，了解如何确保作者的证据是充分的、合理的，了解作为一名诠释证据的作者该如何以令读者满意的方式确立自己的可信度，了解如何在非蓄意持有偏见的前提下使自己的文章具有说服力，了解论文写作的目的是什么，如是要证明一种假设，还是要对它进行检验等。

本书的最终目的是强调在学术写作中具有说服力的论证的重要性。提出议题或论点，对其辩论，这是对所有作者的共同的要求，所有学者的写作都可以看作是这类行为。有些初学者不这样认为，以为写作的任务也不过是收集一些事实材料，对某一主题等进行简单描述和分析。其实，这是对这类文本的狭隘理解。

所谓的国际标准或要求，将会在书中更加详细地展开。在此，需要说明的是：本书作为参照点的标准指的是被公认的具有世界水平的，即一些由国际一流大学、国际上被参考的专业期刊或知名学者们规约以及由学者们所在的学术团体共同遵守的规则、惯例或者要求。这些国际标准可被看作是具有高质量、最有信誉的基准。

学术写作的目的及特征

因为学术写作的目的是提供前所未有的真知灼见、问题的解答和建议，所有作者就要尽可能地用最简洁、合乎逻辑和清晰的语言来撰写学术论文，以便进行思想交流。有些写作新手错误地认为，在写作中可以随便地变换人称，如用"我们"代替"我"，或在文章没有标出出处的情况下使用他人的章节（实质上这属于剽窃）；作者也没有必要在写作过程中空话连篇、夸大其词、措辞晦涩；作为学者，写作要真实，不要用那些很少使用、难懂的语言;也不要写出半页纸那么长的句子,更不要写出又臭又长、自吹自擂的文章。事实上,作者所写的论文的长短取决于需要。值得一提的是,出版的学术论文一般在十页左右(Day,1988,p.129)。科学家和其他的学者通过简练、清晰的学术交流来增加人类的知识,或帮助解决重大问题。因此,学者在写作过程中不要为了单纯地追求如何使文章给人深刻印象而将文章写得过长或失真。要牢记,清晰、简洁和诚实是学者写作的特征和标志。

学术写作作者的任务

所有学术写作作者都需要知道如何利用有限的证据来提出一个观点。所有学术写作作者的任务就是明确地提出一个观点,给出产生这一观点的环境/背景,把这个观点同他人的观点相联系,给出理由阐明为什么自己的观点应该被接受。要用合乎情理的实例、恰当的辩论和定义、确切的术语来为某一观点进行辩护;不能忽视反面证据,而要把它作为一个因素置于辩论之中,这样才能形成具有强劲说服力的、基于证据的学术写作。学术论文的论点不仅要有意义,还必须是原创性的,同时要论证得到位。掌握了这个原则,并将其应用到自己的学术写作中的学者才有可能写出具有说服力的论文,因为这样的论文是建立在一系列强有力的推理的基础之上的。

总结

本书不仅是为了使学术写作符合一些标准(这些标准是有价值的、必要的),而且还力图揭掉那些围绕学者和学术写作的神秘面纱。学术作者必须掌握的技能是提出观点的能力,以及为了支持这一观点并最终使读者接受其观点而组织证据的能力。学术写作的准则、惯例和规定都很重要,因为它们对作者要完成的文本的规模和格式起着约束作用。学术写作这项大型而复杂的工程的核心在于有效的立论和论证。

无论在哪个学科、哪个领域,要想成为一名经验丰富的研究者和作者都要经历大量的实践。很少有人能在不经历这一过程的前提下自然而然地写出高质量的论文。即使是经验丰富的学术写作作者也一定在其职业生涯的某个时段学习过如何撰写学术论文,因此,只要初学者肯于学习,并能够勤勉、系统地练习,就能在学术论文写作中取得成就,特别是初学者要有耐心。

致谢

在此,对给本书内容安排、文字表达提出很多宝贵修改意见的专家和学者,以及提供素材的所有学生表示衷心的感谢,也向关心这本书的读者致以诚挚的谢意。

作者
2023年9月9日

CONTENTS 目 录

第一章 英语学术写作之特点	1
1.1 英语学术文体写作中常见的主要问题	1
1.2 英语学术文体写作之原则	8
1.3 英语学术文体写作之技能培养	13
第二章 撰写科研论文	36
2.1 标题、作者姓名及所在单位的撰写	38
2.2 摘要的撰写	51
2.3 引言/前言的撰写	99
2.4 材料和方法的撰写	106
2.5 结果的撰写	111
2.6 讨论/结论部分的撰写	130
2.7 致谢的撰写	134
2.8 关于参考文献	137
2.9 关于附录	150
第三章 标点符号的用法	152
3.1 标点符号概述	152
3.2 句子标点符号的模式	167
3.3 逗号衔接的错误	169
3.4 标点符号练习(逗号、冒号、分号、破折号)	171
3.5 综合练习:语法、标点符号和惯用语	175
第四章 有效引用的方法	179
第五章 如何避免被指控剽窃	192
5.1 什么是剽窃?	192
5.2 引证的技巧	194
5.3 意译的技巧	196
5.4 原始资料记录	200

第六章 项目/基金申请	201
6.1 项目申请的写作过程	201
6.2 修改科研基金申请	206
6.3 基金申请中预算和期限样本	207
6.4 撰写基金申请的资源	209
6.5 基金申请案例实例(英文版)	210
6.6 基金申请案例实例(中文版)	231
附录Ⅰ 表和图的形式	254
附录Ⅱ 记录原始资料	266
参考文献	268

第一章
英语学术写作之特点

1.1 英语学术文体写作中常见的主要问题

本节旨在检验读者是否能发现下面给出的实例中存在的文体问题。文体风格方面的主要问题如下。

同级标题的结构不平行	词语使用过于复杂
部分之间的转换强度不够	名词短语过于复杂
因缺少标点符号引起的含糊	句子过于复杂
因代词引起的指代不清	乱加从句的冗长句子(不用句号、分号等而错用逗号的连写句)
因词序问题引起的不确定	用错动词的时态
句子结构过于单一	主语和谓语不一致
基调问题	用错惯用法

问题实例 1

Discharges of these hazardous substances occur through spills when loading vehicles, spills and over-spills when filling the tanks, leaks from supply pipes and pipe joints, rust holes and cracks in the seams of the tanks themselves.

存在的问题:缺少标点符号引起的含糊。

可改为:

Discharges of these hazardous substances occur through the following: (1) spills when loading vehicles, (2) spills and over-spills when filling the tanks, (3) leaks from supply pipes, and (4) pipe joints, rust holes, and cracks in the seams of the tanks themselves.

这些有毒有害物质的泄漏主要是通过以下几种形式发生的:(1)装车时泄漏;(2)装桶时泄漏或者溢出;(3)输送管道泄漏;(4)管

道连接处、管道锈蚀处以及容器焊缝处破裂等。

问题实例 2

The design of the circuit is shown in Appendix A. The first schematic of the Appendix shows the interface of the EEPROM with the HC11. The decoder and the bit latch were also needed for this circuit. The decoder made sure that the EEPROM responded to address locations $6000 to $7FFF. The latch stored the address lines for the EEPROM when Port C on the EVBU switched from output address lines to input data lines. These integrated chips worked together to give the HC11 the expanded memory.

存在的问题:句子结构过于单一。(所有句子都是由主语开头,后紧跟着动词。)
可改为:

In Appendix A, the first schematic shows the design of the circuit, in which the interface of the EEPROM with the HC11 is shown. The decoder and the bit latch were also needed in the circuit while the decoder made sure that the EEPROM responded to address locations $6000 to $7FFF and the latch stored the address lines for the EEPROM when Port C on the EVBU switched from output address lines to input data lines. These integrated chips worked together to give the HC11 the expanded memory.

附录 A 是第一张电路原理设计图。这张设计图给出了 EEPROM 和 HC11 的电路界面。电路中需要一个解码器和小锁存器,以便使 EEPROM 能随地址区域变化($6000 到 $7FFF 之间);当 EVBU 上的端口 C 从输出地址线路转到输入地址线路时,锁存器为 EEPROM 把地址的线路储存起来。这些集成芯片共同作用来增大 HC11 的记忆存储量。

问题实例 3

Report Title: *Loading Dock Boxcar Stop Viscous Damping Values*

存在的问题:名词短语过于复杂。(注:本实例的修改须要首先看原文。)
可改为:

Damping Values for Limiting Oscillations of a Boxcar Stopping System
火车刹车系统的振动所需要的阻尼参数

问题实例 4

Standalone Operation. This involved both hardware and software....

存在的问题:部分之间的转换强度不够。
可改为:

Standalone Operation. Operation of the HC11 microprocessor in the standalone mode involved both hardware and software.

自行操作。HC11 微处理在自行操作的模式下运行时不仅需要硬件,还需要软件。

问题实例 5

The objective of this endeavor is to develop a commercialization strategy for solar energy systems by analyzing factors impeding early commercial projects (i. e. , SOLAR ONE) and by identifying the potential actions that can facilitate the viability of the projects.

存在的问题:词语使用过于复杂。
可改为:

This study will consider why current solar energy systems, such as Solar One, have not reached the commercial stage and will find out what steps we can take to make these systems commercial.

这项研究需要探讨为何现行的太阳能系统,如 Solar One,未能进军商业领域,并找到使其商业化的措施。

问题实例 6

It has come to my attention that your sport utility vehicles are not as technologically advanced as they could be! Microprocessors are more than just a booming technological buzzword; they are something that can be seamlessly implemented into existing vehicles and will add countless dimensions to their capabilities.... These are of course tiny examples in a grander scheme of things that can be accomplished with microprocessors. There are much more useful and innovative things that could be done to improve both the mechanical and ergonomic aspects, which would put you light-years ahead of your closest competitors, all the while fattening your pockets.... I enthusiastically look forward to meeting with you!

存在的问题:基调问题。(基调问题由黑体字标出。)
可改为:

It has come to my attention that your sport utility vehicles are not as technologically advanced as they could **be**! Microprocessors are more than just a **booming technological buzzword**; they are something that can be **seamlessly implemented** into existing vehicles and will add **countless dimensions** to their capabilities.... These are **of course tiny examples in a grander scheme** of things that can be accomplished with microprocessors. There are much more useful and innovative things that could be done to improve both the mechanical and ergonomic aspects, which would put you light-years ahead of your closest competitors, all the while fattening your pockets.... I enthusiastically look forward to meeting with you!

我已经注意到你的运动型多用途运载车在技术上已经不如过去那样先进了。微处理器已不仅仅是一个时髦的技术术语，它完全可以被用于现有汽车之中，并使其各方面功能得到增加……当然，这些例子只不过是微处理器所能实现的众多功能中的极小一部分。微处理器在机械性能和人类环境改造等方面有着很多创新的用途，它会使你远远超过那些危险的竞争对手；同时也会使你的腰包鼓起来……我在热切地期盼着与你相见。

问题实例 7

Enormous mining companies are both continuing operations at old gold mines, such as the case of the Homestake Mine in Lead, South Dakota, which has operated continuously since 1877 and is continuing to increase its operations [Hinds and Trautman, 1983], and opening new gold mines, often in very disturbing locations, such as the proposed, and for now, postponed, New World Mine, whose proposed location was about 2.5 miles from the border of Yellowstone National Park, near Cooke City, Montana.

存在的问题：句子过于复杂。

可改为：

Enormous mining companies are both continuing operations at old gold mines and proposing the opening of new gold mines. An example of a mine continuing its operations is the Homestake Mine in Lead, South Dakota. This mine has operated continuously since 1877 and is increasing its operations [Hinds and Trautman, 1983]. An example of a proposed new gold mine is the New World Mine, whose proposed location is about 2.5 miles from the border of Yellowstone National Park, near Cooke City, Montana. Like other proposed gold mines, the New World Mine has been postponed because it is in an environmentally sensitive region.

许多大型采矿公司在继续开发旧金矿的同时提出开发新金矿的建议。南达科塔州国有金矿公司就是这样一个连续运作的例子。这家金矿公司从1877年就开始并拓展金矿开采（西德斯，特曼，1983）。新世界金矿则是一个新提议开发的金矿，这家被提议开采的矿场位于距黄石国家公园约2.5英里处，临近蒙大拿州的库克城。和其他被提出开采的金矿一样，从环境角度出发，由于其所处区域敏感，提议开采的新世界金矿的开发已被延缓。

问题实例 8

Most people are diagnosed with phenylketonuria at birth.

存在的问题:因词序问题引起的不确定。

可改为:

Most people with phenylketonuria are diagnosed at birth.

多数的苯丙酮尿症患者在出生时就是能被诊断出来的。

问题实例 9

Since the invention of the catalytic converter, one problem that has baffled people involved with emission control is their lack of effectiveness in oxidizing CO and HC until the engine is warm.

存在的问题:因代词引起的指代不清。

可改为:

Since the invention of the catalytic converter, one problem that has baffled people involved with emission control is the converter's lack of effectiveness in oxidizing CO and HC until the engine is warm.

自发明催化转化器以来,困扰从事控制排放工作者的一个棘手的问题是怎样能使转化器在引擎变热前有效地使 CO 和 HC 氧化。

问题实例 10

Procedures for Design. The procedures for this part of the laboratory began with the ASM command. This command was used to disassemble code. This disassembly began at the specified memory address. This command was useful in examining the code predefined by the Buffalo Disassembler. The ASM command was used at the start of address ＄E000. It listed the first three instructions at location ＄E000. Table 1 shows both the machine code and the disassembled code for these instructions.

存在的问题:句子结构过于单一。(所有句子都是由主语开头,后紧跟着动词。)

可改为:

Procedures for Design. The procedures for this part of the laboratory began with the ASM command which was used to disassemble code and was useful in examining the code predefined by the Buffalo Disassembler. This disassembly began at the specified memory address. The ASM command was used at the start of address ＄E000 and the first three instructions were listed at location ＄E000. Table 1 shows both the machine code and the disassembled code for these instructions.

设计步骤:本实验这一部分是从 ASM 操作开始的,用以分解编码,还用于对 Buffalo 分解器预先确定的编码进行检查。ASM 操作的使用是在＄E000 地址开始的,在此给出了前三个指令。表一给出了这些指令的机器编码和分解的编码。

问题实例 11

To provide spill protection all tanks were to include catchment basins and automatic shutoff devices or overfill alarms or ball float valves.

存在的问题:因缺少标点符号而引起的含糊。

可改为:

To provide spill protection, all tanks were to include catchment basins and one of the following: automatic shutoff devices, overfill alarms, or ball float valves.

为防止溢流,所有容器都需要加设汇水池,或下述中的一种:自动关闭装置、溢流警报器或者浮球阀。

问题实例 12

Introduction
Background
Origin of Computer Viruses
Destruction by Computer Viruses
Example (Burleson Virus)
Barriers to Computer Viruses
Physical
Antiviral Barriers
Conclusions
Recommendations

存在的问题:同级标题的结构不平行。

可改为:

1. Introduction
   1.1   History of Computer Viruses
      1.1.1   Where Do Viruses Originate?
      1.1.2   What Damage Have Viruses Caused?
2. Ways to Combat Computer Viruses
   2.1   Physical Barriers
   2.2   Antiviral Barriers
3. Conclusions
4. Summary
5. Recommendations

1. 引言
    1.1   计算机病毒的历史
        1.1.1   计算机病毒的起源
        1.1.2   计算机病毒的危害
2. 计算机病毒抵御措施
    2.1   物理屏障
    2.2   抗病毒屏障
3. 结论
4. 总结
5. 提议

问题实例 13

Each time we wired the hex display, we placed it in a different location on the bread board. Unfortunately, each time the hex display would show a different reading. The third time proved to be the charm as the hex display read all of the numbers correctly.

存在的问题：基调问题。（基调问题由黑体字标出。）

可改为：

Each time we wired the hex display, we placed it in a different location on the bread board. Unfortunately, each time the hex display would show a different reading. The third time **proved to be the charm** as the hex display read all of the numbers correctly.

不幸的是，每当我们连接十六进制显示，并把它置于不同的区域面板上时，它给出的读数都是不同的。而第三次出现了奇迹，它准确地读出了所有数字。

问题实例 14

Interfacing the Matrix Keyboard. Here, a 4×4 matrix keypad and TIL-311 hex display to be added to the hardware wired in the previous section.

存在的问题：部分之间的转换强度不够。

可改为：

Interfacing the Matrix Keyboard This section of the laboratory assignment called for a 4×4 matrix keypad and TIL-311 hex display to be added to the hardware wired in the previous section.

矩阵键盘的连接这一部分的实验任务要求将一个 4×4 的矩阵键盘和 TIL-311 十六进制显示器加到已经连接在前一部分中的硬件上。

问题实例 15

Title: Vertical Linear Actuators Position Measurement and Repeatability NIF Bottom Loading Insertion System Test Procedure

存在的问题:名词短语过于复杂。(由于只有标题,本标题不好修改;此标题的修改需要依据上下文,也要视读者而定。)

1.2 英语学术文体写作之原则

通常,多数人在读到一篇文章的时候,会凭直觉辨别文体的好坏以及哪些句子读起来是冗长、晦涩的。尽管人们能够毫不费力地把那些糟糕的句子挑出来,但却不容易说出为什么某个句子达不到其应有的表达效果,特别是那些语法上正确的句子。那么,问题出在哪里?

什么样的句子是好句子? 在回答这个问题时,重要的一点是把自己放在读者的位置上。首先,读者希望在句子里发现的是信息,是清晰、明确的信息。其次,语言也要流畅、雄辩。读者不想绞尽脑汁地去理解句子,他期望看到的是相互衔接的观点,从而能毫不费力地感受作者语言的轻重缓急和表述的重点。作为读者,他想读到的句子是有说服力的、直截了当的、清晰明了的。

下面提供英语学术文体写作的一些基本原则。

原则 1:把关注点放在施动者及其行为上。

要想写出好句子,记住下面这个原则很重要:句子的基本层面是施动者及其行为,因此句子的主语要直指施动者,句子的动词应该描述其重要的行为。

这个原则看上去很简单,似乎没有进一步讨论的必要。然而仔细想一想,再看看下面的句子,就会发现很多问题。

There was uncertainty in the CEO's mind about their intention to cut the financial budget.

这个句子没有语法错误,但显然这个句子既冗长,又没有力度。再看看下面的句子:

The CEO remained unconvinced that they intend to cut the financial budget.

总裁对他们欲缩减财务预算始终持怀疑态度。

上面的句子有什么变化呢? 主要变化有:去掉了 there be 句型;用更有力度的 remained unconvinced 取代了无力的 uncertainty;用有力度的动词 intended 取代了抽象的名词 intention。但是,这样的变化有什么规约吗? 确切地说就是前面提到的,即句子应由施动者做主语,句子中的行为应由具有力度的动词来说明。

每当你觉得你的写作乏味、令人困惑、难以理解的时候,找找句子的施动者在哪儿,施动者是否是句子的主语,行为是否由动词体现,如果不是,就要改写句子。

原则2：要具体。

有些作者过度依赖抽象名词,而忽略了对动词的运用。例如:不用有力度的动词 expect,而用抽象名词 expectation;不用更具生动性的动词 evaluate,而用抽象名词 evaluation。为什么在能用动词就能很好地表达意思时不用动词,却用抽象的名词? 究其原因,就在于有些作者错误地认为抽象名词会使他们的写作看上去更具"学术性"。而事实是,当作者使用大量的抽象名词写作的时候,不但可能会使读者感到困惑,而且可能在句法上使自己陷入困境,原因如下。

(1) 名词常常需要介词与其搭配使用。

如果句子中有过多的介词短语,其读起来就会很困难。而动词可独立使用,且使语义更清晰,下面的句子可说明这一点。

> *An evaluation of the tutors by the administrative staff is necessary in servicing our clients.*

你会发现在这些名词的要求下,句子使用了大量的介词短语;如果用动词,就大不一样了,试看下面使用动词的句子。

> The administrative staff evaluates the tutors so that we can better serve our clients.

这个句子读上去要容易得多。

(2) 抽象名词的使用。

抽象名词常常需要与 There is 结构搭配使用,试看下面这个句子。

> *There is much discussion in the department about the upcoming tenure decision.*

如果把它改写为:

> The faculty discussed who might earn tenure.

句子表达得更直接,更易读。

(3) 抽象名词太具概念化。

过多使用抽象名词会使写作看上去浮泛、缺乏根基,而使用具体的名词,犹如使用了动词一样,能有力地传递你的思想和观点。

(4) 抽象名词会扰乱逻辑关系。

下面的句子使读者感到很难跟上作者的推理思路。(下面把可以改为动词或形容词的名词都用黑体字标示出来。)

> **Decisions** with regard to **the dismissal** of tutors on the basis of **their inability** to detect grammar errors in the papers **of students** rest with the Director of Composition.

再看下面改过的句子:

When a tutor fails to detect grammar errors in student papers, the Director of Composition must decide whether or not to dismiss her.

还要注意:使用抽象名词会使你不得不使用笨拙的短语,如 on the basis of 或 in regard to。如果把上面句子中的逻辑衔接词改为 when,句子会更简洁、流畅。

原则 2 的例外,何时使用抽象名词?

当然,作者也发现抽象名词有时对句子而言是至关重要的。抽象名词有时起到提及前句的作用(these arguments、this decision 等)。它们还可以起到使句子简洁的作用(her needs 相对于 what she needed 要简洁得多)。抽象名词在句中有时表述的是一个概念,它在你的辩论中起到重要作用,如表述自由、爱、创新等概念的抽象名词。需要注意的是,如果在对写出的作品进行仔细检查的过程中发现过多地使用了抽象名词,那么,去掉那些不必要的抽象名词,这样会使写作既"瘦身"又得体。

原则 3:简洁。

在写作中,有时使作者感到烦恼的是不知如何做到简洁。作者常使用原本一个词就能表达的短语,或者用原本一个形容词或一个动词就可代替的形容词短语或动词短语。他们也会反复重复一件事,以为这样更能达到目的。

结束这种不理智的行为,一旦你能够冷静地对待这件事,就会毫不吝惜地把它们(指短语)从文章中去掉。

你真的需要 actually、basically、generally 等词语吗?如果不需要,为什么还让它们在那儿?你是不是在使用原本可以用一个词就能表达的两个词?你不觉得 first and foremost 累赘吗?future 在 future plans 中有什么意义?你为什么总是用 in my opinion 这样的短语?难道读者不知道这是你文章中的观点、是基于你的观点吗?

有时,修改冗长的句子并非是删除一些词语或短语就能达到的,可能需要重写整个句子。比如下面这个句子:

Plagiarism is a serious academic offense resulting in punishments that might include suspension or dismissal, profoundly affecting your academic career.

它的意思很简单,就是下面的表达:

Plagiarism is a serious offense with serious consequences.

为什么不这样说呢?这样不是更简洁吗?

原则 4:连贯。

文体讨论到现在,我们已经从把句子与句子之间的关系看作是互不相关的单位,发展到把句子之间看作是要相互适应的一个整体。连贯的问题是初学者在写作中遇到的一个普遍问题。有时你会遇到这样的文章:文章中包含了所需要的所有的观点,但这些观点却难以让人领会;文章好像是混乱地堆在一起的东西,推理的思路也不是线性的。你也许会问,难道就不能将文章写得易懂些吗?

尽管探讨连贯的问题不是一件容易的事,我们还是能提供一些有效的方法来帮助作者把句子写得更加流畅。"你应该把你的句子装扮得像新娘子一样:既要'穿戴上'新的,也要有旧的",这样比喻听上去可能有点可笑,但事实就是如此。也就是说,每个句子开头用已知信息,即与前一句有关的内容,然后再向读者展现新的内容,这样才能易于读者跟上作者的推理思路。

这个建议听上去很简单,但事实上并不容易做到。下面我们来具体地说明该怎么做,以便更好地了解如何"装扮"句子。

首先要注意句子的开头,文章是否连贯,在很大程度上取决于句子是如何开头的。我们都知道"良好的开头是成功的一半",写作亦如此。

万事开头难,开始写文章时,要注意以下三点。

(1) 句子的主题是否就是句子的主语?

有时句子之所以缺乏连贯,原因就在于作者没有注意到句子的话题也应该是句子语法意义上的主语。比如,如果话题是关于约翰逊讲话的技巧,那么就要将语法意义上的主语体现出来,正确的表达方式应该是:

Johnaon's skill as a speaker was far more crucial to the rise of the party than was his skill as a politician.

相反,如果把主题放在从句之中,效果就不一样了,显然,在下面这个句子中,主题变得晦涩难懂了,不如上面的句子那样主题突出。

Johnaon's rise to power, an event which came about because of Johnaon's skill as a speaker, was not due to any real political skill.

(2) 句子的主题/主语都是始终如一的吗?

主题/主语不一致的例子:

A gestation period of between 10 and 14 months is required for the baby whale, or calf, to be born (depending on the whale species). The mother returns to the breeding grounds in which she conceived the baby so that the calf can be born in the warmer waters during winter. Birth is carried out closer to the water's surface. This is so that the water pressure is optimal, as it can become very intense and constrictive in the deeper areas, and because the water at the top is warmed by the sun. The place where the calf is born is the most important, as it provides opportunity for the calf to have only a short way to travel to take its first breath of fresh air.

要想使段落做到连贯,多数句子主语都应该是一样的。检查一下是否做到了这一点,从一篇文章中选一个段落,把所有句子的主语都列出来,看所有的主语是否合适。如果你写的段落是关于鲸鱼生活的,就要看是否多数句子的主语都反映这个主题,或者句子中的一些主语是否都是由 *baby whale*、*calf*、*water's surface* 来承担。尽管 *gestation* 的确在文章中占有一席之地,但如果段落所讨论的中心内容不是这个主语,读者便会感到困惑,这时你就要改写句子(或者是整个段落),以达到连贯的效果。

修改后的例句:

> The baby whale, or calf, is born after a gestation period of between 10 and 14 months (depending on the whale species). The mother returns to the breeding grounds in which she conceived the baby so that the calf can be born in the warmer waters during winter. Birth is carried out closer to the water's surface. This is so that the water pressure is optimal, as it can become very intense and constrictive in the deeper areas, and because the water at the top is warmed by the sun. Most importantly, the calf is born closer to the surface to allow for it to have only a short way to travel to take its first breath of fresh air.

> 幼鲸在母亲怀孕 10~14 个月后出生(怀孕期限取决于鲸的种类)。母亲返回到她怀孕的繁殖地,以便幼鲸在冬季时候能出生在更温暖的海域。分娩是在更接近水面的地方完成的。这是因为这时的水压是最适宜的,在较深的水域水压会变得更强,而接近表面的水受到日晒变得暖和。幼鲸的出生地是至关重要的,如果幼鲸出生在更接近水面的地方,就可以使它在不需要游很长的路途的情况下很快地呼吸到第一口新鲜空气。

(3)在所表述的观点之间是否恰当地使用了过渡词?

连贯体现在是否把当前的句子同前面的句子很好地衔接起来。使用如 however 或 therefore 等过渡词把句子有效地连接起来;有时也要用转换词来提示读者有什么重要的或令人沮丧的事要出现了,如 it is important to note that、unfortunately 等;有时可能要在议论中提到时间、地点等,就会用到 then、later、earlier、in my previous paragraph 等过渡词。

也要注意不要过多使用过渡词。有些作者认为过渡词本身能够在议论中起到引导读者的作用。的确,有时整个段落需要的仅是一个 however,议论的内容就由此而明确了。然而,有关连贯的问题,更多时候不是由缺少过渡词造成的,而是作者在表述不同层次的含义时没能够把观点间的内容衔接表达清楚。不要过分地依赖过渡词,再多的过渡词也无法使你凌乱的写作变成意思完整的文章。

原则 5:有力度。

我们已经探讨了句子和句子的开头。那句子和结尾呢?

如果说句子的开头要回头看看过去都说了些什么,句子的结尾就要向前看(指未来),引出新的话题或观点。要知道正是句子的结尾体现出你的胆识,发挥强调的作用,在组织句子的结构时,要在结尾时出重拳。

要使句子有力度,就要遵循下面的原则:

(1)如上所述,把重要的观点放在句末,把次要的移到句子开头。

(2)修整句子的结尾。

不要越写越无意义;不要重复说过的话;如果不是迫不得已,不要对讲过的内容加以修饰;单刀直入地阐述你的观点,往下写。

(3)用从句来表达次要的观点。

所有重要的观点都应放在主句中,所有次要的观点都放在从句中。如果你要在同一个句子里表达两个同样重要的观点,使用并行结构或分号。这两种技巧要比其他有关方法更能有效地表达在两种同样重要观点之间保持平衡的思想。

原则 6:控制好句子的长度。

如果读者发现他读的句子始终看不出有结束的迹象,就说明作者对写作失去了控制,难以驾驭他的写作了。在写作的时候,如果发现句子看上去冗长、没完没了,第一件要做的事就是把长句子分成两个或更多的短句,这是最简单的解决办法。但有时这也不是最合理的做法,这样做的结果是句子变短了,但却不连贯了。而且,如果你在这种情况下的做法就是把句子分成两个,那你将永远也不会知道长句子和复杂句子的妙用。在不违反学术写作原则的条件下,长句子和复杂的句子也是有很多好处的。

因此,当你遇到一个太长的句子时该怎么办呢?首先应考虑句子表达的意思,通常在这种情况下,要表达的观点不止一个。思考要表达的观点以及这些观点之间的联系,然后才能确定选用什么样的语法结构来达到目的。

(1)要表达的观点同等重要。

这时意思之间用并列连接词或分号来连接,恰当的时候还可用并行结构。

(2)要表达的观点并非同等重要。

这时意思之间用从属分句或关系从句来连接。

(3)要表达的意思适合做插入语。

插入语要放在逗号或破折号之间,也可放在恰当的句子的括号之间。

(4)一些观点是否都属于同一个句子。

如果是,用一个句子;否则,写成两个句子。

原则 7:写得优雅得体。

如果想要写出更好的文章,就要注意以下这些要点:具体的比例和布局要合理、匀称,有高潮,有重点,有平行结构,有韵律,有隐语和足够的语言表达力度等。如你对这些修辞方式感兴趣,可参考有关文体风格的书,如 Williams 的作品 *Style*: *The Basics of Clarity and Grace*,你会从中获取很多有价值的建议。

1.3 英语学术文体写作之技能培养

1.3.1 简洁的技能

写作中的简洁是指有效地使用词语。写得简洁并不总是指词语使用得越少越好,而是指使用了最该使用、最能表达要阐述的语义的词语。作者常常使用原本可以省略或可被替换的、表达力不强或不必要的词语。词和短语的使用要慎重,以尽其用。当剩下的都是能有效表达语义的词和短语时,句子就会非常简洁,可读性就更强。

下面是达到简洁的建议,以及修剪句子的具体策略。

1. 用表达力强、具体的词语代替那些含糊不清的词语

有时作者使用一些意义不确定的小词或模棱两可的词语来表达一个概念,结果不但浪费了精力,也没能达到用几个具体的词语就能更好达到的效果。通常的规则是:越具体的词语,越能使写作达到简洁。因为名词、动词和形容词具有多样性,以及很多事物之间的描述都密切相连,所以选词不能孤立地从个别词语出发,要集思广益,从整体把握。下面给出的是意义更加准确、用词更加简洁的例子。

冗长:*The politician talked **about several of the merits of** after-school programs in his speech.*(14 words)

简洁:*The politician **touted** after-school programs in his speech.*(8 words)
政治家在演讲中赞扬了课外活动计划。

冗长:*Suzie **believed but could not confirm** that Billy **had feelings of affection for** her.*(14 words)

简洁:Suzie **assumed** that Billy **adored** her.(6 words)
苏西认为比尔爱慕她。

冗长:*Our website **has made available many of the things you can use for making a decision on** the best dentist.*(20 words)

简洁:Our website **presents criteria for determining** the best dentist.(9 words)
我们网站给出了评价最佳牙医的标准。

冗长:*Working as a **pupil under someone who develops photos** was an experience **that really helped me learn a lot.***(19 words)

简洁:Working as a **photo technician's apprentice** was an **educational** experience.(10 words)
在照片技师手下学徒是一个具有教育意义的经历。

冗长:*I am disinclined to acquiesce to your request.*(8 words)

简洁:No.(1 word)

冗长:*I utilized a fork to ingest my comestibles.*(8 words)

简洁:I used a fork to eat.(6 words)
我是用餐叉吃饭的。

2. 审视句中每一个词

核实每一个词以保证每一个词对句子来说都是重要的、不可缺少的。如果是无关紧要的,就删掉它或将其替换成其他词。本书的其他地方还要更详细探讨这一观点,在此先提供一些可以删除词语的例子。

冗长:*The teacher demonstrated some of the various ways and methods for cutting words from my essay that I had written for class.*(22 words)

简洁:The teacher demonstrated methods for cutting words from my essay.(10 words)
老师以我的短文为例示范说明如何在写作中做到简洁。

冗长:*Eric Clapton and Steve Winwood formed a new band of musicians together in 1969, giving it the ironic name of Blind Faith because early speculation that was spreading everywhere about the band suggested that the new musical group would be good enough to rival the earlier bands that both men had been in, Cream and Traffic, which people had really liked and had been very popular.*(66 words)

简洁:Eric Clapton and Steve Winwood formed a new band in 1969, ironically naming it Blind Faith because speculation suggested that the group would rival the musicians' previous popular bands, Cream and Traffic.(32 words)
埃里克和史蒂夫在 1969 年创立了一个新乐队,称其为 Blind Faith,他们猜测这个乐队能和他们之前参加的流行乐队 Cream 和 Traffic 相竞争。

冗长:*Many have made the wise observation that when a stone is in motion rolling down a hill or incline that moving stone is not as likely to be covered all over with the kind of thick green moss that grows on stationary unmoving things and becomes a nuisance and suggests that those things haven't moved in a long time and probably won't move any time soon.*(66 words)

简洁:A rolling stone gathers no moss.(6 words)
滚石不生苔(见异思迁的人终无所获)。

冗长:*The question as to whether fish can experience pain is an important one.*(13 words)

简洁:Whether fish experience pain is important.(6 words)
鱼是否有痛感很重要。

冗长：It has not often been the case that any mistake has been made. （13 words）

简洁：Few mistakes were made. （4 words）
很少犯错误。

3. 句子组合

有些信息并不需要单独的句子来传递，完全可以在不失掉其价值的同时将其置于另一个句子中。

冗长：Ludwig's castles are an astounding marriage of beauty and madness. By his death, he had commissioned **three castles**. （18 words）

简洁：Ludwig's **three castles** are an astounding marriage of beauty and madness. （11 words）
路德维格的三座城堡是美丽与激情的完美结合。

冗长：The supposed crash of a UFO in Roswell, New Mexico aroused interest in extraterrestrial life. This crash is rumored to have occurred in **1947**. （24 words）

简洁：The supposed 1947 crash of a UFO in Roswell, New Mexico aroused interest in extraterrestrial life. （16 words）
传说发生在1947年美国新墨西哥州罗斯韦尔的UFO撞毁事件引起了人们对外星球生命的兴趣。

4. 可去掉的词语

（1）去掉那些显而易见或包含过多细节的解释性词语。

无论在初稿还是修改稿阶段，都要时刻想着读者。如果所解释或描述的内容对读者来说是显而易见的，就要把这些内容去掉或重新措辞。读者在补充那些不重要的叙述性内容上是很内行的，如下面最后那个例子（由77个词组成的句子改为由11个词组成的句子）。

冗长：I received your inquiry that you wrote about tennis rackets yesterday, and read it thoroughly. Yes, we do have.... （19 words）

简洁：I received your inquiry about tennis rackets yesterday. Yes, we do have.... （12 words）
我昨天收到了你询问有关网球拍的信。是的，我们确实有。

冗长：It goes without saying that we are acquainted with your policy on filing tax returns, and we have every intention of complying with the regulations that you have mentioned. （29 words）

简洁：We intend to comply with the tax-return regulations that you have

mentioned.（12 words）
我们要按照你提到的纳税申报条例去做。

冗长：*Imagine a mental picture of someone engaged in the intellectual activity of trying to learn what the rules are for how to play the game of chess.*（27 words）

简洁：*Imagine someone trying to learn the rules of chess.*（9 words）
想象一下有人在尝试学习如何下国际象棋。

冗长：*After booking a ticket to Dallas from a travel agent, I packed my bags and arranged for a taxi to the airport. Once there, I checked in, went through security, and was ready to board. But problems beyond my control led to a three-hour delay before takeoff.*（47 words）

简洁：*My flight to Dallas was delayed for three hours.*（9 words）
我乘坐的飞往达拉斯的航班延迟了3小时。

冗长：*Baseball, one of our oldest and most popular outdoor summer sports in terms of total attendance at ball parks and viewing on television, has the kind of rhythm of play on the field that alternates between times when players passively wait with no action taking place between the pitches to the batter and then times when they explode into action as the batter hits a pitched ball to one of the players and the player fields it.*（77 words）

简洁：*Baseball has a rhythm that alternates between waiting and explosive action.*（11 words）
棒球具有一种等待和爆发性动作相交替的节奏。

(2) 去掉不必要的限定词和修饰语。

有时作者在写作中加入了多余的词或短语，这些多余的词或短语看上去好像对名词的含义起到了修饰或限定作用，但实质上根本没有任何意义。尽管这些词或短语在恰当的场合具有一定的意义，但它们常常被用作"填充物"，是可以去掉的。

冗长：*Any particular type of dessert is fine with me.*（9 words）

简洁：*Any dessert is fine with me.*（6 words）
什么甜点我都吃。

冗长：*Balancing the budget by Friday is an impossibility without some kind of extra help.*（14 words）

简洁：*Balancing the budget by Friday is impossible without extra help.*

(10 words)
如果没外援,不可能在周五做完平衡预算。

冗长:For all intents and purposes, American industrial productivity generally depends on certain factors that are really more psychological in kind than of any given technological aspect. (26 words)

简洁:American industrial productivity depends more on psychological than on technological factors. (11 words)
美国工业生产力更多是依赖于心理方面的因素,而不是技术方面的因素。

冗长:A surprising **aspect** of most labour negotiations is their friendly **quality**. (11 words)

简洁:Most labour negotiations are surprisingly friendly. (6 words)
大多数的劳务谈判是在极其友好的气氛下进行的。

冗长:The **fact** of the war had the **effect** of causing many changes. (12 words)

简洁:The war caused many changes. (5 words)
战争引起很多变化。

以下是一些可从句子中修剪掉,从而使句子变得更加明了的词和短语:kind of、sort of、type of、really、basically、for all intents and purposes、definitely、actually、generally、individual、specific、particular。

(3)去掉重复性的用语。
避免写出那些意思相近而导致重复的短语或较长的段落。那些与句子或段落内容不相关的词语几乎都没有什么用,要去掉。

冗长:I would appreciate it if you would bring to the attention of your drafting officers the administrator's dislike of long sentences and paragraphs in messages to the field and in other items drafted for her signature or approval, as well as in all correspondence, reports, and studies. Please encourage your section to keep their sentences short. (56 words)

简洁:Please encourage your drafting officers to keep sentences and paragraphs in letters, reports, and studies short. Dr. Lomas, the administrator, has mentioned that reports and memos drafted for her approval recently have been wordy and thus time-consuming. (37 words)

请让你的起草人员将信函、报告和研究论文中的句子和段落保持简短。管理者洛马斯博士提到最近让她审批的报告和备忘录写得啰里啰唆,读起来很费时。

冗长:*The supply manager considered the correcting typewriter an unneeded luxury.* (10 words)

简洁:The supply manager considered the correcting typewriter a luxury. (9 words)

设备经理认为纠错打字机就是一种奢侈品。

冗长:*Our branch office currently employs five tellers. These tellers do an excellent job Monday through Thursday but cannot keep up with the rush on Friday and Saturday.* (27 words)

简洁:Our branch office currently employs five tellers, who do an excellent job Monday through Thursday but cannot keep up with Friday and Saturday rush periods. (25 words)

我们这个部门最近雇用了 5 位出纳员,他们周一至周四工作得都很出色,但是在周五、周六繁忙的高峰期就不行了。

(4) 去掉冗余、成对使用的词语。

有些成对使用的词语相互包含,*finish* 含有 *complete* 的意义,因此在多数情况下,短语 *completely finish* 是冗余的。

以下成对使用的词语也是冗余的:past memories、various differences、each individual、basic fundamentals、true facts、important essentials、future plans、terrible tragedy、end result、final outcome、free gift、past history、unexpected surprise、sudden crisis、mutual agreement、future prospects、consensus of opinion、reconsider。

与此相关的一个表达法 very unique 与其说是冗长,还不如说是不合乎逻辑。由于 unique 的含义是"独一无二的",加上表程度的修饰语 very、so、especially、somewhat、extremely 等就不合乎逻辑了。unique 表明的含义只能是二者选一:要么是唯一的,要么是不存在的,因此不存在等级、层级上的差异。

冗长:*Before the travel agent was completely able to finish explaining the various differences among all of the many very unique vacation packages his travel agency was offering, the customer changed her future plans.* (33 words)

简洁:Before the travel agent finished explaining the differences among the unique vacation packages his travel agency was offering, the

customer changed her plans. (23 words)
在这个旅行代理还没有解释完他们旅行社所提供的旅游套餐之间的区别之前,那个客户就改变了她的计划。

(5) 去掉冗余的表示类别或种类的词语。

具体的词包含了他们的类别或种类,因此我们不必同时阐述两者。我们知道 a period 表示的是一段时间,pink 表示的是颜色,shiny 表示的是外观。

以下短语中表示类别或种类的术语都可以去掉,只需留下具体的描述性词语:large in size、often times、of a bright color、heavy in weight、period in time、round in shape、at an early time、economics field、of cheap quality、honest in character、of an uncertain condition、in a confused state、unusual in nature、extreme in degree、of a strange type。

冗长:During that time period, many car buyers preferred cars that were pink in color and shiny in appearance. (18 words)

简洁:During that period, many car buyers preferred pink, shiny cars. (10 words)
那段时间,许多购车者喜欢选择粉色、有光泽的汽车。

冗长:The microscope revealed a group of organisms that were round in shape and peculiar in nature. (16 words)

简洁:The microscope revealed a group of peculiar, round organisms. (9 words)
显微镜下可见一群奇异、圆形的生物。

5. 变换短语

(1) 把短语变为单独的词,如一个形容词。

如果使用了短语来表达那些仅仅需要一个词就能表达的意思,就显得冗长,此时就该尽可能把短语换成单独的词。

冗长:The employee with ambition.... (4 words)

简洁:The ambitious employee.... (3 words)
雄心勃勃的雇员……

冗长:The department showing the best performance.... (6 words)

简洁:The best-performing department.... (3 words)
效率最高的部门……

冗长:Jeff Converse, our chief of consulting, suggested at our last board meeting the installation of microfilm equipment in the department of data processing. (23 words)

简洁：At our last board meeting, Chief Consultant Jeff Converse suggested that we install microfilm equipment in the data processing department. (20 words)
在我们上次董事会会议上，首席顾问杰夫·康威建议在数据处理部门安装缩微拍摄设备。

冗长：*We read the letter we received yesterday and reviewed it thoroughly.* (11 words)

简洁：We thoroughly read the letter we received yesterday. (8 words)
我们把昨天收到的信认真地读了一遍。

冗长：*As you carefully read what you have written to improve your wording and catch small errors of spelling, punctuation, and so on, the thing to do before you do anything else is to try to see where a series of words expressing action could replace the ideas found in nouns rather than verbs.* (53 words)

简洁：As you edit, first find nominalizations that you can replace with verb phrases. (13 words)
在编辑时，你首先要找出并去掉可以由动词短语所取代的动名词。

（2）把不必要的 that、who 和 which 从句变成短语。

使用从句来表达原本可以用短语甚至一个词就能表达的内容，这同样会使句子变得冗长。此时，在可能的情况下，把从句修改为短语或单独的词。

冗长：*The report, which was released recently....* (6 words)

简洁：The recently released report.... (4 words)
最近发表的报告……

冗长：*All applicants who are interested in the job must....* (9 words)

简洁：All job applicants must.... (4 words)
所有的求职者必须……

冗长：*The system that is most efficient and accurate....* (8 words)

简洁：The most efficient and accurate system.... (6 words)
最有效、最准确的系统……

冗长：*The novel,* **which is** *entitled Ulysses, takes place....* (8 words)

简洁：The novel *Ulysses* takes place.... (5 words)
小说《尤利西斯》发生在……

冗长：It was Confucius **who** said.... (5 words)
简洁：Confucius said.... (2 words)
孔子说……

冗长：*I think that* X is the case.... (7 words)
简洁：X is the case,.... (4 words)
证据表明 X 是这样：……

冗长：There is a tendency among many writers **who may be seen** to display **certain signs of lack of** confidence that their sentences **will be overloaded** with relative clauses and other words **which are** generally useless **in function**. (37 words)
简洁：Many hesitant writers overload their sentences with relative clauses and other useless words. (13 words)
许多踌躇的作者在句子中使用了关系从句和其他没用的词语，结果他们写出的句子变得冗长。

(3) 变被动动词为主动动词。
有关这个主题的更多参考可见一些语法教科书（见参考文献书目）。

冗长：*An account was opened by Mrs. Simms.* (7 words)
简洁：Mrs. Simms opened an account. (5 words)
西姆斯太太开了一个账户。

冗长：*Your figures were checked by the research department.* (8 words)
简洁：The research department checked your figures. (6 words)
研究部门检查了你给出的数字。

冗长：*It is felt that an exercise program should be attempted by this patient before any surgery is performed.* (18 words)
简洁：The patient should attempt an exercise program before surgery. (9 words)
这个病人在手术之前应该尝试一下康复锻炼计划。
简洁：I recommend that the patient attempt an exercise program before surgery. (11 words)
我建议病人在手术前尝试一下康复锻炼计划。

(4) 去掉不必要的 to be 和 being。

  冗长：*The program is considered **to be** effective.*（7 words）
  简洁：The program is considered effective.（5 words）
     这个计划被认为是有效的。
     The program is effective.（4 words）
     这个计划有效。

  冗长：*because of the terrain **being** rough*（6 words）
  简洁：because of the rough terrain（5 words）
     由于地形崎岖不平

6. 需要避免的事项

(1) 避免在句子开头过多使用填充语或虚词。

  填充语是指短语"it + be-verb"或"there + be-verb"。在有些场合，这类表达式的修辞效果是不容置疑的，但如果过多或在不必要的情况下使用了这类结构，你的写作会变得冗长。如句子："It is imperative that we find a solution."，同样的意思可以用更简洁的措辞来表达："We must find a solution."。但由于这类结构把表示重要性的词语放在句子靠前的位置，因此有利于突出紧要的情况，在有些场合还是适用的。

  但你还是要避免过多或不必要地使用上述提到的这种句子结构。这种最常见的不必要的结构会紧跟着出现一个名词和以 that、which 或 who 开头的关系从句。多数情况下可以这样去开头的填充词，修改后可以更加简洁：用名词做句子的主语，再去掉没必要的关系代词。

  冗长：*It is the governor who signs or vetoes bills.*（9 words）
  简洁：The governor signs or vetoes bills.（6 words）
     州长签署或者否决法案。

  冗长：*There are four rules that should be observed:....*（8 words）
  简洁：Four rules should be observed:....（5 words）
     要遵守的规则有四条：……

  冗长：*There was a big explosion, which shook the windows, and people ran into the street.*（15 words）
  简洁：A big explosion shook the windows, and people ran into the street.（12 words）
     大爆炸震动了窗户，之后人们都跑到了街上。

(2) 避免过多使用动词的名词化形式。

可能的情况下使用动词，而不是由动词转化而来的名词，即动名词。使用动名词的句子通常要用 be 的结构来充当动词。使用隐藏在动名词中的行为动词作为主要动词,而不是 be 结构,这样能避免你的写作变得乏味。

to have an expectation, hope, wish, understanding, etc.
(to expect, hope, wish, understand, etc.)
to make an arrangement, plan, decision, inquiry, acquisition, etc.
(to arrange, plan, decide, inquire, acquire, etc.)

冗长:The function of this department is the collection of accounts. (10 words)

简洁:This department collects accounts. (4 words)
这个部门负责收账。

冗长:The current focus of the medical profession is disease prevention. (10 words)

简洁:The medical profession currently focuses on disease prevention. (8 words)
目前医学界的重点是疾病防御。

(3)避免使用不必要的不定式短语。

有些不定式短语可以变成限定动词或简洁的名词短语。这样的改动有时还常常能把 be 动词结构变为行为动词。

冗长:The duty of a clerk is to check all incoming mail and to record it. (15 words)

简洁:A clerk should check and record all incoming mail. (9 words)
办事员需检查并记录所有收到的邮件。

冗长:A shortage of tellers at our branch office on Friday and Saturday during rush hours has caused customers to become dissatisfied with service. (23 words)

简洁:A teller shortage at our branch office on Friday and Saturday during rush hours has caused customer dissatisfaction. (18 words)
在周五、周六高峰时段我们办公室缺少出纳员,引起了客户的不满。

(4)避免表述时转弯抹角,要直截了当。

迂回表述,就是通常说的转弯抹角。这样的表达方式自然要比简洁的表述所使用的词语更多。我们常常忽略了这一点,这可能是由于已经养成了这种讲话习惯。但在写作中,要避免使用类似的表达,因为这样增加的只是词语,而不是意思。当然,偶尔出于修辞上的考虑,也可使用填充语式的结构,而不是更简洁的结构。因此这里所提的建议只是一般性的指导，不是绝对的规则。

俗套语改为一个词或省略：

for the purpose of (to), due to the fact that (because), at this point in time (now), in the near future (soon), with regard to (about), in view of the fact that (because), as the case may be (—), basically (—)

冗长：*At this/that point in time....*（5 words）
简洁：Now/Then....（1 word）
现在/那时……

冗长：*In accordance with your request....*（5 words）
简洁：As you requested....（3 words）
按照你的要求……

下面是其他一些词语，可用来简化迂回的表达。

because/since/why =
the reason for/for the reason that/owing/due to the fact that/in light of the fact that/considering the fact that/on the grounds that/this is why

when =
on the occasion of/in a situation in which/under circumstances in which

about =
as regards/in reference to/with regard to/concerning the matter of/where... is concerned

must/should =
it is crucial that/it is necessary that/there is a need/necessity for/it is important that/cannot be avoided

can =
is able to/has the opportunity to/has the capacity for/has the ability to

may/might/could =
it is possible that/there is a chance that/it could happen that/the possibility exists for

冗长：*It is possible that nothing will come of these preparations.*（10 words）
简洁：Nothing may come of these preparations.（6 words）
这些准备可能是徒劳的。

冗长：*She has the ability to influence the outcome.*（8 words）
简洁：She can influence the outcome.（5 words）
她可以影响到结果。

冗长：*It is necessary that we take a stand on this pressing issue.*（12 words)

简洁：We must take a stand on this pressing issue. (9 words)
对于这个紧迫的问题我们必须表明自己的立场。

1.3.2 清晰的技能

为什么我们要关注句子的清晰问题？
(1) 以便与读者进行有效的交流；
(2) 以便使自己的写作具有说服力；
(3) 以便表明作者的学术可信度和学术权威性。

1. 由已知信息到新信息

从给读者提供他们已知信息开始，逐步把读者引向你要向读者展示的"宏伟画面"，这样读者才能把他们熟悉的与你提供给他们的新信息联系起来。随着新信息成为已知信息，再由此已知信息进一步引出新信息。

下面的例句属于表述清晰、可被理解的句子，因为新信息是由已知信息过渡而来的。

Every semester after final exams are over, I'm faced with the problem of what to do with books of lecture notes (new information). They (old) might be useful some day, but they just keep piling up on my bookcase (new). Someday, it (old) will collapse under the weight of information I might never need.

每个学期在期末考试后，我都面临如何处理像书一样的课堂笔记的问题（新信息）。这些笔记（已知信息）在某一天可能会有用，但问题是它们在书架上越堆越高（新信息）。总有一天，书架（已知信息）会在我可能永远也不会需要的信息资料的重负下坍塌。

下面这个例句的意思就不明确，它的表述是由新信息到已知信息。

Lately, most movies I've seen have been merely second-rate entertainment, but occasionally there are some with worthwhile themes. The rapid disappearance of some folk culture (new) is the topic of a recent movie (old) I saw.

你是否发现第二个句子既难读又难懂，原因在于已知信息是在新信息之后出现的。下面是修改后的句子，是从已知信息开始，然后过渡到新信息，句子更易读懂。

Lately, most movies I've seen have been merely second-rate entertainment, but occasionally there are some with worthwhile themes. One recent movie (old) I saw was about the rapid disappearance of some folk culture. (new)

最近大部分我看过的电影属于二流水平的娱乐片，但是偶尔也能看到一些主题有意义、值得一看的影片,其中有一部是关于某一民俗文化快速消亡的影片。

2. 要注意从句的位置
如果主句中加入的从句会引起语义混乱,此时就要避免在主句中置入从句。

中间嵌入从句引起混乱的例句:

Industrial spying, because of the growing use of computers to store and process corporate information, is increasing rapidly.

语义清晰的例句(从句在句尾):

Industrial spying is increasing rapidly because of the growing use of computers to store and process corporate information.

语义清晰的例句(从句在句首):

Because of the growing use of computers to store and process corporate information, industrial spying is increasing rapidly.

由于越来越多地使用计算机来存储和处理企业信息,工业间谍正快速增长。

3. 注意修饰语的位置
语义含混的例句(修饰语的位置不当):

Jennifer called her adorable kitten opening the can of tuna and filled the food bowl.

语义清晰的例句(修饰语的位置适当):

Opening the can of tuna, Jennifer called her adorable kitten and filled the food bowl.

Jennifer, opening the can of tuna, called her adorable kitten and filled the food bowl.

Jennifer opened the can of tuna, called her adorable kitten, and filled the food bowl.

詹尼弗打开金枪鱼罐头,把她可爱的小猫咪唤过来,然后将食物放在碗里。

语义不明确的例句(修饰语的位置不当):

Portia rushed to the store loaded with cash to buy the birthday gift.

语义清晰的例句(修饰语的位置适当)：

  Portia, loaded with cash, rushed to the store to buy the birthday gift.
  Loaded with cash, Portia rushed to the store to buy the birthday gift.
  拿上钱，波西亚急匆匆地奔向商店去买生日礼物。

注意：不同位置的修饰语，意义也不同。辨别下面每个句子的意思。
哪个句子表明班级所有的人都考试不及格？

  Almost everyone in the class passed the calculus exam.
  几乎班上所有的人都通过了微积分考试。
  Everyone in the class **almost** passed the calculus exam.
  班上所有的人都没通过微积分考试。

哪个句子表明约翰挣了些钱？

  John **nearly** earned $100.
  约翰差点挣到那一百美元。
  John earned **nearly** $100.
  约翰挣了差不多一百美元。

4. 使用主动语态

  主动语态的句子比被动语态的句子要好理解，因为主动语态能让我们清晰地看出行为执行者。此外，把被动语态的句子改为主动语态的句子，会使句子更加简明。因此，除非有特殊理由，否则使用主动语态。如果你不想让读者关注行为者，或者行为者不重要、自明或不清楚，或者被动语态是读者惯用的风格等，这时应使用被动语态。

行为者不十分明确的例句(被动语态)：

  A decision was reached to postpone the vote.

语义清晰的例句(主动语态)：

  The committee decided to postpone the vote.
  委员会决定推迟选举。

行为者不十分明确/语义含混的例句(被动语态)：

  The decision that was reached by the committee was to postpone the vote.

语义清晰的例句(主动语态)：

  The committee reached the decision to postpone the vote.
  The committee decided to postpone the vote.
  委员会决定推迟选举。

行为者不十分明确/语义含混的例句(被动语态):

The disk drive of the computer was damaged by the electrical surge.

语义清晰的例句(主动语态):

The electrical surge damaged the disk drive of the computer.

The electrical surge damaged the computer's disk drive.

电涌损坏了计算机光驱。

5. 指向不明的修饰语

指向不明的修饰语是指读者无法确定身为修饰语的词或短语在句中所要修饰的是哪一个词或短语。

无法指出修饰语 having finished dinner 在句中修饰哪个词或哪个短语:

Having finished dinner, the football game was turned on.

修改后:

(1) 你可以把修饰语的逻辑主语用作独立子句的主语:

Having finished dinner, Joe turned on the football game.

(2) 你也可以还原指向不明的短语中的行为主语:

After Joe finished dinner, he turned on the football game.

乔晚餐后,打开电视看足球赛。

指向不明的修饰语的例句:

Playing solitaire on the computer for three hours, Michael's paper was not completed.

修改后:

Playing solitaire on the computer for three hours, Michael did not complete his paper.

由于在电脑上玩了三个小时的单人纸牌游戏,迈克没有完成他的论文。

Because Michael played solitaire on the computer for three hours, he did not complete his paper.

因为迈克在电脑上玩了 3 个小时的游戏,他没有完成他的论文。

指向不明的修饰语的例句:

Locked away in the old chest, Richard was surprised by the antique hats.

修改后:

Locked away in the old chest, the antique hats surprised Richard.

藏于旧箱子里的老式帽子令理查德感到惊奇。
The antique hats locked away in the old chest surprised Richard.
藏于旧箱子里的老式帽子令理查德感到惊奇。

指向不明的修饰语的例句：

To work as a loan officer, an education in financial planning is required.

修改后：

To work as a loan officer, one is required to have an education in financial planning.

要想成为一名信贷员,就应接受过财务策划方面的教育。

指向不明的修饰语的例句：

Being a process that still needs to be refined, scientists are searching for a more effective plan for chemotherapy treatment.

修改后：

Scientists are searching for a more effective plan for chemotherapy treatment, a process that still needs to be refined.

科学家正在寻求一个更为有效的化学疗法的治疗方案,这个方法仍须进一步完善。

指向不明的修饰语的例句：

Carrying a mouse in its mouth, John saw the cat enter the room.

修改后：

John saw the cat enter the room carrying a mouse in its mouth.

约翰看见猫进屋了,嘴里还叼着一只老鼠。

指向不明的修饰语的例句：

While unable to master grammar, the English teacher had to explain the use of adverb phrases to me again.

修改后：

Since I could not master grammar, the English teacher had to explain the use of adverb phrases to me again.

由于我没能掌握好语法,英语老师只得又给我解释了副词短语的用法。

指向不明的修饰语的例句：

By using this premise, it makes Hume's argument more plausible.

修改后：

> By using this premise, Hume makes his argument more plausible.
> 休姆利用这个前提，使他的论证更可信。

6. 使用平行结构

如果你使用了系列的词、短语、从句，那么把它们置于平行结构之中（即相似的语法结构），以便读者能更确切地识别它们之间的连接关系。

不十分明确的例句（结构不相似）：

> *We had no alcohol. We also did not have drugs.*

修改后更清晰（平行结构）：

> We had neither alcohol nor drugs.
> 我们既没有酒，也没有毒品。

不十分明确的例句（结构不相似）：

> *Guns are for family protection, to hunt dangerous or delicious animals, and keep the King of England out of your face.*

修改后更清晰（平行结构）：

> Guns are for *protecting* your family, *hunting* dangerous or delicious animals, and *keeping* the King of England out of your face.
>
> The purpose of guns is to *protect* your family, *hunt* dangerous or delicious animals, and *keep* the King of England out of your face.

不十分明确的例句（结构不相似）：

> *In Florida, where the threat of hurricanes is an annual event, we learned that it is important (1) to become aware of the warning signs. (2) There are precautions to take, and (3) deciding when to take shelter is important.*

在上段话中，没有把第二句话中提到的要关注的一系列事件置于平行结构之中，同第一个句子相比，第二个句子对读者来说更容易理解。

修改后更清晰（平行结构）：

> In Florida, where the threat of hurricanes is an annual event, we learned that it is important (1) to become aware of the warning signs, (2) to know what precautions to take, and (3) to decide when to seek shelter.
> 在佛罗里达，飓风每年都要发生，我们意识到注意飓风前兆、采取预防措施、决定何时躲避都很重要。

7. 避免使用一连串的名词

尽量不要一起使用一连串的名词,因为这样理解起来很困难,修改的方法之一是把其中的一个名词改为动词。

不清楚的例句(一连串的名词):

This report explains our investment growth stimulation projects.
这个报告解释我们投资增长的刺激计划。

更清楚的例句:

This report explains our projects to stimulate growth in investments.
这个报告解释我们刺激投资增长的计划。

8. 避免过度使用动词的名词形式

能使用动词的时候尽量不要使用动词的名词化形式,即动名词。

不清楚的例句(使用了动名词):

The implementation of the plan was successful.
计划的执行是成功的。

更清楚的例句:

The plan was implemented successfully.
计划被成功地执行。

9. 避免使用多重否定

尽量使用肯定的形式,而不是多重否定的形式,因为多重否定不易理解。

不清楚的例句(使用了多重否定和被动语态):

Less attention is paid to commercials that lack human interest stories than to other kinds of commercials.
相对于其他商品来说,缺乏有趣故事的商品得到更少的关注。

更清楚的例句:

People pay more attention to commercials with human interest stories than to other kinds of commercials.
相对于其他种类的商品,人们更关注那些具有人文趣味故事的商品。

10. 选用行为动词,而不是 be 的形式

如果可能,在句子和短语中尽量避免采用 be 作为主要的动词。使用 be 动词,就需要伴随使用名词化动词。要关注于你想表达的动作,选择一个合适的动词,而不是使用 be。

不清楚的例句(过度使用 be 结构)：

One difference between television news reporting and the coverage provided by newspapers is the time factor between the actual happening of an event and the time it takes to be reported. The problem is that instantaneous coverage is physically impossible for newspapers.

更清楚的例句：

Television news reporting differs from that of newspapers in that television, unlike newspapers, can provide instantaneous coverage of events as they happen.

与报刊新闻不同，电视新闻能够对事件做出瞬时覆盖的报道。

上述例子表达了两个观点：(1)电视和报刊报道新闻是有区别的；(2)区别的性质。修改后的句子在表述上述两层含义时分别使用了两个动词。

11. 避免使用指代不清的代词

首先，要确定你所使用的代词能明确地指当前或前一句中的某个名词。即使代词所指的是隐含的、没有明示的名词，你也应该改为使用名词，以此来解决代词指代不清的问题。

不清楚的例句(代词指代不清)：

With the spread of globalized capitalism, American universities increasingly follow a corporate fiscal model, tightening budgets and hiring temporary contract employees as teachers. **This** *has prompted faculty and adjunct instructors at many schools to join unions as a way of protecting job security and benefits.*

更清楚的例句：

With the spread of globalized capitalism, American universities increasingly follow a corporate fiscal model, tightening budgets and hiring temporary contract employees as teachers. **This trend** has prompted faculty and adjunct instructors at many schools to join unions as a way of protecting job security and benefits.

随着资本全球化的蔓延，美国许多大学越来越多地遵循企业财政模式，即紧缩预算并雇用临时合同工为老师。这种趋势促使许多学校的教师及其教辅人员加入工会以确保其稳定的工作和利益。

不清楚的例句(代词指代不清)：

Larissa worked in a national forest last summer, **which** *may be her career choice.*

更清楚的例句：

  Larissa worked in a national forest last summer; **forest management** may be her career choice.

  拉丽莎去年夏天在一个国家森林部门工作；森林管理可能成为她选择的职业。

12. 关于如何合并句子

合并句子是指作者用更少的句子来表述几个句子联合表述的内容。合并句子有助于作者构建内容和结构更加复杂的句子。

为什么要了解如何合并句子？
(1)以便使写作更清晰；
(2)以便避免啰唆；
(3)以便避免冗长。

合并句子的关键是什么？
(1)利用形容词；
(2)合理地安排好起修饰作用的从句；
(3)去掉不必要的或只起重复作用的短语。

你将如何修改这段话？

  The boy struggled to ride his bike. The boy is four years old and he is feisty. The bike is new and it is a light blue color. The boy received the bike for his birthday. He struggled for two hours. However, he was unsuccessful in riding the bike.

修改后：

  The feisty four-year-old boy struggled unsuccessfully for two hours to ride his new light blue birthday bike.

  这个仅有四岁的调皮的小男孩的生日礼物是一辆崭新的浅蓝色的自行车，他努力尝试了两个小时都没能学会骑它。

你将如何修改这段话？

  The animal trainer dove into the pool. The trainer was skilled and athletic. She was excited when she dove into the pool. She swam with two dolphins. The dolphins were babies. The dolphins were playful. The trainer swam with the dolphins for over an hour. When the trainer swam with the dolphins, she was happy.

修改后：

  The skilled, athletic animal trainer excitedly dove into the pool and happily swam for over an hour with two playful baby dolphins.

经验丰富的驯兽师情绪饱满地潜入水中,与两只可爱的小海豚一起快乐地游了一个多小时。

你将如何修改这段话?

The blizzard contained strong winds and heavy snow. During the snowstorm, the roof of the town library collapsed. The roof of the post office did the same. The blowing snow covered the county roads. Schools cancelled classes due to the white-out conditions.

修改后:

The blizzard, containing strong winds and heavy snow, caused the roofs of the town library and the post office to collapse, created white-out conditions on county roads, and forced schools to cancel classes.

夹着大风和暴雪的这场暴风雪导致小镇图书馆和邮局的屋顶坍塌,乡间小路一片白茫茫,学校不得不停课。

第二章
撰写科研论文

什么是科研论文,很多作者对此做出了描述,但可能最简明扼要的定义当属 P. Berge 和 C. Saffioti 在其著作 *Basic College Research* 中给出的:"确切地说,科研论文是能够反映科研工作者经过探索就某一特定主题提出的一个观点、主张的书面文本。"

科研论文不同于其他写作之处就在于前一类文本不仅仅是作者自己观点的汇编,它的基础是全面、彻底地查询已发表的、与研究的主题相关的资料。因此,科研论文的关键在于它的质量和如何在论文中准确地以专业的方式对研究发现予以陈述。一篇好的科研论文所提供的所有文献都严格地遵循已确立的准则。有关这些准则见第二章的 2.8 和第四章的文献论述。

就各种文献而言,科学家和工程师们最感自豪的不仅是写出自己的论文,而且是能在使他们随时了解他们所从事的行业发展的最新动态的期刊上发表由他们撰写的科研论文。科研论文是研发或试验项目的最终成果。作者由此向读者提供读者所需的信息:发现了什么,如何发现的,以及这些发现的意义。优秀的科学家和工程师对其论文写作的质量所表现出的关注和兴趣不亚于他们对其他科研工作方面的关注程度。他们深知,如果代表他们科研工作的书面文本不能充分地传递信息,那么,他们在科研技术方面的一切努力几乎是毫无意义的。

要想成为某一领域或学科的一名有经验的研究者和作者,需要经历大量的实践。这一过程对大多数人来说都不会自然而然地来到。即使是经验丰富的学术界前辈,也不得不在其学术生涯的某个时期去学习如何撰写学术论文。因此,只要是勤奋、系统地安排和实践、乐于学习(且不怕犯错误),并有耐心、致力于学习写作的人就会在其科研和写作中取得成就。

各种学术期刊对论文文体的要求有所不同,甚至即使是同一领域的不同期刊,对论文的文体风格要求也会有所不同,因此,在向期刊投稿前,就要首先阅读所投期刊对稿件的组织结构和格式的要求,也可以选读几篇所投期刊已发表过的文章,由此来了解某一特定期刊的文体(包括注脚的格式要求,标题和图、表格的格式,段落的长度以及其他一些特别要求)。

写好科研论文的关键在于把科研和论文融为一体。这也是撰写论文最困难的地方。科研支撑了你的结论,又使你的结论具有了可信度。论文的结论是由坚实的科研做基础的,但科研又不能凌驾于论文之上,不能主宰论文。写作的重心应该是表达你个人的观点,科研起到的是支撑作用。要使用过渡词、转换词和短语,以便使你的思想和参考文献所体现的观点能有效地衔接起来。否则,你的写作会是生硬呆板、牵强、不自然的,文章也将会失去连贯性。要知道,学术论文写作也和其他规范的论文写作一样,应遵循好的写作规则,应该要有引言和主干,也要有结尾和中心,更要有主题充分的展开论述。

尽管不同的期刊对学术文章的文体有不同的要求,但绝大部分的学术文章在其目的和结构方面又有着极其相似的地方。目前大部分的期刊都要求其论文包含标题、作者姓名及所属单位、摘要、引言、方法、结果、讨论、致谢和文献几个部分,与实验过程同时出现在一篇论文中。这也正是本书要遵循的一套学术论文写作的方法。本书将在不同的章节中描述和探讨与每一部分相关的风格、内容以及格式要求和特点。

期刊类论文的各部分是按下述顺序出现的:

研究过程	论文的相应部分
简要说明作者要做什么	摘要
探讨的问题是什么	引言
问题是如何解决的	材料和方法
发现了什么	结果
意味着什么	讨论
谁给予了何种帮助	致谢(可选)
参考了谁的文献	参考文献
附加信息	附录(可选)

引言:引言部分的主要目的是:(1)为全文提供理论基础和依据,对在研主题的展开通常采用的写作过程是由大到小,即讨论过程以由整体到具体问题或具体设想的方式展开;(2)吸引读者对本主题感兴趣。

方法:方法部分在不同程度上对学术研究中所使用的方法、材料和步骤进行描述。

结果:结果部分对研究中的发现进行描述,同时视不同情况对数据进行不同程度的评论。

讨论:讨论部分就本研究的成果(得到了什么)进行推论,推论的进程是由具体到一般,通常以给出一系列的要点来实现,而且有些要点是在引言部分提及过的,全文形成一个首尾相接的整体。

由于学术论文的各章节都已经形成了各自的写作目的,因此,各部分也都形成了自己独特的语言特点。下面,将分别详细地讨论各部分的写作目的和语言特点。

2.1　标题、作者姓名及所在单位的撰写

2.1.1　标题

1. 标题的作用

标题应该是描述性的,不宜过长。标题应与作者的研究相关。编辑索引和摘要的机构完全依据作者的标题来摘录关键词,用于相互参照和计算机搜索。大部分的读者是通过在电子数据库或搜索引擎中键入标题关键词的方式查找文章。标题的好坏,直接关系到你的文章是否会被读者读到。因此,标题要准确、简洁、清晰和具体。有人说标题是摘要的摘要(abstract of abstract),由此可见写好标题的重要性。

标题应该是摘要内容的忠实再现,应尽量表达作者研究的背景和目的。理想的标题一般为 10~12 个单词,包含研究的范围、研究计划和研究目的。通常的做法是把标题写成对研究问题的一种描述,而不是对研究结果或结论的陈述。对已发表论文的研究表明,那些把标题写成陈述式的、概括结果的标题大部分都过分夸大了数据的意义,从技术角度来看不够准确(如标题"Approach X improves oxygenation in ARDS")。摘要的标题也要写得便于读者理解,不要包含难懂的行话或首字母缩略词。标题要包含能描述目前从事的研究工作的关键词。要记住标题已成为当前网络或计算机搜索的依据,因此如果一个标题写得不够充分的话,就会减少这篇文章的阅读量,使渴望读到此类文章的读者与之失之交臂。下面这个标题是有关给小鼠做荷尔蒙实验以观察其某种行为的论文标题。这是个很糟糕的标题,为什么呢?

Mouse Behavior: The Effects of Estrogen on the Nose-Twitch Courtship Behavior

因为这样的标题过于宽泛,可以指任何一种鼠的行为,最好改为:

The Effects of Estrogen on the Nose-Twitch Courtship Behavior in Mice

这样改过以后,从标题关键词能确定某种具体的行为、具体的调节剂,以及实验的有机体。

有可能的话,主要的研究成果也可以体现在标题中,如:

Measurement of Falling Film Thickness Around a Horizontal Tube Using a Laser Measurement Technique

利用激光测量技术测量横管周围的落膜厚度

Advantages of a Combined System for Metering and Regulating Heat Consumption

热耗测定和调节组合系统的优点

此外,注意下面的例子是由两部分组成的。这样写标题有利于读者选取文章,并能在短时间内对文章的大意有所了解。在学术类标题中可以陈述研究的问题、概括主题或研究目的,或利用冒号将标题写成两部分。下面的例子就是由两部分组成的:前一部分给出

文章的背景、讨论的学术问题；第二部分给出文章/作者的观点或看法。

    Entrepreneurial Marketing：The Critical Difference
    企业家的市场化策略：关键的区别
    The Micro-Chamber Thermal Extractor—The latest cost effective solution for rapid materials emissions testing
    小腔热抽取器——用于快速物质排放测试的最新成本效益解决方案

标题可能是较早拟定的，但通常是在全文定稿后修改确定。

2. 格式

标题应居于论文第一页的最上端（惯例是不把标题单独放一页，以节省空间），标题下不要有横线，标题也不要写成斜体字。

实例1 RetinaFace：Single-stage Dense Face Localisation in the Wild
    人脸检测：在户外环境中的单阶段密集人脸定位

实例2 ImageNet Classification with Deep Convolutional Neural Networks
    基于深度卷积神经网络的图像网络分类

实例3 Visual Transfer between Atari Games Using Competitive Reinforcement Learning
    利用竞争性强化学习实现雅达利游戏间的视觉迁移

实例4 A baseline for unsupervised advanced persistent threat detection in system-level provenance
    系统级来源中无监督高级持续威胁检测的基准

实例5 Airport Delay Prediction Based on Spatiotemporal Analysis and Bi-LSTM Sequence Learning
    基于时空分析和Bi-LSTM序列学习的机场延误预测

3. 标题的要求

标题的特征是用词少，对论文内容表述准确。当然，并不是毫无区别地把标题一律缩短，要记住这样做的目的是用最少的词语来传递最大量的信息。

  标题：*An Instrumentation System for Helicopter Blade Flight Research Measurements*
  改为：A Rotor-Mounted Digital Instrumentation System for Helicopter Blade

Flight Research

改过的标题比原来的标题还多了两个词,但看上去更准确,因为仅仅多用了两个词,信息量就增大了。

4. 标题修改策略

(1) 去掉多余的词。

省去下面这些用在标题开头的多余的词语。例如"A study of..." "Investigations/An Investigation of..." "Observations on..." "Study on..." "Discussion on..." "Research on..." "Investigation on..." "The Preparation of..." "The Synthesis of..." "An Analysis of..." "Conference on..."等。其实,根据标题 ABC 三原则(accuracy、brevity、clarity),多数情况下这些词或短语都是可以省去的,这样会使标题更简练些。

实例 1　*A Comprehensive Survey on the Photocatalytic/H_2O_2 Treatment of Oil Field Produced Waters*

可改为:Photocatalytic/H_2O_2 Treatment of Oil Field Produced Waters
油田采出废水的 H_2O_2 光催化处理

实例 2　*Important Significance of Determination of 4 Factors Related to Neutron Multiplication Coefficient k*

可改为:Determination of 4 Factors Related to Neutron Multiplication Coefficient k
与中子增殖系数 k 相关的 4 因子的测定

实例 3　*Discussion on the Problems of the Large Traveling Grate Stocker Hot Water Boilers in Design for Central Heating*

可改为:Problems in the Design of the Large Traveling Grate Stocker Hot Water Boilers for Central Heating
大型链条炉排热水锅炉设计中存在的问题

实例 4　*Research on Effect of Innovative Climate on Organizational Innovation*

可改为:Effect of Innovative Climate on Organizational Innovation
创新气氛对组织创新作用的研究

实例 5　*Study on the Pressure Characteristics of a Pneumatic Jet Pipe*

可改为:Pressure Characteristics of Pneumatic Jet Pipe
气动射流管压力特性研究

实例 6　*Study on the Real Time Navigation Data Model for Dynamic Navigation*

可改为:Real Time Navigation Data Model for Dynamic Navigation

动态导航的实时导航数据模型的研究

实例 7 *A New Approach on Performance Evaluation of University Scientific Research Based on DEA Model and Multi-index Evaluation*

可改为:Performance Evaluation of University Scientific Research Based on DEA Model and Multi-index Evaluation

基于 DEA 模型和多指标评估的大学科研绩效评价

(2)避免过多使用介词。

有时由于加入了一些修饰性的介词短语,标题变得冗长、笨拙,可采取几种方法修改冗长的标题,如把介词短语改成修饰语等。

实例 1 *Analysis of Hydroelastic Vibrations of Shells Partially Filled with a Liquid Using a Series Representation of the Liquid*

可改为: Hydroelastic Vibration Analysis of Partially Liquid-Filled Shells Using a Series Representation of the Liquid

(注:本标题中的 *analysis* 不能省略,因为它被其后的 *using* 所修饰,否则可省略。)

液体系列表示法对部分加载液体的壳体做流体弹性震动分析

实例 2 *A prediction of Performance of Commercial Coal Gasifiers*

可改为: Performance Prediction of Commercial Coal Gasifiers

商业煤气化炉的性能预测

实例 3 *On the Disturbance Properties of High Order Iterative Learning Control Algorithms*

可改为: Disturbance Properties of High Order Iterative Learning Control Algorithms

高阶迭代学习控制算法的扰动性能分析

(3)避免使用过多修饰语。

要注意标题的写作要易于读者理解,一连串的修饰语也会像介词短语一样使标题变得既笨拙、晦涩,又不易理解。在这种情况下,可通过去掉过多修饰语部分来减少介词短语的使用。

实例 *Low-Speed Wind-Tunnel Investigation of Flight Spoilers as Trailing-Vortex-Alleviation Devices on a Medium-Range Wide-Body Tri-Jet Airplane Model*

可改为: Low-Speed Wind-Tunnel Investigation of Flight Spoilers for a Medium-Range Wide-Body Tri-Jet Airplane Model

用于中程宽体三引擎喷气机模型的飞行扰动器的低速风洞研究

（注：这样修改去掉了介词短语，更突出了论文的主题。）

(4) 用动词形式做标题。

使标题具有力度的方式之一是不用由动词转化而来的名词，也就是把由动词转化而来的名词改回到原来的动词形式。

实例 1　*Alleviation of Trailing Vortexes by Use of Flight Spoilers*

可改为：Alleviating Trailing Vortexes by Using Flight Spoilers

利用飞行扰动器来减轻拖动涡旋

实例 2　*Eelectrolyte Materials of Intermedium-temperature SOFC Prepared by Glycine-nitrate Process*

可改为：Preparing Eelectrolyte Materials of Intermedium-temperature SOFC by Glycine-nitrate Process

用甘氨酸-硝酸盐法制备中温 SOFC 电解质材料

(5) 把标题中能删去的冠词删掉。

近年来标题趋向简洁，其中冠词在可用可不用时均可不用。如："A New method..." 可去掉 A；"The problem of..." 可去掉 The；"The Torrent Classification and the Hazard Zone Mapping Information System on GIS" 中的两个定冠词均可去掉；"The Effects of the Patient Age and Physician Training on the Choice and Dose of Anti-melan-cholic Drugs" 中三个定冠词 the 均可删去。

(6) 正确使用标题中的介词。

介词的使用比较灵活，且有很多固定搭配，应注意其用法。这里要特别注意的是介词 of。of 是经常使用的一个介词，但在标题中如果一个 of 套一个 of，连续 3 个 of 出现就容易引起语法结构混乱，甚至会引起读者厌烦。此时，如可能，改用其他介词 on、for 等来代替 of。如果一个句子中需要有两个 of，保留哪一个 of 呢？一般地说，应该保留关系最密切的 of。

实例 1　*Linear Programming Method of Optimization of Systems of Partial Difference Equation*

可改为：Linear Programming Method for Optimization of Partial Differential Equation Systems

也有人在标题里使用所有格。另外，随着现代科技发展，把名词直接当作形容词来使用也是常见的。

实例 2　*Preparation of First PSR Project of Qinshan NPP of China*

中国秦山核电厂的首次 PSR 项目准备

可改为：Preparation of China Qinshan NPP's First PSR Project
Preparation of China Qinshan NPP First PSR Project
Preparation for First PSR Project of China Qinshan NPP
Preparation of First PSR Project for China Qinshan NPP

（7）标题中的缩略词。

随着科学技术的发展，科技名词大量产生。这些名词由多个词构成，无论是在书写、印刷，还是口述中均会有所不便。因此，现多采用缩略形式（abbreviation）来表达，而且多为首字母组成的缩略词（acronym）。但是，在标题中缩略词的使用必须严加限制——只有那些全称较长，缩写已得到科技界公认，且读者群非常熟悉的缩略词才可使用。

  实例 1 LASER（light amplification by stimulated emission of radiation，激光）
  实例 2 DNA（deoxyribonucleic acid，脱氧核糖核酸）
  实例 3 AIDS（acquired immune deficiency syndrome，获得性免疫缺陷综合征，艾滋病）
  实例 4 CT（computerized tomography，电子计算机断层摄影）
  实例 5 NMR（nuclear magnetic resonance，核磁共振）

缩略词的使用范围还受读者群的制约。以上述诸缩略词为例，一般说来，LASER、CT、AIDS 等已为整个科技界所公认并熟悉，可以在各种科技期刊论文标题中使用；NMR、DNA 等已为整个医学界所公认并熟悉，可以在所有医学界期刊论文标题中使用(郑福裕，2003)。

（8）标题中的术语要同摘要及正文中使用的术语相一致。

下面的标题中有的术语同摘要中的术语所指的概念是相同的，但用了不同形式的词语（包括名词单、复数的不一致），其后果是，读者把同一概念的不同表达式当成了两个不同的概念。作者应选择和使用其中之一（更易被学术领域接受的、惯用的表达式），并在以后的使用中保持一致，不要相互交替使用，以免引发混淆。表示同一概念的术语在标题、摘要、关键词乃至正文中的使用要保持一致，而且关键词中出现的词语一定是在标题和摘要中出现过的（例 3 关键词 vector quantization 选择得不合适，因为这个词组并没有出现在标题和摘要中）。

实例 1

Hypervelocity Impact **Acceleration Technology** *and* **Application**

Abstract：**Modern acceleration techniques** *such as two and three stage light gas guns, electrostatic and plasma accelerators, and shaped charge launchers etc., are reviewed and discussed with respect to their projectile mass and velocity ranges and their* **applicability** *for the experimental simulation of*

hypervelocity impacts. The results of spacecraft space debris shield configuration, as well as pressure vessel damage behavior characteristic under hypervelocity impact conditions are presented as **applications**.

Key words: ***acceleration technique***; ***hypervelocity impact***; *spacecraft*; *space debris*

超高速撞击加速技术及其应用研究

摘要：给出了二级轻气炮、三级轻气炮、静电加速器、等离子体加速器和聚能加速器等现代加速技术的原理,讨论了它们的弹丸质量和速度范围以及在超高速撞击实验中的应用。作为应用的例子给出了超高速撞击条件下航天器空间碎片防护结构以及压力容器损伤特性实验研究的结果。

关键词：加速技术；空间碎片；超高速撞击；航天器

修改后的标题、摘要和关键词：

Hypervelocity **Impact Acceleration Techniques** and Their **Application**

Abstract: Modern **acceleration techniques**, such as two and three stage light gas guns, electrostatic and plasma accelerators, and shaped charge launchers etc., are reviewed and discussed with respect to their projectile mass and velocity ranges and their applicability for the experimental simulation of hypervelocity **impact**. The results of spacecraft space debris shield configuration, as well as pressure vessel damage behavior characteristic under hypervelocity impact conditions, are presented as examples of **application**.

Key words: **acceleration techniques**; hypervelocity impact; spacecraft; space debris

实例2

Trajectory Optimization Strategies for **Supercavitation Vehicles**

Abstract: ***Supercavitating vehicles*** *are characterized by substantially reduced hydrodynamic drag with respect to fully wetted underwater vehicles.*

Drag is localized at the nose of the vehicle, where a cavitator generates a cavity that completely envelopes the body....

（修改准则：在 supercavitation 和 supercavitating 中选用一个，选择的标准是看哪一个是行业中惯用的。术语的使用要一致。）

实例3

Joint Source-channel** Coding Suing Residual Redundancy over Noisy **Channels

***Abstract**: The effect of the residual redundancy on the source and channel coding was investigated, and a joint **source/channel** coding **scheme** was proposed based on variable length codes (VLC). This **scheme** utilized the residual redundancy at the output of the source coder to provide error protection for image transmission over noisy **channel**. Comparing with **system** proposed by Sayood K, this **technique** was more universal **because of** utilizing improved convolutional decoding and non-Huffman. Experimental results show that joint coding **system** can achieve higher performance gain than the conventional separate coding system.*

***Key words**: **vector quantization**; variable length codes; error protection; **joint source/channel coding**; residual redundancy*

噪声信道中基于残留冗余的联合信源信道编码

摘要：对残留冗余带给信源信道编码的影响进行了研究，并基于可变长度代码提出了一个联合信源信道编码系统，该系统利用信源编码器输出中的残留冗余为图像传输提供差错保护。与 Sayood K 提出的系统相比，由于该系统利用了改进的联合卷积软解码以及非霍夫曼码的通用可变长码，它更具有普遍性，实验结果表明，联合信源信道编码系统可获得比传统的分离编码系统更高的性能增益。

关键词：矢量量化；可变长编码；差错保护；联合信源信道编码；残留冗余

修改后的标题、摘要和关键词：

Joint Source-channel Coding Suing Residual Redundancy over Noisy Channels

Abstract: The effect of the residual redundancy on the source and channel coding was investigated, and a joint source-channel coding **system** was proposed based on variable length codes (VLC). This system utilized the residual redundancy at the output of the source coder to provide error protection for image transmission over noisy channels. Compared with the system proposed by Sayood K, this **system** was more universal by utilizing improved convolutional decoding and non-Huffman. Experimental results show that the joint coding **system** can achieve higher performance gain than the conventional separate coding system.

Key words: variable length codes; error protection; joint source-channel coding **system**; residual redundancy

实例4

*Power Allocation Scheme for Multiple **Spotbeam** Satellite Communication **Systems** with Coexisting Unicast and Multicast Flows*

Abstract**: A multi-objective optimization power allocation scheme **was** proposed for multiple **spot beam** satellite communication system supporting both unicast and multicast flows. **In consideration of** coherence of each multicast flow in different beams, fairness of different flows sharing uplink **bandwidth and** average transmission rate of all flows, a mathematical model with three objective functions was **constructed, and** a non-dominated sorting genetic algorithm II (NSGA-II) was adopted to solve optimal power set. Simulation results show that this scheme achieves high fairness and multicast coherence, and largely improves average session rate in comparison with the existing schemes. Moreover, the scheme has high convergence speed and **satisfies the situation that network traffic is dynamically changed.

***Key words**: communication; multiple **spot-beam** satellite **system**; power allocation; multi-objective optimization; non-dominated sorting genetic algorithm-II*

单播组播共存环境下的多波束卫星功率优化分配

摘要：针对多波束卫星通信系统单播组播共存情况下的功率分配问题，提出了一种多目标优化设计方案。考虑同一组播流在不同波束下的一致性、数据流之间共享关口站上行链路带宽的公平性以及各个业务流的平均速率，构造了具有三项目标函数的数学模型，并采用了非支配排序遗传算法(NSGA-Ⅱ)来实现最佳功率集。仿真结果表明,同现有的方案相比,该方案在组播一致性、带宽公平性以及平均业务速率方面均取得了较好的性能,而且此算法的收敛速度较快,可适应网络业务量动态变化的需求。

关键词:通信技术;多波束卫星系统;功率分配;多目标优化;非支配排序遗传算法-Ⅱ

修改后的标题、摘要和关键词:

Power Allocation Scheme for Multiple **Spot-beam** Satellite Communication **System** with Coexisting Unicast and Multicast Flows

Abstract: A multi-objective optimization power allocation scheme **is** proposed for multiple **spot-beam** satellite communication system supporting both unicast and multicast flows. **Considering** coherence of each multicast flow in different beams, fairness of different flows sharing uplink bandwidth, and average transmission rate of all flows, a mathematical model with three objective functions **was constructed.** A non-dominated sorting genetic algorithm Ⅱ (NSGA-Ⅱ) was adopted to solve optimal power set. Simulation results show that this scheme achieves high fairness and multicast coherence and largely improves average session rate in comparison with the existing schemes. **The high convergence speed scheme could satisfy the requirements for the dynamically changed network traffic.**

Key words: communication; multiple spot-beam satellite system; power allocation; multi-objective optimization; non-dominated sorting genetic algorithm-Ⅱ

实例5

*Airport Delay Prediction Based on **Spatiotemporal** Analysis and **Bi-LSTM** Sequence Learning*

***Abstract**: The air traffic network is the small-world system whose delay propagates among the entire network quickly. These frequent delays bring huge economic and resources loss. Therefore, accurately predicting the airport delay is essential for the airlines or air traffic controllers to adjust* flight schedules. This paper proposes a **multi-step** deep sequence learning model (**Bi-LSTM+Seq2Seq**) to predict airport delay which considers the **spatial-temporal** correlation of other airports in the network. Firstly, the dataset is processed to analyze the temporal delay correlations of airports based on the complex network theory. The PageRank and K-means **algorithm** are used to **cluster** the behavior of the networks and to know the state of the entire network. Secondly, based on time series data about the current state of the network and delay relationship between airports, the **Bi-LSTM+Seq2Seq** model has been proposed and trained. Through the experiments, the proposed model has better accuracy and stability compared with other prediction algorithms.

Key words: **delay network**; spatiotemporal analysis; **cluster**; **multistep prediction**; Seq2seq+ **Bi-LSTM**

基于时空分析和 Bi-LSTM 序列学习的机场延误预测

摘要:空中交通网络是一个小世界系统,它的时延在整个网络中快速传播。这些频繁的延误带来了巨大的经济和资源损失。因此,准确预测机场延误对于航空公司或空中交通管制人员调整航班时刻表至关重要。本文提出了一种多步深度序列学习模型(Bi-LSTM+Seq2Seq)来预测机场延误,该模型考虑了网络中其他机场的时空相关性。首先,利用复杂网络理论对数据集进行处理,分析机场时间延迟相关性。PageRank 和 K-means 算法用于对网络的行为进行聚类,并了解整个网络的状态。其次,基于网络当前状态的时间序列数据和机场之间的延迟关系,提出并训练 Bi-LSTM+Seq2Seq 模型。通过实验,与其他预测算法相比,该模型具有更好的精度和稳定性。

关键词:延迟网络;时空分析;聚类;多步预测;Seq2seq+ **Bi-LSTM**

修改后的标题、摘要和关键词:

Airport Delay Prediction Based on **Spatiotemporal** Analysis and Bi-LSTM Sequence Learning

Abstract: The air traffic network is a **small world** system whose delay propagates among the entire network quickly. These frequent delays bring huge economic and resources loss. Therefore, accurately predicting the airport delay is essential for the airlines or air traffic controllers to adjust flight schedules. This paper proposes a **multi-step** deep sequence learning model (**Bi-LSTM+Seq2Seq**) to predict airport delay which considers the **spatialtemporal** correlation of other airports in the network. Firstly, the dataset is processed to analyze the temporal delay correlations of airports based on the complex network theory. The PageRank and K-means **algorithms** are used to **cluster** the behavior of the networks and to know the state of the entire network. Secondly, based on time series data about the current state of the network and delay relationship between airports, the **Bi-LSTM+Seq2Seq** model has been proposed and trained. Through the experiments, the proposed model has better accuracy and stability compared with other prediction algorithms.

Key words: **delay prediction**; spatiotemporal analysis; **multi-step prediction**; **Bi-LSTM+Seq2Seq**

5. 标题写作的综合练习
需修改的标题：

(1) *Aerodynamic Performance Analysis of Low Pressure Turbine at Low Reynolds Numbers*
低雷诺数条件下低压涡轮气动性能分析

(2) *A Comprehensive Overview of Unsupervised and Hybrid Methods for Intrusion Detection*
对入侵检测中无监督和混合方法的全面综述

(3) *Research of Identification Method for Irregular-Closed Graphics Based on Contour Measurement Matrix*
基于轮廓测量矩阵的不规则封闭图形辨识方法的研究

(4) *Molecular Dynamics Study on the 60° Dislocation Motion in Si Crystal*
Si 晶体中 60°脱位运动的分子动力学研究

(5) *Performance Analysis of the New Whole-Spacecraft Isolator*
新型全航天器隔离器性能分析

(6) *Study on Phase Centers Calibration of K-band Ranging System*
K 波段测距系统的相位中心校准研究

(7) *Understanding the Impact of Interdependence and Differentiation on Subunits-Level Performance after IS Implementation*
IS 实施后组织单元间的相互依赖和分化对子单元级性能的影响

(8) *How Windows Influence the Expression of Buildings*
窗户对楼房外观的影响

(9) *EI Database and How the Scientific Paper can Be Included by It*
EI 数据库以及科技论文如何被其收录

可供参考的修改后的标题：

(1) The Aerodynamic Performance of Low Pressure Turbine at Low Reynolds Numbers

(2) Overview of Unsupervised and Hybrid Methods for Intrusion Detection

(3) Identification Method for Irregular-Closed Graphics Based on Contour Measurement Matrix

(4) Molecular Dynamics of the 60° Dislocation Motion in Si Crystal

(5) Performance of the New Whole-Spacecraft Isolator

(6) Phase Centers Calibration of K-band Ranging System

(7) The Impact of Interdependence and Differentiation on Subunits-Level Performance after IS Implementation

(8) Window Influence on the Expression of Buildings

(9) EI Database and Its Inclusion of Scientific Papers

2.1.2　作者姓名和所在单位

作者（主要作者）姓名和所在单位要居中写在标题下方，与标题间的间距是双倍，如果是两个以上的作者，姓名之间要用逗号分开，除非最后一个人的姓名和前面的姓名之间有 and。

例如:
Ducks Over-Winter in Colorado Barley Fields in Response to Increased Daily Mean Temperature

Ima Mallard, Ura Drake, and Woodruff Ducque
Department of Wildlife Biology, University of Colorado-Boulder

1. 作者身份(顺序)

尽管第一作者是人人向往的,但作者的先后顺序还是取决于其对科研项目的贡献,如在概念的形成、设计、实施和/或解释中的贡献大小;也取决于是否愿意对研究的后果承担责任。

通常的写法是:
Janet Di Marci, Louis Hernandez, Arthur Smith, and Zhou Wen

2. 作者所在单位和相关作者

实例(两个作者及其所在的单位)
Chu Wen[1]* and John Done[2] $
Departments of Biostatistics[1] and Chemistry[2]
University of the Atlantic Baltimore, MD
* current address: Dept. of Chemistry, University of the Pacific, Palo Alto, CA
$ to whom correspondence should be addressed

2.2 摘要的撰写

摘要是你对你的工作的一个完整、准确而又内容丰富的叙述,也就是说,它浓缩了全文的内容,使读者在不借助全文的情况下就能对全文的主要内容有一个完整的了解。它不仅对全文的内容起导航的作用,而且也是论文的缩略本,包含了读者可以用以确定如下内容所需要的所有信息:

(1)研究的目的是什么?
- 你要研究的问题(或目的)(来自论文的引言部分);
- 在开头的第一、二句中清楚地阐述研究的目的。

(2)研究是如何进行的?
- 实验设计和使用的方法(来自论文的方法部分);
- 清楚地表明基本的研究方案;
- 说明或简要描述使用的基本方法,但不要过细,只指出使用的主要技术。

(3) 获得的研究结果是什么？
- 主要的发现，包括重要的定量性结果或趋势/倾向（来自论文的结果部分）；
- 报道那些能回答你所提出的问题的结果；
- 指出趋势、相关的变化或不同之处等。

(4) 得出的结果所表明的意义是什么？
- 简单地概述一下你对上述研究结果的解释和得出的结论（来自论文的讨论/结论部分）；
- 明确地说明你的研究成果所回答的问题、意味着什么或可能产生的影响。

每一篇科技论文，包括你在课堂以及会议上的演讲，开头的时候都有一个摘要，以便读者充分了解你的文章内容，从而做出决定：是否值得进一步阅读或聆听你的文章。摘要也会出现在全文不出现的参考书中，以便读者在阅读了这类参考书后确定是否需要向摘要的作者索要全文。此外，随着摘要数据库或目前广泛使用的在线出版数据库的出现，很多读者读到的也许会是与全文相脱离的摘要，因此，写出一篇优秀的摘要对于激励读者去索要你的原文、阅读你的原文、引用你的文章都是至关重要的。由此可以看出，与一二十年前相比，写好一篇摘要已经变得更加重要。除了上述原因之外，由于科学家常常可以通过各类计算机从提供摘要服务的部门获取摘要，因此摘要的写作就更要谨慎，更要简洁，用尽量少的文字获得最大的效果。

摘要不是概要。概要可以出现在文章的结尾，而且是对重要发现和结论的一种重述；不同于摘要，概要不包括经过提炼的诸如研究背景、目的或方法等方面的信息。也不要把摘要混同于书评，摘要中不包含有对文章的评论或评价。

尽管摘要出现在文章的开头，但多数作者是在写完论文的最后一部分之后才开始写摘要的。

在2.1.1一节中我们曾经指出过，标题只是作者对文章的内容做的最简单的陈述，而摘要给作者提供了就文章的每一重要部分做出阐述的机会。摘要的长度通常在200～300字之间（这是典型的标准期刊中摘要的长度）。要尽可能地把你对文章主要部分（如目的、方法、结果等）的阐述限制在两三句话内。因为摘要有助于读者确定是否会继续去读文章的其他部分，或确定是否把摘要看作是他们通过电子文献搜索或在已出版的摘要汇编中查找所要的资料的唯一依托，所以摘要不能遗漏重要的信息（如主要结果、观察到的事实、从中发现的倾向等）。这样才能使摘要有针对性地服务于那些需要了解你的研究动态的人。

2.2.1 摘要的功能

同时兼有双重目的的摘要无论是对专业人员还是对非专业人员都是十分重要的。摘要既概述了文章的内容，又同时起着为文章做宣传的作用。在很多时候，学术刊物中的摘要都与原文分离，摘要也就成了唯一为大家所熟知的永久记录科研成果的文本，因此它应该具有独立性。

摘要通常会包含下列要素：背景知识、材料和方法、研究结果和结论/讨论。现在越来越多的期刊和会议明确提出使用"结构式摘要"，即要有标题（参看后面的摘要例文）。其他类型的摘要在格式上的要求可能没有那么严格,但也都要求具有信息性、完整性、清晰性、准确性和结构的严谨性。

摘要通常是由文章的作者来完成的,但有时由作者写出的摘要也可能被从事摘要节录的机构选用,重新摘录,如现在越来越多的科研领域习惯把摘要单独发表在硬拷贝(hard copy)或电子数据库(electronic databases)中。研究者通过浏览这类数据库来阅读摘要,从而决定是否需要阅读全文。有些期刊的摘要不单单用一种语言,如一些中文和日文的刊物会用两种语言来发表摘要。

因此,摘要应具有下面的功能。

1. 有助于筛选文献

摘要首先起到筛子的作用,它以快捷的方式帮助读者了解原文的内容,以便读者能在最短的时间内决定是否要进一步去读原文。由于通读全文十分耗时,因此,一篇写得好的、能够提供充足信息的摘要有助于读者节省宝贵的时间和精力。

2. 体现独立、完整文本的特征

摘要的另一重要作用是它可以作为独立的文本来使用。如果读者在阅读完摘要后觉得不值得去阅读全文,但值得记住以便之后参考,那么读者就可以把这类摘要存储在其文档中,以备以后之用,甚至可能在不阅读全文的情况下摘用其中的某些内容。

3. 发挥预览的作用

即使读者认为有必要去阅读全文,写好摘要也是有很多好处的。好的摘要发挥着导读的作用,它使读者能够了解文章的整体结构,使读者在重要观点出现时有一个心理准备。

4. 有助于索引的编排

摘要的另一功能在于它有助于索引的编排。索引的编排(无论是单位内的图书馆,还是大型公共图书馆,如国家级的图书馆)常常依据作者写的摘要来选定用于对照索引(for cross-indexing)的关键词和短语。文章摘要写得好坏直接关系到作者的文章是否能被合理地编入索引,进而直接关系到该文章是否能被需要此类信息的研究者阅读到。

在信息"爆炸"的时代,很多研究者常常会只读文章的摘要。

2.2.2 有效摘要所具有的特征

一篇摘要总是同标题一起被阅读,因此摘要不该重复标题(包括内容相同、措辞不同的标题)。由于摘要很可能与文献的其他部分分开来被阅读,因此摘要要写得独立、完整,要用简练、完整的句子,要迅速切入主题。由于摘要的长度在 200~300 字之间,因此摘要通常为一段。

(1)摘要中不要涉及文本中没有涉及的信息。

(2)摘要中尽量回避商标(trade names)、首字母缩写词、缩写词、符号等。否则,你需要对它们进行解释,这样会占用很大篇幅。

(3)使用文本中的词做关键词。关键词的选用要慎重,因为关键词是给原素材做索引用的。因此,关键词的选用要便于他人有更多的机会引用你的文章。

（4）展开到位的摘要应该是统一、连贯、简洁、自成一体的。

（5）采用引言/主要部分/结论式的结构,以此来体现文章的目的、结果、结论和建议这样的结构特征。

（6）要严格遵循原文的展开顺序。

（7）所含信息之间要使用逻辑衔接词来连接。

（8）不要加入与原文无关的新信息,只对原文进行概述。

（9）做到大多数读者能读懂。

（10）摘要中不应包含过多的背景知识,无关文献的参考,省略的或不完整的句子,会使读者感到困惑的缩写词或术语,各类图解、图形、表格及与其相关的内容。

2.2.3 摘要的类型

目前被广泛使用、描述的摘要的类型有很多。尽管有一种学派认为,只有指示型摘要和信息型摘要才算得上是真正的摘要,本书也会评论性地介绍一些其他类型的摘要,如指示-信息型摘要、评论型摘要、袖珍型摘要、结构型摘要以及学位论文型摘要。要记住,无论在何种情况下,选择摘要类型的标准是:原文的性质是什么,你想要原文发挥什么样的作用,以及可能的读者是谁。因此,我们将在此探讨不止一种类型的摘要。还有一点需要说明,摘要的类型并不仅限于我们讨论的这些,而且有时一篇摘要体现了不止一种摘要类型的特征。

1. 指示/描述型摘要

指示型摘要(有时也叫作描述型摘要)向读者传递的是原文包含了哪方面的信息,如有关目的、方法以及研究范围等。指示型摘要不提供详细而精确的数据、研究结果、结论或建议。这类摘要要写得简短,读者从中可以决定他们是否需要进一步地去阅读整篇论文。这类摘要要做的就是向读者介绍论文的主题是什么。而要想了解作者的研究结果、结论或建议的读者就必须去阅读全文。

指示型摘要中不会写出下面这类句子:

> Based on an exhaustive review of currently available products, this report concludes that none of the available grammar-checking software products provides any useful function to writers.
>
> Table 1 shows that the most common source of infection is disks brought from home.

(这是你在信息型摘要中才会发现的摘要类型。)

相反,指示型摘要要写成:

> This report provides conclusions and recommendations on the grammar-checking software that is currently available.

本报告包括对现有的语法校验软件调查后的结论和建议。

> Table 1 shows the most common modes of infection.

表一列举了最常见的计算机病毒感染类型。

指示型摘要的例子:

实例 1

Pattern Recognition Using Pulse-coupled Neural Networks Anddiscrete Fourier Transforms

Abstract: A novel method for pattern recognition using discrete Fourier transforms on the global pulse signal of a pulse-coupled neural network (PCNN) is presented in this paper. We describe the mathematical model of the PCNN and an original way of analyzing the pulse of the network in order to achieve scale- and translation-independent recognition for isolated objects. We also analyze the error as a result of rotation. The system is used for recognizing simple geometric shapes and letters.

Key words: pattern recognition; pulse-coupled neural networks; Discrete Fourier transforms

利用脉冲偶合神经网络和离散傅立叶变换的模式识别

摘要:本文提出了一种新的模式识别方法,即在脉冲偶合神经网络(pulse-coupled neural network,PCNN)的全局脉冲信号使用离散傅立叶变换来进行模拟识别。介绍 PCNN 模型和分析网络脉冲最初方法,以完成对单个物体尺度和平移独立的识别。我们也分析了旋转带来的误差。此系统可用于识别简单的几何图形以及字母。

关键词:模式识别;脉冲偶合神经网络;离散傅立叶变换

实例 2

Customer Segmentation Framework Model Based on Data Mining

Abstract: Data mining techniques are broadly used in Customer Relationship Management (CRM) more often than ever, which enhances the capacity of customer segmentation to a new level. Since there is no unified framework model for customer segmentation by now, we review recent studies and propose one based on data mining, which is composed of space model, process model, and DFM (Data, Function, Method) model. The exploratory work in this paper provides a referential platform for further study on customer segmentation based on data mining.

Key words: customer segmentation; framework model; space model; process model; DFM model

基于数据挖掘的客户细分框架模型

摘要：数据挖掘技术在客户关系管理领域的应用日益广泛，使客户细分的能力达到了新的高度。针对目前客户细分研究中缺乏统一研究框架这一问题，本文在概括和总结现有研究的基础上提出了基于数据挖掘的客户细分框架模型。该模型主要包括空间模型、过程模型和DFM（数据、功能、方法）模型。本探索性研究工作为今后基于数据挖掘的客户细分研究提供了参考性框架平台。

关键词：客户细分；框架模型；空间逻辑模型；实现过程模型；DFM模型

实例3

Correlation between Digital Tooling and the Advancement in Architecture

Abstract: Design is a reflection of a form conceived in the designer's mind. The design process is the construction of the imagination with the assistance of some sort of tool—a drawing, physical scale model, computer model, virtual simulated animation or even mental model. The unfolding of the designer's imagination is reflective of how one reads the physical world through his/her personal experiences. Advancement in architecture is directly related to the advancement of the designer's perceptions about an ever-changing world.

While design perceptions are phenomenal and psychological, the methods or tools used to realize them are tangible and measurable. By studying the tools currently in use and those under development, we are able to depict or predict how architecture will advance in the future. This paper investigates the historical development of design tools and the current dilemma in using digital tools in design. It takes RHIKNOWBOT, a newly developed knowledge-based parametric design system, as a point of departure to examine this correlation between tool development and the development of architecture. The goal of this paper is to search the potential answers to the question most architects are asking: what is the future of architecture?

Key words: design tools; knowledge-based parametric design system; the future of architecture

<h2 style="text-align:center">数字工具与建筑设计进步的相互关系</h2>

摘要:建筑设计体现的是设计师头脑中对建筑的构造形式。建筑设计的过程是一个借助某种工具对某一想象进行构建的过程,建筑设计工具包括制图、物理尺度模型、电脑模型、虚拟模拟动画甚至是思维模型。设计师想象的呈现反映了他是如何通过个人经历来解读面对的现实世界,建筑的进步与设计师对不断变化的世界的认识密切相关。

尽管设计观念是非凡的,属于精神层面的,但是实现设计理念的方法或工具是真实的、可测量的。通过对现在应用中的和正处于开发阶段的设计工具的研究,我们可以描述或者预测未来设计将如何发展。本文研究了设计工具发展的历史,并对当今设计领域对数字工具使用的问题进行了研究。以一套新开发的、基于参数设计系统的自动化设计工具——RHIKNOWBOT——为起点,来研究数字工具的发展和建筑发展之间的关系。本文的目的就是要为大多数建筑设计师都会提出的问题寻找答案:建筑设计的未来是什么。

关键词:设计工具;基于知识的参数设计系统;建筑设计的未来

实例4

<h2 style="text-align:center">Overview of Unsupervised Methods: From Intrusion Detection to Attacker Attribution</h2>

Abstract: Over the last five years there has been an increase in the frequency and diversity of network attacks. This holds true, as more and more organizations admit compromises on a daily basis. Many misuse and anomaly based intrusion detection systems (IDSs) that rely on either signatures, supervised or statistical methods have been proposed in the literature, but their trustworthiness is debatable. Moreover, as this paper uncovers, the current IDSs are based on obsolete attack classes that do not reflect the current attack trends. For these reasons, this paper provides a comprehensive overview of unsupervised and hybrid methods for intrusion detection, discussing their potential in the domain. We also present and highlight the importance of feature engineering techniques that have been proposed for intrusion detection. Furthermore, we discuss that current IDSs should evolve from simple detection to correlation and attribution. We descant how IDS data could be used to reconstruct and correlate attacks to identify attackers, with the use of advanced data analytics techniques. Finally, we argue how the present IDS attack classes can be extended to match the modern attacks and propose three new classes regarding the outgoing network communication.

Key words: Anomaly IDSs; Correlation and Attribution; Attack Reconstruction; Digital Forensics; Network Forensics; Data Analytics; Unsupervised Learning; Feature Selection

无监督法综述：从入侵检测到攻击者属性

摘要：近五年来，网络攻击的频率和多样性不断增加。越来越多的组织不得不在日常生活中妥协已是事实。文献中提出了许多基于误用和异常的入侵检测系统（IDSs），它们依赖于签名、监控或统计等方法，但它们的可信性值得商榷。此外，正如本文揭示的，目前的入侵检测系统基于过时的攻击类，这些攻击类不能反映当前的攻击趋势。因此，本文对入侵检测中的无监督和混合方法进行了全面的综述，并对其在领域的应用进行了讨论。同时，我们还介绍并强调了特征工程技术在入侵检测中的重要作用，进一步论述了当前入侵检测应该从简单检测发展到相关性和属性。我们描述了如何使用先进的数据分析技术，利用IDSs数据来重建和关联攻击以识别攻击者。最后，我们讨论了如何扩展现有的IDSs攻击类以匹配现代攻击，并提出了三个新的种类来实现对外网络通信。

关键词：异常入侵检测；相关性和属性；攻击重建；数字取证；网络取证；数据分析；无监督学习；特征选择

2. 信息型摘要

信息型摘要是指示型摘要的扩展。除了关于目的、研究范围和使用的方法外，信息型摘要还要给出原文的研究结果、结论和建议。给出的结论、结果和建议要具体，要给出主要的数据、具体的结果和方法。如果使用的是新的研究方法，要提供新方法运作的原理和范围。信息型摘要包含主要的统计细节，对原文每个重要章节的重要信息都要进行概述。

信息型摘要中要去掉：
（1）介绍性的说明（除非那是论文主干部分的焦点）；
（2）定义和其他背景性的信息（如果这些内容不是论文的主要焦点）；
（3）表明所借用的原始资料来源的说明；

(4)与结论和建议有关的细节;
(5)图表、曲线图或表格。

信息型摘要的例子:

实例1

Surface Modification of Nanophase Hydroxyapatite with Chitosan

Abstract: Nanophase hydroxyapatite (Hap) particles were aged in 0~2.5 wt% chitosan acetate solutions for 30 days to evaluate the influence of chitosan on Hap surface chemistry. The Hap characterization results from Fourier transform infra-red spectroscopy (FTIR), thermal gravimetric analysis (TGA), Carbon-Hydrogen-Nitrogen (CHN) analysis, and BET N_2 adsorption revealed measurable changes in the Hap surface chemistry after aging in the chitosan acetate solutions. The TGA mass loss exhibited by Hap increased from 3.3~6.5 mass% as the chitosan acetate gel concentration increased from 0~2.5 mass%. The CHN analysis revealed an increase in C and H contents with increasing chitosan acetate concentration while the N concentration remained relatively constant (0.30~0.32 mass%). Chitosan interaction with Hap caused an increase in specific surface area from 85 m^2/g up to 160 m^2/g for Hap aged in 1.5 mass% chitosan acetate solution (Hap 1.5). Chitosan exhibits strong adsorption interactions with Hap and enhances colloid stability for processing of chitosan/hydroxyapatite nanocomposites.

Key words: Surface modification; Hydroxyapatite; Chitosan; Nanocomposites; Adsorption

壳聚糖修复羟基磷灰石纳米颗粒表面

摘要:羟基磷灰石纳米颗粒在浓度0~2.5 wt%的壳聚糖酸溶液里时效处理30天,来评价壳聚糖对羟基磷灰石表面化学性能的影响。傅立叶红外光谱分析、热重量分析、碳-氢-氮分析和吸附氮气的分析结果显示,在壳聚糖醋酸溶液中时效的羟基磷灰石纳米相表面化学性质有可测量的变化。热质量分析的质量损失表明,随壳聚糖醋酸胶体浓度从0~2.5%开始增加,羟基磷灰石纳米相质量从3.3~6.5%开始增加。碳-氢-氮分析结果显示随壳聚糖醋酸胶体浓度的增加和氢的含量增加而氮的浓度相对恒定(质量百分比为0.30~0.32),在浓度为1.5%(质量分数)壳聚糖醋酸溶液中时效的羟基磷灰石,由于壳聚糖与羟基磷灰石纳米相的相互作用,表面积从85 m^2/g 增加到160 m^2/g。壳聚糖羟基磷灰石纳米相之间强吸附作用,能明显增加壳聚糖羟基磷灰石纳米化合物胶体的稳定性。

关键词:表面修正;羟基磷灰石;壳聚糖;纳米化合物;吸附

实例2

Effects of Radiated Cotton Cellulose on Properties of Nitrocellulose

Abstract: The aim of the determination is to study effects of radiated cotton cellulose by high energy electron on properties of nitrocellulose (NC). The nitrocellulose was prepared by the $N_2O_5-HNO_3$ system and then radiated by high energy electrons. The viscosity of NC was determined by viscometry, and the nitrogen content was determined by polarizing microscope method, respectively. Results indicate that the viscosity of NC changes from 0.598 Pa·s to 0.036 Pa·s as the absorption dose varies from 0 kGy to 14 kGy, while the nitrogen content of NC is retained basically. The emperic relationship between the viscosity of NC and doses of absorption was obtained; it is $\eta = 354.8 D^{-0.97}$. Under a certain nitrating condition, the nitrogen content and homogeneity of NC are retained basically with different doses of absorption.

Key words: Radiated Cotton Cellulose; Properties of Nitrocellulose; high energy electron

高能电子辐射处理过的棉纤维素对硝化纤维素性能的影响

摘要:本测定的目的是要研究用高能电子辐射预处理精制棉纤维素对制备的硝化纤维素性能的影响。硝化纤维素是用 $N_2O_5-HNO_3$ 体系制备并受高能电子辐射的。用黏度计法和偏光显微镜法分别测定硝化纤维素的黏度和含氮量。实验结果表明,当棉纤维素的吸收剂量由 0 kGy 变为 14 kGy 时,硝化纤维素的黏度从 0.598 Pa·s 降至 0.036 Pa·s,含氮量保持不变。棉纤维素的吸收剂量与硝化纤维素的黏度之间存在定量关系 $\eta = 354.8 D^{-0.97}$。在硝化条件一定时,不同的吸收剂量对硝化纤维素的含氮量及氮量均匀性没有影响。

关键词:辐射处理过的棉纤维素;硝化纤维素性能;高能电子

3. 信息-指示型摘要

信息-指示型摘要结合了信息型摘要和指示型摘要。它概括性地引入了主要的观点或具体的方法和发现,给出了足够的信息,如背景知识和条件、方法和分析以及具体的数据和研究得出的结论,以便读者参考并就此进行检验。这类摘要常常用于撰写科研论文和学位论文(但学位论文的结构略有不同)。

信息-指示型摘要的例子:

实例1

Microscopic Characterization of a TiB_2-carbon Material Composite: Raw Materials and Composite Characterization

Abstract: Titanium diboride (TiB_2) is a very attractive material for the aluminum industry, because it is readily wetted by molten aluminum and combines good physical properties (electrical conductivity), chemical (fairly resistant to dissolution by molten aluminum), and mechanical (wear resistance) properties. In this article, both raw materials (anthracite, pitch, and TiB_2 powder) and TiB_2-carbon composites (TCC) were characterized. Inclusions of aluminosilicate and iron oxide types were found in the anthracity aggregates. X-ray diffraction (XRD) analysis allowed differentiation between two types of aggregates: stratified (LC = 44 nm) and nonstratified (LC = 15 nm). The principal impurity found in the TiB_2 powder was TiCN and surface analysis of the particles revealed the presence of a contaminant layer composed of C, N, O, and Ti; the thickness of this layer varied from 5 to 15 nm. Characterization of the TiB_2 particles in the composite showed important surface modifications compared to their initial state. Evidence seen on the particles' surfaces showed that a TiC-(Otraces) formed preferentially on the side of particles rather than on top surface. The thickness of this TiC-(Otraces) layer was evaluated to 30 nm.

Key words: TiB_2-carbon material composite; Raw materials and composite characterization

TiB_2 碳基复合材料的微观特征:原材料和复合物特征

摘要:硼化钛(TiB_2)在制铝业中是一种很受欢迎的材料,因为它易于被熔融的铝润湿,而且具有好的物理性能(导电率)、化学性能(很好地抵御被熔融的铝分解)和机械性能(耐磨性)。本文讨论了原材料(无烟煤、沥青和 TiB_2 粉末)及 TiB_2 碳基复合材料(TCC)的特征。在无烟煤聚合体中发现了铝矽酸盐和铁的氧化物,由 X 射线衍射分析(XRD)可得两种聚合物的区别:层积的(LC=44 nm)和未层积的(LC=15 nm)。TiB_2 粉末中发现的主要杂质是 TiCN。另外,颗粒表面分析可见由 C、N、O 和 Ti 组成的污染层。这个污染层厚度为 5 至 15 nm 不等。复合物中 TiB_2 颗粒的特征,表明了与初始状态相比而言有很重要的表面修正。颗粒表面所见的迹象显示 TiC-(Otraces)优先在颗粒的边缘而不是顶表面形成。这个 TiC-(Otraces)层厚度据估计有 30 nm。

关键词:TiB_2 碳基复合材料;原材料和复合物特征

实例 2

A Model of Wood Flash Pyrolysis in Fluidized Bed Reactor

Abstract:With a view of exploiting renewable biomass energy as a highly efficient and clean energy, liquid fuel from bio pyrolysis, called bio-oil, is expected to play a major role in future energy supply. At present, fluidized bed technology appears to have maximum potential in producing high-quality bio-oil. A model of wood pyrolysis in a fluidized bed reactor has been developed. The effect of main operation parameters on wood pyrolysis product distribution was well simulated. The model shows that reaction temperature plays a major important role in wood pyrolysis. A good agreement between experimental and theoretical results was obtained. Particles less than 500 μm could achieve a high heating-up rate to meet flash pyrolysis demand.

Key words:Wood; Pyrolysis; Model; Fluidized Bed Reactor

流化床反应器闪速热解木材的数学模型

摘要:以开发高效、洁净可再生的生物能源为目的,在高温下分解生物质而得到的液体燃料,称为生物质油。它将在未来的能源供应上扮演主要角色。目前来看,在生产高效的生物质油的各种设备中,流化床显示出了巨大的潜在能力。一种木材高温分解流化床反应器模型已经建成。在模拟木材高温分解时产品各组分的主要参数构成上得到良好的结果。此模型显示了在木材高温分解中,反应温度为主要的影响因素,并且理论结果与实验结果具有良好的一致性。同时,粒径小于 500 μm 的粒子通过高速升温的途径,能达到闪速热解的需要。

关键词:木材;闪速热解;模型;流化床反应器

4. 结构式摘要

结构式摘要与传统摘要明显不同之处在于行文中使用了醒目的标题(黑体、全部大写、黑体全部大写或斜体),直接标出目的/背景、方法、结果、结论等。目前,结构式摘要在保健、航空等科学领域已得到普遍的认可,在临床期刊中成为主要的摘要形式。很多科学领域的期刊,如行为科学、社会科学、生物科学以及基础医学期刊也越来越多地采用这一摘要的形式。它的主要优点是便于搜索和提取到所需要的信息,因此,结构式摘要越来越受到欢迎。MLA(Modern Language Association,美国现代语言协会)在 2003 年的年会上就强烈建议使用结构式摘要,还建议当时的参会者们在下一年的年会使用这一形式提交论文。

结构式摘要能更好地提供与期刊和数据库要求相一致的信息。读者和研究者也能更有效地通过数据库找到他们所需的论文。过去作者写的摘要在内容和质量上都有很大差别,结构式摘要解决了这一问题。

针对期刊和数据库所写的结构式摘要通常要覆盖论文的主要内容,其中的四个方面是必须有的,即目的、方法、发现、价值,其他两个方面,即研究的局限性、研究的意义和应用性,可以视论文的具体情况确定有无。

具体地说,结构式摘要要能:

(1)使你在写作中做到连贯和清晰;
(2)便于读者对摘要进行评价;
(3)加速对文献研究的速度,即节省读者的时间;
(4)由于这种格式明确地划分了每一部分的内容,便于对关键要素的查寻;
(5)能真正地帮助你针对某一方面的需求获取所需要的学术资料;
(6)便于在图书馆查找到所需文本;
(7)提供从摘要层面对论文价值的评估;
(8)增加了对作为购货窗口的数据库价值量评估的透明度和准确性。

总之,结构式摘要无论是对科研者还是编辑和评审专家都有好处。结构式摘要对科研也是有好处的。它使研究者能够迅速地了解本领域的研究现状,选取那些有利于他们规划自身研究步骤的论文。结构式摘要对研究者从开始构思自己的科研到最后向同行汇报研究结果等都有帮助。结构式摘要给编辑预审论文提供了便捷的方式,也为期刊的评审专家做评审前的纵览提供了方便。

结构式摘要的例子:

实例 1

Raising Taxes to Reduce Smoking Prevalence in the US: Simulation of Anticipated Health and Economic Impacts

Objective: To estimate health and economic outcomes of raising the excise taxes on cigarettes.

Methods: We use a dynamic computer simulation model to estimate health and economic impacts of raising taxes on cigarettes (up to 100% price increase) for the entire population of the USA over 20 years. We also perform sensitivity analysis on price elasticity.

Results: a 40% tax-induced cigarette price increase would reduce smoking prevalence from 21% in 2004 to 15.2% in 2025 with large gains in cumulative life years (7 million) and quality adjusted life years (13 million) over 20 years. Total tax revenue will increase by $365 billion in that span, and total smoking-related medical costs would drop by $317 billion, resulting in total savings of $682 billion. These benefits increase greatly with larger tax increases, and tax revenues continue to rise even as smoking prevalence falls.

Conclusion: Increasing taxes on cigarettes is a unique policy intervention that reduces smoking prevalence, generates additional tax revenue, and results in significant savings in medical care costs.

Key words: Smoking; Tax; Simulation; QALYS; System dynamics; Health and Economic impacts; Price elasticity

以增税方式降低美国吸烟率:对预期健康及经济影响做仿真分析

目的:估算提高香烟的消费税对经济和健康产生的影响。

方法:我们利用计算机动态仿真模型来估算提高香烟税收(使其价格提高 100%)对今后 20 年中所有美国人所产生的健康影响和经济影响。我们还对价格弹性进行了敏感性分析。

结果:税收引致的香烟价格提升如果达到 40%,则吸烟的盛行率将由 2004 年的 21%降到 2025 年的 15.2%,并在今后的 20 年时间里使累计的寿命年和质量调整寿命年有大幅提高(分别为 700 万和 1 300 万)。期间的全部税收收入将达到 3 650 亿美元,同时,与吸烟相关的全部医疗支出将减少 3 170 亿美元,共计节省 6 820 亿美元。随着税率的提高,这笔收入会随之增加,而且在吸烟率下降的情况下,总收益也会随之增加。

结论:对香烟增税是降低吸烟率的唯一政策干预,并可以产生额外的税收收入,同时可以节省相当数量的医疗开支。

关键词:吸烟;税收;仿真;质量调整寿命;系统动态学;健康和经济影响;价格弹性

实例2

Brand Management and Challenge of Authenticity

Purpose—The purpose of this article is to provide an overview of the challenges that the widespread desire for authenticity presents for brand managers.

Design/methodology/approach—To provide a viewpoint essay.

Findings—Authenticity requires brand managers to downplay their overt marking prowess and instead to locate their brands within communities and subcultures. Brands should become members of communities and appeal to more timeless values, while also delivering to members' needs.

Research limitations/implications—Studies of how brands develop images of authenticity are needed. Case histories drawing on multiple sources of data of brands are also needed. Research into how consumers define authenticity is required.

Practical implications—Brand managers must open up their brands to members of a community, downplay their overt marketing prowess, and appeal to the timeless values of that community. Brand managers should decouple and downplay their real business acumen in favor of appealing to social norms.

Originality/value—Brand management models assume that brand marketers provide brands with meaning. This view is challenged, arguing that brand meaning is derived from the day-to-day interactions between the brand and subcultures. The article also challenges the view that marketers should necessarily appear proficient at what they do, instead calling for marketers to downplay their role in order to be more effective.

Key words: Brand management; Brand image

品牌管理对可信赖性的挑战

目的:这篇文章的目的是提出一个挑战性的观点,然后把广为流传的对可信赖性的渴望提供给品牌经理。

设计/方法:提供一篇观点性文章。

结果:可信赖性需要品牌经理淡化他们表面的市场威力,并且在社会群体和亚文化群中定位他们的品牌。品牌应该成为社会群体的成员,在满足成员需求的同时,更要依赖于所在群体的永恒价值。

研究的有限性/建议:需要研究如何发展可信赖的品牌形象,也需要提供更多的建立在有关品牌数据来源基础上的实例,还需要研究消费者是如何定义可信赖性的。

实用性建议:品牌经理必须向其团体成员公开他们的品牌,淡化他们的市场地位,更多地依赖于所在群体的永恒价值,品牌经理应该弱化他们真正的商业洞察,更多地关注于社会的规范。

独创性/价值:品牌管理模式意味着品牌销售者提供的是有意义的品牌。这个观点受到了挑战,因为它提出了品牌的意义来源于品牌和亚文化群之间的日常相互影响的观点。这篇文章也挑战了销售者有必要成为他们所在行业专家的观点,相反,本文提出销售者要想保存实力就要淡化自己的角色的观点。

关键词:品牌管理;品牌形象

实例3

Thermodynamic Properties of Sodium Sulfate-Based Complex Phase-Change Cool Storage System

Abstract: **Aim** To investigate and prepare a new material for cool storage of air conditioner in temperature range of 5℃ ~ 10℃. **Methods** The variation of phase transition temperature with the composition of the cool storage system in which $Na_2SO_4 \cdot 10H_2O$ was selected as the main component was determined, and suitable formulas were defined. Methods for preventing supercooling and segregation were studied. **Results** An eutectic salt hydrate composition comprising 80% of $Na_2SO_4 \cdot 10H_2O$, 2% ~ 8% of KCl, 5% ~ 10% of NH_4Cl, and 1% ~ 5% of $(NH_4)_2SO_4$ has a melting point of 9℃ ~ 10℃. **Conclusion** $Na_2SO_4 \cdot 10H_2O$'s transition temperature was reduced by adding salts such as KCl, NH_4Cl, $(NH_4)_2SO_4$ or NaCl. Adding a nucleating agent and a thickening agent can inhibit supercooling and eliminate segregation.

Key words: Thermodynamic Properties; Complex Phase-Change Cool Storage System

NaSO$_4$·10H$_2$O 复合相变储冷体系的热力学性质

摘要:目的 研究制备相变温度在5℃~10℃之间的新型空调储冷材料。**方法** 测定以 Na$_2$SO$_4$·10H$_2$O 为主要成分的低共熔混合体系的相变温度随组成变化的关系,确定适宜配方,研究抑制过冷和相分层现象的方法。**结果** 由质量分数为80%的 Na$_2$SO$_4$·10H$_2$O、2%~8%的 KCl、5%~10%的 NH$_4$Cl 和1%~5%的(NH$_4$)$_2$SO$_4$ 组成的低共熔水合盐体系的相变温度降至9℃~10℃。**结论** 加入无机盐 KCl、NH$_4$Cl、(NH$_4$)$_2$SO$_4$ 或 NaCl 可降低 NaSO$_4$·10H$_2$O 的相变温度。加入成核剂和增稠剂能抑制过冷和消除相分层。

关键词:热力学性质;复合相变储冷体系

5. 袖珍型摘要

袖珍型摘要是标题的扩展。一个好的标题已经很好地指出了文章的内容和众多的资料检索工具。袖珍型摘要不需要更多的分析,因此编辑起来会很快。在摘要编撰时间紧迫的情况下,袖珍型摘要就显得尤为重要。如在商业信息服务中,由一两句组成的小摘要更有价值;像电报一样简短的袖珍型摘要,由于采用了短信的形式,因而更简明。"电报"型的摘要具有简短而又明确的风格。有些简短摘要的写作采用了非常标准的形式,可以把这样的摘要看作是对计算机搜索系统的高效输入。据对袖珍型摘要使用领域的统计,相对其他领域而言,数学领域更趋向于使用袖珍型摘要。

袖珍型摘要的例子:
实例1

Numerical Solution of Fractional Integro-differential Equations by Collocation Method

Abstract: This paper deals with the numerical solution of fractional integro-differential equations of the type by polynomial spline functions.
$$D^q y(t) = p(t)y(t) + f(t) + \int_0^t K(t,s)y(s)ds, \ t \in I = [0,1]$$
We derive a system of equations that characterize the numerical solution. Some numerical examples are also provided to illustrate the results.

Key words: Integro-differential Equations; Spline functions; Collocation Method

分数阶积分微分方程配置法的数值解

本文利用多项式样条函数处理如下类型分数阶积分微分方程的数值解

$$D^q y(t) = p(t)y(t) + f(t) + \int_0^t K(t,s)y(s)\mathrm{d}s, \ t \in I = [0,1]$$

我们导出表征数值解的方程组,还给出一些数例来说明我们的结果。

关键词:分数阶积分微分方程;样条函数;配置法

实例2

Advantages of a Combined System for Metering and Regulating Heat Consumption

Abstract: Advantages are considered for a combined system for metering and regulating heat consumption, and data are given on the reduction in heat consumption without deterioration in conditions in such a system.

Key words: a Combined System; Metering and Regulating Heat Consumption

耗热量计量与调节应用组合系统的优点

摘要:分析了组合系统在耗热量计量与调节方面的优势,并给出了应用这一系统时在不降低室内品质的情况下减少热量消耗的具体数据。

关键词:组合系统;耗热量计量与调节

6.学位论文摘要

学位论文的产生要经历一个长期、复杂的过程,每一章、每一部分的写作都需要经过缜密的规划和构建,即使是论文摘要的写作也无例外,需要格外的注意。

学位论文的摘要对整个学位论文做一简要的概述,包括作者想要向读者传递的主要思想。通过阅读摘要,读者能理解论文的目的和推理。其写作一定要简洁。要做到这一点,对主题既需要有足够的了解,又要有足够的理解技巧。关于学位论文摘要的篇幅,国内的博士论文英文摘要较长,要在 500 个字以上,但按照 Dissertation Abstract International(专门刊载世界各国博士论文摘要的期刊,各国学校或科研机构可申请加入)的要求,摘要一般不超过 300 个字。

当你在给论文写摘要的时候,要记住,就整个论文而言,摘要很可能是读者最先见到的。因此,写博士论文摘要时,最好满足最基本的学位论文摘要的写作要求。下面是写学位论文摘要时应关注的:

(1)是否明确地提出或至少清楚地暗示出研究的目的?
(2)摘要是否突出了研究方法?
(3)你是否在摘要中给主要的研究方法加上了标题?
(4)是否突出地描述了研究的重点?
(5)如果你的研究是理论性的,是否在摘要中提及了这一理论?
(6)读者是否能从研究方法上看出研究是属于定性的,还是定量的?
(7)总体来说,你的摘要是否能有效地达到你的目的?

博士论文摘要的例子:

Flow-Coupled Hydraulic Transmission with Secondary Regulation Feeding Regenerative Potential Energy to the Mains

Abstract:Hydraulic regulation systems, which consist of devices such as relieve valves, throttle valves, and hydraulic motors among others, are widely used to control hydraulic drives or actuators (pumps, motors, cylinders, etc) in industrial, commercial, and residential applications. The methods of control used by these devices have been found to have resulted in much energy wastage and poor performance of hydraulic systems.

Moreover, some hydraulic vertical transport or lift systems are usually not provided with a counterweight to balance the system load. Besides, the electric motors of most hydraulic systems are oversized during design to power many loads, and whenever this machine powers less load, energy is wasted. Some of these motors in industries and commercial sectors run at a constant speed, thereby continuously using energy even during idling. In addition, the fear of near exhaustion and depletion of the naturally deposited fossil energy in future has continuously led to the rising cost of energy throughout the world. It was, as a result, these and other unmentioned problems that contribute to this project that was conceived and carried out with the aim of solving some of the probelems mentioned above.

The main objective of this research is to convert hydraulic energy to electrical energy and regenerate it back to the power line or mains. The work would also explore all the possible methods of effectively reducing or eliminating undesirable energy consumption in the system's drives and driven parts in order to improve the system regenerative energy and energy wastage. This work is supported by the national science foundation of China under Grant Number 50375033. Theoretical analysis of the past research works on energy conversion and saving in hydraulic system is presented in this dissertation. The experimental system of inverter-controlled flow coupled hydraulic transmission system with secondary regulation feeding regenerative potential energy to the mains consists mainly of 12 kW induction motor, GY A4V40 hydraulic pump/motor, and M-D 114 inverter with inbuilt filters and was constructed to verify the validity of the analytical and simulation results.

The modeling and prediction of the induction motor velocity stability at the appropriate speeds during load acceleration and deceleration are the main steps for achieving efficient stable regenerative energy that is fed to the mains. The system modeling which is mainly in three parts includes induction motor/inverter modeling, servovalve, and secondary units modeling. These predict the behavior of the system drives, particularly the velocity stability of induction motor, when subjected to different speeds and loads. The level of energy regeneration to the mains at different speeds, loads and time is also predicted during upward and downward movement of the load cylinder. The SPWM inverter modeling predicts that it helps in regenerating sinusoidal pulse waveform power to the mains as well as reducing the system harmonics, pressure surges as well as smooth starting and stopping of the system drives, hence overall improving the system process control and component life. The direction of the induction motor torque during acceleration and deceleration of the load cylinder is also presented.

The simulation of the active and reactive powers of the induction motor was performed within a periodic time during acceleration and deceleration of the load cylinder. These whole system model and simulations were carried out using PID and neural network (NN) controllers in order to evaluate their performances, and the results are presented. Our approach is also analyzed by mathematical equations to calculate the rate of energy saving and consumption of the system during the load acceleration and deceleration using experimental data measured by the three-phase electrical integrated instrument HB-33001.

During the experiments, five different tests were conducted in order to know the effects of varying system parameters such as the inverter frequency, the swash plate angle of the pump/motor, and the load stroke speed to the energy regeneration to the power line. Results showed that variation of different parameters of the system has significant regenerative energy effect.

Energy efficiencies between standard induction motors and pumps in driving flow coupled hydraulic transmission system are compared. Their values and advantages in terms of operation cost, maintenance cost, and energy saving cost are presented; and finally a novel method is considered as the best solution.

The comparison of pressure and flow coupled system is described with reference to working principle, energy saving, merit, and demerit including modeling of the pump flow rate.

Comprehensive types of adjustable speed drives (ASD) with special emphasis on variable speed drives (VSD) and energy saving techniques of VSD are also presented.

Finally, the comparison of the system performance was made using PID and NN controllers and the results showed that NN controller has a better performance in all aspects.

Key words: Energy saving; variable speed drives (VSD); SPWM; energy regeneration; hydraulic pumps/motors

基于二次调节静液传动流量耦联技术的势能回馈电能研究

摘　要

在工业、商业和建筑业中,由溢流阀、节流阀和液压马达等组成的液压控制系统广泛用于控制液压元件,来完成预定的任务。但是在实际使用过程中发现,液压设备不仅能源浪费严重,而且有些液压系统的性能较差。

有些液压垂直运输或提升系统通常不安装配重去平衡系统的负载。此外,为满足最大负载的要求,大部分液压系统的功率在设计时就是偏大的,当负载较小时,能源就浪费了。在工业和商业部门,有一些以恒定转速工作的电机,即使是在空转也在不断地消耗能源。同时,目前人们惧怕自然界储存的矿物能源加速枯竭,这使得在整个世界范围内能源价格不断地上升。正是由于这些原因,本论文提出了相应的研究课题,以便解决这些问题。本研究的主要目的是将垂直负载中下降时的重力势能转换为电能,并返回到电网中。这项工作也在寻求一切可能的方法,有效地减少或消除系统中驱动器和驱动部件中不良的能源消耗,以提高系统的能源回收和减少能源的浪费。这项研究是由中国国家自然科学基金资助的,资助号:50375033。本文综述了液压系统能源转换和节能方面的理论。相应的实验系统为基于二次调节技术的流量耦联系统。该系统能实现将回收的能量反馈至电网。该系统主要由 12 千瓦电动机、GY A4V40 液压马达/泵、内置滤波器的 M-D 114 变频器等组成。

在负载加速和减速的时候,对电机在某一适当速度下的速度稳定性的准确建模和预测是实现高效稳定的能量回收的关键。该系统建模主要围绕三个关键元件展开,即电机/变频器、电液伺服阀和液压马达/泵。该模型可以预测系统驱动特性,特别是电机在不同速度和负载时的速度稳定性。它还可预测负载液压缸在不同的速度和负载条件下的能量回收能力。变频器的建模有助于将回收的能量以正弦脉冲波形的形式回馈至电网,以及可以减少系统谐波和压力突变,有助于平稳启动和停车,从而提高了该系统的过程控制品质,延长了组件的寿命。在负载液压缸加速及减速时,电机扭矩的方向也可计算出来。

本文完成了在负载液压缸周期性加速和减速过程中的电机的仿真工作。为评估该系统的性能,本文分别使用了 PID 和单神经网络(NN)两种控制器进行建模和仿真。实验数据是通过三相集成装置 HB-33001 测得。通过对这些数据的分析,最终计算出了在负载加速和减速时能量的回收和利用比例。

实验测定了变频器的频率、液压马达/泵斜盘倾角、负载液压缸的运动速度对能量回收效果的影响。实验表明在负载减速、变频器以最小输出频率工作时,系统具有最好的能量回收能力。实验结果还表明,负载越大,系统压力越高,回收能量越多。另外,在负载减速时,其加速度的大小对能量回收的影响显著。

本文对电机和液压泵在流量耦联系统中的驱动效率进行了比较,并列出了它们在运行成本、维修成本及节能效果等方面的数据和优点,最终给出了此类系统的最优解决方案。

本文从工作原理、节能、系统的优缺点等方面,比较了二次调节静液传动压力耦联和流量耦联系统。

本文综述了调速驱动器(ASD)的类型,并特别强调了可变速驱动(VSD)及其节能技术。

最后,对 PID 和单神经网络控制器在本系统中的性能进行了比较,研究结果表明 NN 控制器在各方面都表现出了更好的性能,并通过实验验证了理论分析和计算机仿真结果的正确性。

关键词:节能;可变速驱动(VSD);正弦脉宽调制(SPWM);能量再利用;液压泵/马达

7. 会议论文摘要

会议论文摘要与其他类型的摘要有什么不同呢？会议论文摘要的写作是为了能在专业会议上宣读论文。它的长度由会议的组织者来确定,一般很少超过500字。这类摘要最好是在全文完成后再写,但有时,作者不得不在全文还未完成的情况下先写摘要,特别是在会议要求的摘要迫在眉睫的情况下。由于有时会议论文评审委员会只读摘要,而不是全文,那么你就要把摘要写得自成体系,即独立完整;要完全按照专业委员会的要求去做;要选择符合会议的主题(如,为了强调你的摘要与会议主题是密切相关,你可以在你的摘要中使用摘自于会议给出的题目或征文的词语);要仔细研究征文说明。会议征文会详细规定摘要的长度、具体的格式要求,也会说明摘要是否会被发表在会议论文集或会议录中等。不按照会议要求格式去写的论文一般不会被会议录用,因此要注意会议要求。

按照表述性摘要的基本要求,会议论文摘要也要有几句有关提交的论文与会议主题相关的话。如会议征文的主题是"19世纪的科学与文学",你要有一两句涉及你在探讨的理论方面的句子,指出对你产生影响的具体文献。如果你能把 join、junction 或 disjunction 这样的词加入到你的标题或摘要中,就会增加你论文被接收的机会,因为这样写能明确地表明你的论文与会议的主题是相吻合的。会议摘要的结尾最好是有关论文宣读的内容,如"本论文的宣读需要20分钟"等,因为会议主席最怕论文过长或过短。组织者也需要知道宣读论文时是否有特殊的技术要求,因此结尾时可以写上"本论文宣读需要20分钟,需要用×××设备播放剪辑片"等,这些都是行业内所十分欣赏的。

会议论文摘要要做的是向会议组织者通报有关你已经完成或正在进行的研究工作的情况。

(1)完整的会议论文摘要(包括标题和姓名)不要超过一页A4(21 cm×29.5 cm),页边的空白不少于2.5 cm。

(2)除非容许另一种语言,通常国际会议和研讨会上提交的摘要都用英文写。

(3)摘要必须提交电子版或者直接用电子信函寄往会务部门或某相关刊物,不交电子稿的将被拒收,当今人们很少愿意接受由计算机输出的打印件。

(4)摘要的结构形式要遵循征文提供的范例格式。

(5)多数被接收的论文的字体都用 Times New Roman,字号大小一般为10 point(有时为12 point),空间大小和长度都要符合规定(如宽为14 cm或5.5 inches,长为10 cm或4 inches)。

(6)摘要的全部内容都要写在会议要求的空间内(包括标题、作者姓名、单位、城市、省、国家、邮政编码等)。

2.2.4 摘要的组成

尽管摘要从字数上看并不多,但它却发挥着摘要后面由多页组成的论文的作用。也就是说,在多数情况下,它应该包括下面即将论述的部分,每一部分一般是一句话,当然有时也不止一句,可能要用几句。你不妨把下面讲的当作检查你所写的摘要的清单。

1. 标题

标题要简短,但应是描述性的。它指出的是与你所研究的问题相关的问题。

标题要严格地遵循摘要的内容,尽量多地传递有关研究的前后关系以及目的、内容,理想的长度是 10~12 个词,应包括研究的范围、研究计划和目标。通常最好把标题写成是对研究了什么的描述,而不是对研究结果或结论的陈述。在对已发表过的科研论文的研究中发现,那些概述研究结果的标题大部分都过度地论述了其数据的寓意(如"Approach X improves oxygenation in ARDS"),从学术上来说,这样的论述是不正确的。摘要的标题应便于读者的理解,不应该含有行话或不熟悉的首字母缩写词,例如:

Effect of Time Spent on Homework on Student Performance in Physics

2. 作者、日期、地址

K. Couch Breitbach, September 6th, 1996, General Physics, NUHS

3. 摘要中的关键词

摘要中的关键词是至关重要的。标题和摘要都要被归入电子档案中,编纂索引和录用摘要的机构也要使用关键词。因此,摘要中必须有能反映文章重要内容的关键词,以便他人能从中检索到相关的信息。

有些出版物要求有关键词,其目的有二:一是便于关键词的检索(尽管目前由于网上摘要文本搜索的广泛使用使其重要地位有所减弱),二是以此来确定论文该分配给哪位评委或编者来审阅,因此,关键词决定着文章的命运。在选择关键词的时候,一定要确定所选的关键词有助于文章被归入到该归入的类别。

关键词选得好有助于文章被合理地利用。想一想那些通过搜索五六个短语和关键词来找你文章的人是如何做的,一切就不言而喻了。要保证摘要中的关键词确实属于关键的词,这样,这些关键词才会首先出现在搜索结果的清单上。

4. 主要动机/主题/背景

用一句话来描述你要研究的主题及研究的重要性;简要地确立研究背景及其相互关系、研究的基本原理和意义。在这样的背景下表述你所研究的问题是什么、为什么关心这个问题、其结果会是什么。如果要研究的问题看上去不是大家所"十分关心"的问题,最好先表明其研究动机;但如果研究工作的重要性属于正在不断被大家所认识的范围,那么最好首先论述你要研究的问题是什么,以便指出你研究的侧重点、突破点。本部分应包括你的工作的重要性,其难点是什么,会带来什么影响等,如:

Many research papers have noted that the amount of instructional time and study time devoted to a particular school subject can influence student performance.

通常一篇论文所发表的期刊就是这篇论文产生的环境(如关于计算机的杂志 *IEEE*

通常刊载有关计算机技术方面的文章），但如果你的文章将要发表在不是通常该发表的刊物上，那么你一定要在叙述你要研究的问题同时说明你的研究可应用的研究领域是什么。

5. 具体研究的问题或相互关系（或问题的陈述）

用一两句话来描述你选定研究的问题或与本研究相关的问题：你的研究所要解决的问题是什么？你的研究规模有多大（通常采用的方法或具体适用的范围）？小心不要用过多的行话。有时把问题的陈述放在对研究动机的叙述之前，但这样的顺序安排一般是在多数读者对问题的重要性已经有所了解的前提下，如：

I investigated the effect of time engaged in homework by students on their overall performance in physics.

我研究了学生花在家庭作业上的时间对在物理专业上的表现的影响。

6. 步骤或方法

概述一下你用以进行问题研究和解决的步骤或方法；描述一下研究的广度，你做了什么或测量了什么，以及你是如何进行的；详细说明你的研究地点和时间，你如何着手于问题的解决，或者如何在你所研究的问题上取得进展；你是用仿真、分析模型、构建原型，还是为实际的产品做野外数据分析的，你的工作的广度有多大（如你的着眼点是一个应用程序还是一百个程序）；你所控制、忽略或测量了哪些重要的变量。

7. 结果

答案是什么？多数优秀的论文都会在结尾的时候具体地说明什么比什么快了百分之多少、便宜了百分之多少、小了百分之多少或好了多少，也就是用数字来表示结果。给出的重要数据要具体，不要含糊。尽可能量化给出的具体数字，少用这样的术语，如 most、some、very、small 或 significant。如果必须含糊，也只能用在改进的数量级这样的话题上。陈述那些重要的解释和发现、你的发现与最初的研究问题是如何相关联的、研究结果的局限性以及由此而得出的建议等。需要提醒的是，不要提供容易产生误解的数字。另外，摘要中也没有足够的空间来让你解释所有的建议。

8. 结论或含义

结尾的时候要对你的工作的贡献及其意义加以陈述。你的研究工作可能对相关问题或以前的研究具有意义，如你的发现表明有必要对先前的模型重新加以解释；你的结果具有普遍的应用性，还是特殊的实用性；你的答案所具有的含义是什么，它是否会改变世界，是重大的"胜利"还是仅为一次很好的尝试，或只起路标、导向的作用，或表明沿着这条路研究下去就是浪费时间（**要知道，得出上述所有的结果都是有价值的**）；你得到的结果是普遍、概括性的，还是只适用于特殊情况；等等。

也要明确表明所取得的研究结果的局限性，表明局限性的动词为 might、could、may 和 seem。

上述讲到的摘要结构适合于学术和学位论文。会议、研讨会和回忆录的摘要有时更具有不定性或描述性，不遵循这个结构。

简言之,摘要应回答下述问题:
你为什么要做这个研究或项目?
你做了什么,是如何做的?
你的发现是什么?
你的发现意味着什么?
如果你的论文是关于一个新方法或新仪器的,最后两个问题应改为:
这个方法或仪器的优点是什么?
它好在什么地方?

摘要包含的应该是你希望读者读过后能够记住的内容,即使你的读者读了全文后早已把细节忘掉,但却仍记得摘要中仅有的那几件重要的事。

为了写好摘要,你要先仔细阅读和研究他人的摘要,然后练习写自己的摘要。你可以读期刊或学位论文中的摘要,或者访问摘要数据库(如科学引文索引)。读摘要的时候,要细读,以便能更好地判断它是否具备信息性,写得好不好。你必须能辨别摘要的好坏。在写自己的摘要时,留出足够的时间修改摘要的初稿;要以读者的身份去读自己的摘要,这样才能找出存在的问题。

2.2.5 写好摘要的步骤

尽管摘要是全文的第一部分,但因为摘要是对全文的概述,应该是最后写的。开始的时候,可以按顺序从论文的每一章中摘取可概括全章的完整的句子或重要的短语,然后开始修改或增加词语使其变得连贯、清晰。

反复阅读你的全文,但心里要想着写摘要的事,重点看论文的主要部分:目的、方法、研究范围、结果、结论和建议。如果你写的是他人文章的摘要,就从文章的序言和概要部分开始。这些地方通常包含全文的重点,读完全文后,写摘要的草稿,写完前不要看你写了些什么。不能仅仅是从文章中抄写关键的句子。如果这样做,你很可能摘取了过多的信息或过少的信息。不能依赖原材料在文章中的措辞方式去写摘要,要用一种新的方法来概述信息。

关于较长的论文

有时被迫用尽量少的词语来表述要论证什么,这时你会发现你正在写的同你已经写完的是不同的,很容易与复杂的论证相脱离。你可以尝试多种形式的摘要,从中发现用什么样的方式才能提炼你的思想或重新组织你的论证。在写文章的时候,要养成一个习惯,就是习惯性地写摘要,并与你的草稿做比较。有时摘要文本会更好,因为摘要文本更能真正代表你的思想以及这些思想的逻辑结构。如果论文中失去了这些,说明你该回过头来修改你的论文。

修改

如果你发现最后修改的摘要文本与最早写的草稿摘要存在区别,又不确定该如何在这两者之间进行协调,最好的解决方法是与你的教授或同行一起来对你的材料进行回顾,尤其是当你所从事的写作计划是一项很大的工程时,最好在提交论文之前先写出最后定稿的摘要。如果你写出的摘要既连贯又清晰,而且又与论文相一致,那么你可以确信你写的文章也是清晰和连贯的。

修改草稿
- 修正结构和组织上的不足；
- 改进观点之间转折语的使用；
- 去掉不必要的信息；
- 把遗漏的重要信息加进去；
- 去掉多余的词；
- 修改语法、拼写和标点符号方面的错误。

核对工作

摘要一经写完,就要核对摘要中的信息是否与论文中的相吻合。要确定摘要中出现的**任何**信息都在论文的主要部分中出现过。

语态

"科学家多年来一直致力于寻找恰当的手法来讨论他们的发现。"此意应该写成下面的哪一种呢?

> We measured ion concentration in the blood.

或

> Ion concentration in the blood was measured.

现代学术文体倾向于采用主动语态。摘要常常也不例外,除非被动语态能减少字母和单词的总数。

2.2.6 撰写摘要的技巧

摘要必须是对全文完整而又简洁的描述,不能设想(或试图驱使)读者在只有浏览了全文之后才能获知摘要中某些含糊的陈述是什么意思。摘要必须自身意义完整,包含下述的要点:

(1)遵守字数的要求。如果摘要过长,一是可能被拒收,二是可能会被他人给修剪成规定的长度。摘要的目的只能通过作者本人的艰辛努力和剪辑才能很好地实现。作者的目的不可能由只关心把字数减少到规定的范围内的人来实现,因为他人不可能像你那样那么关心怎样才能把努力成果表现出来,所以投稿时不要超过字数的要求。通常摘要在 100～300 字之间。

(2)避免使用冗长、复杂的句子。

(3)避免过多地使用行话,可能的话,避免使用商标、首字母的缩写词、缩写词或符号。否则,你就要对此进行解释,那就会需要占用过多的空间。

(4)要确保摘要中包含所有关键词(以用于搜索数据库)。

(5)短的摘要(100～300 字)通常写成一个段落,长的摘要可写成几个段落。

(6)不要在摘要中对原文的各章节进行解释说明。

(7)避免把句子的结尾写成"...is described""...is reported"或者"...is analyzed"。

(8)摘要中不能涉及原文中没有出现的信息。

(9)用清晰、简练的方式陈述结果和结论。

（10）语言要简短，句子的开头不要写成 it is reported that、it is suggested that、it is believed that 或者 it is indicated that，因为用这四个短语开头的方式破坏了**简洁**。结果、结论或发现等的陈述要做到既清晰又简洁。在表明使用的方法时，不要对某一具体方法讲得过细。

（11）少用人称，如果你不是本领域的名人或杰出专家，尽量少用第一人称 we 和 I，少用人称以便读者更加关心你的研究、方法和结果，而不是你个人。

（12）为了体现学术性，避免使用口头语言和非正式的表达，如 get rid of、in this way、deal with 等。

（13）避免用 "Research on..."、"Study on..."、"Development of..." 等方式开头。

（14）去掉不必要的转折语，如 on the one hand、on the other hand、if... when、furthermore、at first、at last 等，避免冗长，避免由于不恰当地使用现在分词而出现无依着修饰语的句子。

（15）不要评论，不应有对文章评论或评价的内容。

（16）内容不要重复，也不要重复标题中已出现的信息。

（17）要具有信息性，提供足够的数据来支持你的结论。

（18）摘要中不能用引用语来显示所使用的原始资料；也不要有涉及有关文章的图表、表格、图形等，更不能出现原文中未出现过的任何信息。

（19）要详细说明原文包含的内容，但出于简洁的考虑，避免过细，如：

过细的实例：

> The article provides a brief background on computer technology in education, describes the Musical Instrument Digital Interface (MIDI), and covers budgeting, hardware and software needs, and facility design. It also offers additional resources for those who want more information.

（20）摘要写得要严谨。摘要被拒收的一个普遍原因就是因为写得不够严谨。有些陈述只会使人产生怀疑，以为研究还未完成，如 results will be presented、the implications will be discussed 等，写出这样的摘要是不可原谅的，一定要避免，因为将来时会使读者困惑：你的研究结果是否已经得出。摘要一旦完成，结果以及其意义都要写得十分清楚；应使用意义明确的动词，而不是那些语义含糊的词，如 deal with、developing or development 等，因为它们违反了**精确**的基本原则。

（21）如果作者认为，在摘要中提及研究步骤是至关重要的，也应仅限于对方法或使用的过程的类型加以辨识（不要过细地对使用的某一具体方法加以说明）。

（22）不要直接从原文的章节中摘取句子，而是要对重要章节中的内容或信息加以综合或重新措辞，清晰、简洁地陈述，使读者提早了解原文的内容。

（23）句子要写得完整，不要为了节省空间而省略诸如冠词之类的小词。

（24）摘要的第一句应该是关于论文的主题和范围的，接着是论文的论题或作者的关注点，然后是对每章中重要内容的概述，包括方法、步骤、结果和结论。

本节结论：写出一篇有效的摘要是一项艰苦的工作，但你会从中得到回报：会在你所从事的研究领域产生越来越大的影响，越来越多的人会读你的出版物。记住，在你的下一篇摘要中一定要包含那些好的摘要所应拥有的成分和要素。

2.2.7 标题和摘要的练习

需修改的原文 1：

Effect of Rhizobium Trifoli on the Plant Growth

*Rhizpbia are bacteria capable of inducing nitrogen-fixing modules on specific legumes. Rhizobium infections are normally restricted to specific plant species (**Djordjevic, 1987**). In this experiment, four, eight, sixteen, and twenty-four drops of Rhizobium trifoli specific to white clover were added to four different sets of white clover. We expect the set with the twenty-four drops of Rhizobium trifoli to produce the **most** mass and highest number of nodules. The mass and the number of nodules were determined after five weeks. **The sets with four and sixteen drops of Rhizobium trifoli produced the poorest result. The sets of eight and twenty-four drops produced the best result. They have the most mass and the highest number of nodules.** The **result shows** that there is a limit to how much Rhizobium trifoli can be added to allow the plant to grow to its maximum capacity.*

***Key words**: Rhizpbium trifoli; the plant growth*

根瘤菌三叶草对植物生长的影响

摘要： 根瘤菌这种细菌能诱使氮固块在特定豆科植物上产生。根瘤菌感染通常仅限于特定植物种类。在实验中,把白三叶草特有的根瘤菌三叶草分别向四组白叶草中滴入四滴、八滴、十六滴和二十四滴,我们预期二十四滴那组的小瘤产生的数量和质量都会最多。五周后我们对小瘤的数量和质量进行了测定,发现就植物性能而言,滴入四滴和十六滴根瘤菌三叶草那两组的结果最差,而滴入八滴和二十四滴的那两组结果最佳。研究结果表明,加入多少根瘤菌三叶草才能使植物生长得最好,是有一定限量的。

关键词： 根瘤菌三叶草;植物生长

修改稿:

Effect of Rhizobium Trifoli on the Plant Growth

Rhizobia are bacteria capable of inducing nitrogen-fixing modules on specific legumes. Rhizobium infections are normally restricted to specific plant species (**don't cite in the abstract**). In this experiment, four, eight, sixteen, and twenty-four drops of Rhizobium trifoli specific to white clover were added to four different sets of white clover. We expect the set with the twenty-four drops of Rhizobium trifoli to produce the **highest** mass and highest number of nodules. The mass and the number of nodules were determined after five weeks. The sets with four and sixteen drops of Rhizobium trifoli produced the poorest **results**; while the sets of eight and twenty-four drops produced the best results, in terms of plant performance. The **results show** that there is a limit to how much Rhizobium trifoli can be added to allow the plant to grow to its maximum capacity.

Key words: *Rhizpbium trifoli*; *the plant growth*

需修改的原文2:

Compact Fullk-rotundity in Some Banach Spaces

Abstract: *It is known that a Banach space X is kR (resp. LkR) if and only if it is CkR (resp. CLkR) and R. This paper gives a new method to study the properties of CkR and CLkR in Banach spaces. Some relationships between compact full k-rotundity, compact local full k-rotundity and some other geometric properties in Banach spaces are discussed.* ***It is also proved that*** *in Orlicz function spaces equipped with the Orlicz norm, the notions of compact full k-rotundity and compact local full k-rotundity coincide.* ***Moreover, it is shown that*** *Orlicz spaces equipped with the Orlicz norm are compactly fully k-rotund if and only if they are reflexive and rotund.*

Key words: *k-rotundity*; *Compact full k-rotundity*; *Property (S)*; *Local uniform rotundity*; *Orlicz spaces*; *Orlicz norm*

一些 Banach 空间中的紧全 *k*-凸性

摘要:当且仅当 **Banach** 空间 X 是紧 *k* 凸(特别是紧局部 *k* 凸)和

R 时,Banach 空间 X 是 k-凸(特别是局部 k-凸)。本文给出了一种研究 Banach 空间中紧 k-凸性和紧局部 k-凸性的新方法,并讨论了 Banach 空间中紧全 k-凸性、紧局部全 k-凸性以及其他几何特性之间的关系。在赋有 Orlicz 标准的 Orilicz 函数空间中,紧全 k-凸性与紧局部全 k-凸性是相同的,赋有 Orlicz 标准的 Orilicz 空间只有当且仅当其是自反和凸性时才是紧全 k-凸性的。

关键词:k-凸性;紧全 k-凸性;(S)性质;局部一致凸性;orlicz 空间;Orlicz 标准

修改稿:

Compact Fullk-rotundity in Some Banach Spaces

Abstract: A Banach space X is kR (resp. LkR) if and only if it is CkR (resp. CLkR) and R. This paper gives a new method to study the properties of CkR and CLkR in Banach spaces. Some relationships between compact full k-rotundity, compact local full k-rotundity, and some other geometric properties in Banach spaces are discussed. In Orlicz function spaces equipped with the Orlicz norm, the notions of compact full k-rotundity and compact local full k-rotundity coincide. Orlicz spaces equipped with the Orlicz norm are compactly fully k-rotund if and only if they are reflexive and rotund.

Key words: k-rotundity; Compact full k-rotundity; Property (**S**); Local uniform rotundity; Orlicz spaces; Orlicz norm

需修改的原文 3:

*Aerodynamic Performance **Analysis** of Low Pressure Turbine at Low Reynolds Numbers*

Abstract*: This paper calculates and analyzes the last stage of the low pressure turbine of an aero-engine at different Reynolds numbers and compares the aerodynamics performances. **By the calculations and analyses, it can be seen** that the efficiency and the load decreases greatly, the loss increases, the boundary layer gets thicker, and the loss of horseshoe vortex enhances compared with the condition at high Reynolds numbers.*

Key words: low Reynolds number; low-pressure turbine; efficiency loss

低雷诺数条件下低压涡轮气动性能分析

摘要：本文对某型航空发动机低压涡轮末级进行了不同雷诺数条件下的计算分析，对比了不同雷诺数条件下该级涡轮的气动性能。计算和分析表明，同高雷诺数条件相比，在低雷诺数条件下，低压涡轮效率和负载明显降低，损失增大，附面层变厚，马蹄涡损失增加。

关键词：低雷诺数；低压涡轮；效率损失

修改稿：

Aerodynamic Performance of Low-Pressure Turbine at Low Reynolds Numbers

Abstract: This paper calculates and analyzes the last stage of the low pressure turbine of an aero-engine at different Reynolds numbers and compares the aerodynamics performances. Calculations and analyses show that, compared with the condition at high Reynolds numbers, the efficiency and load of low-pressure turbine decrease greatly; the loss increases; the boundary layer gets thicker; and the loss of horseshoe vortex enhances under the condition of low Reynolds numbers.

Key words: low Reynolds numbers; low-pressure turbine; efficiency loss

需修改的原文4：

Research on Stability of Rotor-bearing System with Different Sliding-bearing

Abstract: **Takes** the 600MW turbine generator group model test rig rotor sustained by different bearing types as research object, this paper sets up the dynamic model of this rotor **system**, and analyzes the linear and non-linear dynamic characteristics of this rotor system sustained by cylindrical bearing, elliptical bearing and tilting pad **bearing respectively**. **It also investigates** the difference between linear and non-linear dynamic characteristics and contrastively **analyzes** the affection on rotor system in *different bearing conditions. Meanwhile, after conducting experiment research on the oil film vortex movement and vibration of the rotor system sustained by different bearing type, this paper gets the instable rule of the oil film in different bearing conditions and this is compared with the theoretical analysis result. The research result can be the reference of project design and the safety operation of turbine generator group.*

Key words: *Sliding bearing*; *Rotor-bearing system*; *Non-linear dynamic characteristics*; *Oil whirl*; *Oil film*

不同滑动轴承型式对转子系统稳定性影响研究

摘要：以不同滑动轴承形式支承的600 MW-轴承汽轮发电机组模型实验台转子为研究对象,建立了其转子-轴承系统动力学模型,分别对圆柱瓦、椭圆瓦和可倾瓦轴承支承下的转子-轴承系统进行了线性及非线性动力学特性分析,研究了线性和非线性动力学特性的差别,并对比分析了不同轴承对转子-轴承系统动力学特性影响。同时,对不同型式轴承支承下转子-轴承系统油膜涡动和油膜振荡进行了实验研究,得到了不同支承下转子-轴承系统油膜失稳规律,并与理论分析结果进行对比。研究结果为工程设计及机组安全运行提供参考。

关键词：滑动轴承;转子-轴承系统;非线性动力学特性;油膜

修改稿：

Stability of Rotor-bearing System with Different Sliding-bearing

Abstract: Taking the 600 MW turbine generator group model test rig rotor sustained by different bearing types as the research object, this paper sets up the dynamic model of this rotor system and analyzes the linear and non-linear dynamic characteristics of the rotor system sustained by cylindrical bearing, elliptical bearing, and tilting pad bearing, respectively. The difference between linear and non-linear dynamic characteristics is investigated and the affections on rotor system in different bearing conditions are also analyzed. After conducting experimental research on the oil film vortex movement and vibration of the rotor system sustained by different bearing types, the instable rule of the oil film in different bearing conditions is obtained. The rule is compared with theoretical analysis results. The results can be taken as the reference to project design and the safety operation of turbine generator group.

Key words: Sliding bearing; Rotor-bearing system; Non-linear dynamic characteristics; Oil film

需修改的原文5:

Research of Identification Method for Irregular-Closed Graphics Based on Contour Measurement Matrix

Abstract: It is a key algorithm in the field of computer vision recognition **that get** binary image and form the basis of final interpretation after pretreatment to image in the Image Pattern Recognition. **Sum up invariant on behalf of the characteristics and realize interpretation from the simple binary image**, which is the final core steps of the completion of the **identification**. A self-defined contour measurement matrix and identification method for irregular-closed graphic is proposed in this paper. The matrix optimally describes the outline geometry characteristic of graphic **outline**, a group of eccentric-rate parameter based on the matrix is **defined**, the probability density function of parameters is considered as the basis of groups. **Combining with Bayes theory, minimum-error probability classification design method is proposed. Demonstrated by application, the algorithm doesn't limited by the identified region's area, can detailed expressed characteristic of outline. It is designed to be quite flexible, reliability and operational efficiency are both good.**

Key words: Contour Measurement Matrix; Outline Geometry Characteristics; Eccentric-Rate parameters; Minimum-Error Probability

基于轮廓测量矩阵的不规则封闭图形辨识方法研究

摘要:图像模式识别中对图像进行预处理之后得到二值图像,并在图像模式识别中预处理图像后为最终解释提供依据是计算机视觉识别领域的一项关键算法。完成识别的最终核心步骤是从最简的二值图像中归纳得到能代表特征的不变量并实现解读。本文提出了一种适用于不规则封闭图形的自定义轮廓测度矩阵和识别方法。自定义轮廓测度矩阵从轮廓形态上很好地描述了不规则封闭图形的几何轮廓特性,并基于该矩阵对偏心率族参数进行了定义。把该参数的概率密度函数作为确定偏心率族参数的依据。结合 Bayes 理论论述了达到最小误差概率的设计方法。实际应用显示,该方法不依赖于辨识对象的绝对面积,故能很好地描述图形的轮廓特征形态,具有很强的适应性、可靠性和操作效率。

关键词:轮廓测度矩阵;几何轮廓特性;偏心率;最小误差概率

修改稿:

Identification Method for Irregular-Closed Graphics Based on Contour Measurement Matrix

Abstract:It is a key algorithm in the field of computer vision recognition to obtain binary image and form the basis of final interpretation after pretreatment to image in the Image Pattern Recognition. The final core steps of the completion of the identification are to sum up invariants on behalf of the characteristics and realize interpretation from the simple binary image. This paper presents a self-defined contour measurement matrix and identification method for irregular-closed graphics. The matrix optimally describes the outline geometry characteristics of graphic outline, and a group of eccentric-rate parameters based on the matrix is defined. The probability density function of parameters is considered as the bases of the groups. The minimum-error probability classification design method is proposed based on Bayes theory. Application shows that the algorithm is not limited by the identified region's area and thus can express characteristics of outline in detail with good flexibility, reliability, and operational efficiency.

Key words:Contour Measurement Matrix; Outline Geometry Characteristic; Eccentric-Rate parameters; Minimum-Error Probability

需修改的原文 6:

Discrete Ordinate Solutions of Radiative Transfer Equation

Abstract:*The discrete ordinate method of three-dimensional radiative transfer equation in absorbing-scattering medium is expounded. The **selection** of quadrature sets of in-scattering term are analysed. The causes about the formation of false scattering and ray effect and its influence on the* accuracy of solutions are also analysed. **By detailed comparison, it is shown that false scattering and ray effect exact** not only in discrete-ordinates method, but also in zone method, discrete transfer method, etc., and the influence of false scattering and ray effect on solution accuracy of radiative transfer equation can be reduced by decreasing grid size and increasing the number of solid angle discretation. The process of radiative heat transfer in a **three-dimension** rectangular furnace is simulated using discrete-ordinates method. **By comparison with zone method and discrete transfer method, it is found that** discrete-ordinates method **has** a good accuracy, **and recently is** one of the best method to simulate the process of radiative heat transfer in furnace.

Key words: radiative heat transfer; numerical simulation; discrete ordinate method

求解辐射传递方程的离散坐标解法

摘要:阐述了吸收散射性介质中三维空腔内辐射传递方程的离散坐标解法。讨论了入射散射项积分格式的选取,以及假散射和射线效应对解精度的影响。详细的比较表明,假散射和射线效应只存在于离散坐标方法中,不存在于区域法和离散传递法中;而且可以用减少网格规模和增加实角离散的方式来降低伪散射和射线对辐射传递方程解精度的影响。区域法和离散传递法比较说明,离散坐标法具有较好的精度,是目前燃烧室内辐射传热过程数值模拟的一种较好的方法。

关键词:辐射传热;数值模拟;离散坐标方法

修改稿:

Discrete Ordinate Solutions of Radiative Transfer Equation

Abstract: The discrete ordinate approximation method of three-dimensional radiative transfer equation in absorbing-scattering medium is expounded. The selections of quadrature sets of in-scattering term are analyzed. The causes of the formation of false scattering and ray effect and its influence on the accuracy of solutions are also analyzed. Detailed comparison shows that false scattering and ray effect exist not only in discrete-ordinate method, but also in zone method and discrete transfer method, etc.; and the influence of false scattering and ray effect on solution accuracy of radiative transfer equation can be reduced by decreasing grid size and increasing the number of solid angle discretation. The process of radiative heat transfer in a three-dimensional rectangular furnace is simulated using discrete-ordinates method. Comparison between zone method and discrete transfer method indicates a good accuracy of the discrete-ordinates method as one of the best method to simulate the process of radiative heat transfer in furnace.

Key words: radiative heat transfer; numerical simulation; discrete ordinate method

需修改的原文 7：

Post-process Method for Business Card Recognition Based on Fuzzy Reasoning

Abstract: *Most of the processing methods for card information use the semantic analysis, and much information is very simple on the card,* ***no semantic relation, the use of semantic analysis is not appropriate. In order to solve this problem,*** *in view of the characteristics of card information and the low recognition rate of OCR, a new **post-processing methods** based on fuzzy reasoning is proposed. This method analyzed results of text information and candidate text information gained by OCR system and the typeset page is analyzed by image-syncopated parameters provided by OCR system.* ***In the above process,*** *the fuzzy reasoning method is applied to the typeset analysis.* ***Furthermore,*** *a new type of intersection operator is designed **which is used** in fuzzy reasoning.* ***Then the final results are obtained by fusing the above information.*** *The **algorithms** on the sides of correct classification rate and identified rate **is** better than several other **commonly** business card system's,* ***this*** *method improved the accuracy of the OCR recognition and post-processing results.*

Key words: *fuzzy reasoning; the OCR; post process of recognition; classification*

基于模糊推理的名片识别后处理方法

摘要：对名片上的信息进行处理大多采用语义分析，而名片上信息多为简单信息,无语义关系,因此采用语义分析方法是不合适的。为解决这一问题,针对名片信息特点和 OCR 识别方法识别率低的问题,给出一种新的基于模糊推理的后处理方法。该方法通过对 OCR 识别得到的文本信息和候选文本信息进行文本内容分析,通过 OCR 过程中的图像切分参数进行版面分析,在分析中均采用模糊推理的方法,同时,提出一种新的模糊运算的交型算子,应用于模糊推理运算中。最后综合上述内容分析和版面分析的结果得到最终的信息分类结果。该方法在名片识别和分类正确率方面明显优于其他几种常用名片系统采用的算法,本方法提高了 OCR 识别的正确率和经后处理以后的名片信息的识别正确率。

关键词:模糊推理;OCR;后处理方法

修改稿:

Post-processing Methods for Business Card Recognition Based on Fuzzy Reasoning

Most of the processing methods for card information use the semantic analysis, but the excessive simple information on card also indicates that the use of semantic analysis is not appropriate due to the absence of semantic relation. To solve this problem, in view of the characteristics of card information and the low recognition rate of the optical character recognition (the OCR), a new post-processing method is proposed based on fuzzy reasoning. This method analyzed results of text information and candidate text information gained by OCR system, and the typeset page was analyzed by image-syncopated parameters provided by OCR system. The fuzzy reasoning method was applied to the typeset analysis. A new type of intersection operator was designed for fuzzy reasoning. The final results were obtained by fusing the above information. The algorithms on the sides of correct classification rate and identified rate are more accurate than those of several other commonly used business card systems, thus improving the accuracy of the OCR and post-processing results.

Key words: post-processing methods; fuzzy reasoning; the OCR; post precess of recognition

需修改的原文 8：

Guaranteed Cost Reliable Control with Actuator Failures

Abstract：***the*** reliable design of guaranteed cost for linear systems with actuator failures was concerned. A practical and general model of actuator failures was given. On the basis of considered influence of actuator failures, a sufficient condition of asymptotic stability with guaranteed cost control was presented. A dynamic feedback controller was designed by applying algebra Ricatti equation. ***Furthermore, when the actuators failures do not occur, the system is asymptotic stability and the performance index is good, when the actuator failures occur, the system is still asymptotic stability.*** A simulation example is given to illustrate the effectiveness of the result.

Key words：actuator failures；guaranteed cost reliable control；dynamic feedback controller；Ricatti equation

执行器故障时的保成本可靠控制

摘要：针对线性定常系统，在涉及不确定性的保成本问题基础上，提出了带有执行器故障扰动的保成本可靠控制问题（范围）。给出了更实际、更一般的故障模型。鉴于执行器故障的考虑，给出了确保成本控制的渐进稳定度的充分条件。通过求解代数 Ricatti 方程完成动态反馈控制器的设计，在执行器故障时，系统渐近稳定且具有良好的保成本指标。当系统的执行器发生故障时，系统仍保持渐近稳定且性能指数是理想的；而在无执行器故障时，系统仍然处于渐近稳定。仿真实例验证了本文的结果的有效性（方法和结果）。

关键词：执行器故障；保成本可靠控制；动态反馈控制器；Ricatti 方程

修改稿：

Guaranteed Cost Reliable Control with Actuator Failures

Abstract：The reliable design of guaranteed cost for linear systems with actuator failures was proposed. A practical and general model of actuator failures was given. In light of the influence of actuator failures, a sufficient condition of asymptotic stability with guaranteed cost control was presented. A dynamic feedback controller was designed through algebra Ricatti equation. With the actuator failures, the system is asymptotically stable, and the performance index is ideal; while without the actuator failures, the system is still asymptotically stable. Simulations verify the effectiveness of the results.

Key words: actuator failures; guaranteed cost reliable control; dynamic feedback controller; Ricatti equation

需修改的原文 9：

Method Based on Expected Value for Fuzzy Multi-sensor Information Fusion

Abstract: *Based on fuzzy multiattribute decision theory, characteristic index value and observation value of sensors are expressed with triangular fuzzy number.* ***Aimed at*** *the type recognition problem in which the characteristic values of object types and measurement of sensors are in the form of triangular fuzzy numbers, a new fusion method is proposed. The method transforms the triangular fuzzy numbers elements of decision matrix into the expected value elements. After solving the single object programming of minimizing the total deviation between the object types and the unknown object, the weights of the attributes are obtained. The result of recognition for the unknown object is given by the comprehensive attribute expected values. This method can avoid the* ***objectivity*** *of selecting attributes weights. It is straightforward and can be performed on computer easily.* ***Finally, a simulated example is given to*** *demonstrate the feasibility and practicability of the proposed method.*

Key words: *multi-sensor; information fusion; triangular fuzzy number; expected value*

基于期望值的模糊多传感器信息融合方法

摘要：利用模糊多属性决策理论，本文以三角模糊数来表征特征指标值和传感器的观测值。针对目标类型的特征指标值和传感器的测量值均为三角模糊数的多传感器类型识别问题，提出了一种新的融合方法。该方法将三角模糊数决策矩阵元素转化为期望值，通过求解目标类型与未知目标属性偏差最小的优化问题得到属性的权重，根据各目标类型的综合属性期望值给出未知目标识别结果。较好地避免了属性权重选取的主观性,计算简单,易于计算机上实现。仿真实例表明了提出的方法的有效性和实用性。

关键词:多传感器;信息融合;三角模糊数;期望值

修改稿:

Expected Values Based Information Fusion for Fuzzy Multi-sensor

Abstract: Based on fuzzy multi-attribute decision theory, the characteristic index values and the observation values of sensors are expressed with triangular fuzzy numbers. In light of the type recognition problem in which the characteristic values of object types and measurement of sensors come in the form of triangular fuzzy numbers, a new fusion method is proposed. The method transforms the triangular fuzzy number elements of decision matrix into the expected value elements. After solving the single object programming of minimizing the total deviation between the object types and the unknown object, the weights of the attributes are obtained. The results of recognition for the unknown object are given by the comprehensive attribute expected values. This method can avoid the subjectivity of selecting attributes weights. It is straightforward and can be performed on computer easily. Simulations demonstrate the feasibility and practicability of the proposed method.

Key words: multi-sensor; information fusion; triangular fuzzy numbers; expected values

需修改的原文 10:

Performance Analysis of the New Whole-Spacecraft Isolator

Abstract: *Whole-spacecraft vibration isolation is a direct and effective method **to reduce** the dynamic loads while actually launching. In this paper, a new type of isolator is designed without **any change of** the existing satellite hardware. The dynamic equations and the finite element model are given to calculate the transmissibility of the isolator with spacecraft, **and the isolating effect of different dampers is obtained**. The results show that the new type of isolator can isolate the spacecraft vibration loads effectively.*

Key words: *Isolator*; *Whole-spacecraft*; *Damper*

新型整星隔振器隔振性能分析

摘要：对整星进行振动隔离是降低作用于卫星上振动载荷的有效方法。在不改变现有卫星硬件的条件下，设计了一种新型圆盘隔振器。通过建立隔振器动力学方程及有限元模型，分析了卫星-圆盘隔振器耦合系统的复模态、振动传递率及不同阻尼对隔振效果的影响。结果表明，在不改变星箭结构条件下，新型圆盘隔振器能有效地隔离振动载荷。

关键词：隔振器；整星；阻尼

修改稿：

Performance of the New Whole-Spacecraft Isolator

Abstract: The whole-spacecraft vibration isolation is a direct and effective method for reducing the dynamic loads while actually launching. In this paper, a new type of isolator is designed without changing the existing satellite hardware. The dynamic equations and the finite element model are built to calculate the transmissibility of the isolator with spacecraft to obtain the isolating effect of different dampers. The results show that the new type of isolator can isolate the spacecraft vibration loads effectively.

Key words: Isolator; Whole-spacecraft; Dampers

需修改的原文11：

Study on Phase Centers Calibration of K-band Ranging System

Abstract: *The range and range rate between linter communication satellites can be obtained from measurement between the phase centers of K-band raging system. In practice, the phase centers could be drifted due to the difference environment between pre-launch and in-flight phase as well as vibration during launch phase et al.* **Considering this characteristic**, *the phase centers calibration of K-band ranging system during in-flight phase based on nonlinear Kalman filter was researched in detail* **while the centers** *of mass of satellites were known precisely. The associated computational simulation demonstrated that the calibration accuracy is high if appropriate parameters of sensors were designed.*

Key words：*K-band ranging system*； *phase centers*； *nonlinear Kalman filter*

星间微波测距系统相位中心在轨标定研究

摘要：星间微波测试系统能够精确测量其相位中心之间的伪距和伪距变化率，从而获得双星质心之间的距离和距离变化率。然而实际上，由于卫星的地面环境和空间环境存在差异，以及卫星发射段和入轨段的震动等原因会导致星间微波测距系统相位中心发生变化。针对这一情况，研究了当卫星质心已精确确定后，基于非线性卡尔曼滤波理论的星间微波测距系统的相位中心在轨标定。仿真结果表明，设定合适的敏感元件的参数，该方案具有较高的精度。

关键词：星间微波测距系统；相位中心；非线性卡尔曼滤波

修改稿：

Phase Centers Calibration of K-band Ranging System

Abstract：The range and range rate between linter communication satellites can be obtained from measurement between the phase centers of K-band raging system. In practice, given that the phase centers could be drifted due to the different environments between pre-launch and in-flight phase as well as vibration during launch phase, etc., the phase centers calibration of K-band ranging system during in-flight phase based on nonlinear Kalman filter was researched in detail under the condition that the centers of the mass of the satellites were known precisely. The associated computational simulations demonstrate that the design of appropriate parameters of sensors can improve the calibration accuracy.

Key words：K-band ranging system; phase centers; nonlinear Kalman filter

需修改的原文12：

An Empirical Analysis on the Impact of Real Estate Macro-control Policy

Abstract: A VAR model was formulated to study the policy **impacted** on the supply, demand and price of real estate. The currency supply and land supply were chosen in Macro-control policy study. **The study on supply and demand of real estate market chooses real estate investment and the commercial residential building selling index to build a** 3 **VAR model system that consisted of the real estate supplying, demanding and house price.** The impulse response function and variance decomposition method were used to analyze the time delay, duration and intensity of the impact on real estate supply, demand and price induced by micro-control policy. The study indicates: ① for impact on real estate supply, land supply is the most important factor; the second important factor is the interest rate, while money supply has little impact; ② for real estate demand, all the three policies have little impact; ③ for real estate price, land supply is the most important, and the other two have little impact. **As a result**, the recent key problem of real estate macro-control is land supply, **thus** the government should properly increase land supply.

Key words: real estate macro-control policy; VAR model; impulse response function; variance decomposit

我国房地产宏观调控政策效果的实证分析

摘要：利用向量自回归（VAR）模型研究宏观调控政策对我国房地产市场供需和房价的实际影响。选取利率、货币供应量和土地供给量为宏观调控政策指标；把房地产投资和商品房销售面积作为房地产市场供求指标。依据这些指标，建立了房地产供给、需求和房价3个VAR模型。利用脉冲响应函数（IRF）和方差分解（Variance Decomposition）来分析微控政策分别对房地产市场供需和房价的影响时滞、持续时间和作用强度。研究结果表明：① 就对房地产供给的影响而言，土地供给量影响最大，利率影响其次，货币供给量影响很小；② 就对房地产需求的影响而言，三种政策影响都很小；③ 就对房价的影响而言，土地供给量影响最大，其余两个政策影响都很小。结合我国当前房地产宏观调控的实践，土地供给为关键要素，建议政府适当放松土地供给量。

关键词：房地产宏观调控政策；VAR 模型；脉冲响应函数；方差分解

修改稿：

An Empirical Analysis on the Impact of Real Estate Macro-control Policy

Abstract：A VAR model was formulated to study the policy impact on the supply, demand, and price of real estate. The data of interest rate, currency supply, and land supply were chosen as the Macro-control policy indicators. The data of the real investment and the commercial building sale area were chosen as the supply and demand indicators of the real estate market. Three VAR models, including the real estate supplying, demanding, and house price, were built on the basis of these indicators. The impulse response function and variance decomposition method were used to analyze the time delay, duration and intensity of the impact on real estate supply, demand, and price induced by micro-control policy. The study indicates the following three. First, for impact on real estate supply, land supply is the most important factor; the second important factor is the interest rate, while money supply has little impact. Second, for real estate demand, all the three policies have little impact. Three, for real estate price, land supply is the most important, and the other two have little impact. As the land supply now is the the key problem of the real estate macro-control, the government should properly increase land supply.

Key words：real estate macro-control policy；VAR model；impulse response function；variance decomposition

需修改的原文 13：

The Effects of The Electrode Structure on the Properties of Contactless Conductivity Detector

Abstract：*The performance of contactless conductivity detector（CCD） depends greatly on the electrode structures. However, at present many discussions* **about** *the effects of electrode on the performance are* ***inclined to be*** *based on experimental results, and analyses in theory are relatively not* enough. In this paper a novel equivalent circuitry model of cell was presented consisting of a network of resistors and capacitors. The aim of the work reported in this contribution was a more thorough theoretical investigation of the effects of electrode structure on the performance of CCD. Through the simulation on the equivalent circuitry model, the detection sensitivity is relative to the effective length of the electrode. It was found that Faraday shield eliminates very well nonlinearity of analytes' conductance response of output current under high frequency, which optimizes the stability of current response for different analytes and detection limits. It was also found that a plateau region appears on the curve of frequency dependence of output current under effects of Faraday shields, therefore anti-jamming capability of the detector is improved. This paper will be helpful to give some theoretical guidance to improve the overall performance of CCD.

Key words: *Contactless conductivity detector*; *Electrode*; *Equivalent Circuit*; *Parameter*; *Sensitivity*

电极结构对非接触电导检测性能的影响

摘要：非接触电导检测的检测性能与检测池的电极结构密切相关。目前，电极对检测性能的影响主要从实验的角度进行讨论，缺乏理论的分析。本文提出了一种新的由电阻和电容组成的非接触电导检测池的等效电路模型，用以从理论上全面了解电极结构对非接触电导检测性能的影响。通过对检测池等效电路的仿真，发现检测灵敏度与电极的有效长度有关；法拉第屏蔽电极能够很好地消除高激发频率下低待测溶液电导值的输出电流幅值/溶液电导曲线的非线性，提高了待测溶液电导的均匀性和最低检测限，使输出电流幅值/激发频率曲线形成稳定的平台区，很好地提高了检测系统的抗干扰能力。本文对提高非接触电导检测的性能具有一定的理论指导作用。

关键词：非接触电导检测；电极；等效电路；参数；灵敏度

修改稿：

The Effects of the Electrode Structures on the Properties of Contactless Conductivity Detector

Abstract: The performance of contactless conductivity detector

(CCD) depends greatly on the electrode structures. At present, while many discussions concerning the effects of electrode on the performance are based on experimental results, analyses in theory are relatively not enough. In this paper a novel equivalent circuitry model of cells was presented (consisting of a network of resistors and capacitors) for the purpose of a more thorough theoretical investigation of the effects of electrode structures on the performance of CCD. The simulations of the equivalent circuitry model show that the detection sensitivity is relative to the effective length of the electrode. Faraday shield eliminates very well nonlinearity of analytes' conductance response of output current under high frequency, which optimizes the stability of current response for different analytes and detection limits. A plateau region appears on the curve of frequency dependence of output current under the effects of Faraday shields, improving anti-jamming capability of the detector. This paper provides some theoretical guidance for improving the overall performance of CCD.

Key words: Contactless conductivity detector; electrode; equivalent circuit; parameter; sensitivity

需修改的原文 14：

Understanding the Impact of Interdependence and Differentiation on Subunits-Level Performance after IS Implementation

Abstract: Based on the organizational information processing theory, this paper discusses the impact of interdependence and differentiation on subunits-level performance after IS implementation. **Its research points that** *the interdependence and the differentiation among subunits cannot influence the performance of subunits directly, but bring some intermediate benefits after IS implementation. In order to* **confirm** *the theoretical model and the supposition* **which this article proposed**, *this research collected data from 22 enterprises in China* **in the form of** *questionnaires and received 581 effective papers.* **It used the single factor variance analysis method to examine the outer factor influenced the interdependence on subunits-level performance and used the structure equation model (SEM) to examine the paths and hypothesis by the data collected.** *We confirmed and supplemented predecessors' theories, and presented some new conclusions and discovery.*

Key words: *Organizational Information Processing*; *Subunits*; *Performance*; *Interdependence among Subunits*; *Structure equation model*

IS 实施后单元间的相互依赖和差异对单元级绩效产生的影响

摘要:本文以组织信息处理理论为基础,探讨了单元间相互依赖和差异在单元实施 IS 后对单元级绩效的影响。单元间的相互依赖和差异不会直接对单元间绩效产生影响,但在 IS 实施后会带来一些"中间利益"。为验证本文提出的理论模型及假设,本研究通过发放问卷的方式从全国 22 家企业收集了数据,共回收有效问卷 581 份。对单因素方差进行分析,来检验外部影响因素对单元级绩效间相互依赖的影响,采用结构方程(SEM)来分析所收数据的路径和假设。验证和补充了前人的理论,并得出一些新的结论和发现。

关键词:组织信息处理理论;单元;绩效;单元间相互依赖;结构方程模型

修改稿:

The Impact of Interdependence and Differentiation on Subunits-Level Performance after IS Implementation

Abstract:Based on the organizational information processing theory, this paper discusses the impact of interdependence and differentiation on subunits-level performance after IS implementation. The interdependence and the differentiation among subunits cannot influence the performance of subunits directly, but bring some intermediate benefits after IS implementation. In order to verify the theoretical model and the supposition proposed in the article, this research collected data from 22 enterprises in China through questionnaires and received 581 effective papers. The single factor variance is analyzed to examine the outer factor influence on the interdependence between subunits-level performances. The structure equation model (SEM) is used to examine the paths and hypothesis by the data collected. We confirmed and supplemented predecessors' theories and presented some new conclusions and discovery.

Key words: Organizational Information Processing theory; Subunits; Performance; Interdependence among subunits; Structure equation model

2.3 引言/前言的撰写

引言部分引导读者由对研究领域的概括性了解深入到对研究领域具体问题的了解。引言的导航作用体现在引言首先让读者了解文章所讨论问题目前的发展状况,使读者由已发表的前期研究结果和结论,进而理解目前作者的研究的重要性,理解为什么作者目前的研究值得学术领域去关注。

很多作者会发现撰写结构式引言是他们开始撰写全文的良好开端。结构式引言使作者把必要的精力投向研究如何有效提高论文质量上。通常作者不会从前言开始,而是从后面,即作者认为知道得最多和较熟悉的部分开始。因为引言部分的结构要求非常高,因此实际上引言部分总是最后写或定稿。

1. 引言的作用

(1)为所报道的研究工作确立一个发生的背景,方法是通过对相关文献进行论述,概述一下对正在探讨的问题的理解。

(2)用提出设想、疑问或问题的方式来论述研究工作的目的。

(3)必要时,要简要地解释一下所采用的基本原理和方法,以及研究可能得出的研究成果。

实际上,引言部分必须回答下述问题:本作者目前研究的问题是什么?为什么这个问题是重要的问题?本作者之前,他人对此问题已经研究到了何种程度?本研究会如何促进学科的发展?

2. 引言的文体

尽量用主动语态。有时可以用第一人称,但应避免过多使用第一人称。

3. 引言的结构

可把引言部分的结构看作是倒置的三角形——最宽的部分在上,代表着最具概括性的信息,逐渐聚焦到所研究的具体问题。在组织引言部分的内容时,先从有关主题的概括性的信息开始;然后缩小范围,过渡到具体的能够提供有关主题背景方面的信息的内容;最后是对研究目的和基本原理的论述。也可采用另一种论述方法,即和上一种方法相反,先从具体目的开始,然后确定研究所涉及的问题产生的学术背景。这样就能很好地判断引言部分应该在什么样的学术背景、什么样水平的背景下开始。

4. 引言部分应该包括的内容

(1)首先明确地指出你所感兴趣的学科领域。方法是把标题中的关键词用在引言开头的前几句中,以便恰到好处地突出主题、确保不偏离重点、快速进入主题。如在一篇有关小鼠行为的文章中,就应该在引言的前一两句出现这样的词语:hormones 和 behavior。

(2) 简要而又恰到好处地回顾本学科已有的、已发表过的相关文献，以便使读者了解研究是在什么样的背景下进行的。关键在于要概述一下对要开始的实验或研究的具体问题你都已经知道了些什么。但不要过细，解释得也不能过繁，因为很可能在讨论部分你要进行更详细的说明。当然，什么是概括性的，什么是详细的，两者的区分本身不是一件容易的事，但随着对文献的不断阅读和了解，你会对你的读者或听众有更好的把握。如在有关小鼠行为的文章中，先从鼠类在某一行为方面的一般表现开始，过渡到具体行为，如荷尔蒙对行为的调节作用等。以从文献回顾的一般性的论述到你所感兴趣的具体问题的论述的方式，把读者的注意力引向对研究问题的目的、设想等的陈述上（从大的画面如荷尔蒙对行为调节作用的描述，到具体的如再生荷尔蒙的影响，特别是雌激素对性别行为的调节作用等）。

(3) 在对研究问题进行文献查询时要弄明白应该寻找什么样的文献，才能有助于了解某问题目前的研究现状。要把你的努力放在寻求第一手资料来源的科研期刊上，即那些发表原始科研论文的期刊上。尽管你可能要读一些综合、基础性参考资料（如百科全书、课本、实验指南、设计手册等），以便熟悉学科领域，但你的引证不能出自于这些材料，因为这类资料提供的信息都属于学科领域中最基本的或"普遍"的知识。应引用那些出自报道具体的研究结果而且与你的研究密切相关的文章。要尽快学会如何查找原始文献（科研期刊）和评论性的文章，而不是依赖于参考书。良好开端应该是从查阅论文结尾部分相关文献中的文章开始的。大部分的图书馆都提供引证索引，使你能及时地了解、跟踪你所研究的领域的最新进展。目前一些较新的搜索引擎实质上都会提醒你又出现了什么你可能感兴趣的文章。要注意，评论性文章特别有用，因为它们概述了特定研究领域在特定时间内的研究现状（一年至几年内的状况）。

(4) 条理清晰地论述调查研究的目的和/或假设是什么。如果你是写学术论文的新手，不妨依照惯例，使用这样的一些套话，如"The purpose of this study was to...."或"We investigated three possible mechanisms to explain the...."等。最好把目的的论述放在引言部分快结束的地方，它常常是引言部分中最后一段的主题句。由于 hypothesis 或 null hypothesis 这样的词语比较含蓄，而你对目的和预期的论述又是明确的，因此没必要使用这样的词。

(5) 要明确地给出用于解决研究问题的方法的基本原理。引言的最后部分应该论述目的和设想，这样就能很好地过渡到材料和/或方法部分。

你可能会这样写：

Our objective was to determine if the relationship between legumes and nitrogen-fixing bacteria is species-specific. We hypothesized that legumes would grow best when infected by the same *Rhizobium* species that it occurs within the field.

简要地论述你是通过什么途径解决问题的（如你可写"I studied oxidative respiration pathways in isolated mitochondria of cauliflower."）。通常这会出现在引言部分最后一段中对目的的论述之后。论述一下你为什么要选择此种实验或实验方案，此种模型系统在科研上有什么价值，它为你提出的问题的解答会带来什么好处。但在此不该讨论你在研究中采用的实际技术方法或草案（这些内容应该出现在材料和方法部分）。你的读者也会十分熟悉你的研究领域采用的是何种惯例的技术方法和手段,如果你采用的是**新技术或新方法**(过去没有采用过的),那么在引言部分应当说明采用的新技术或新方法相对于以前采用的方法有什么优点。

5. 一个非常好的、结构完整的引言范例

Entrepreneurial Marketing: The Critical Difference

In an article *The Harvard Business Review*, John A. Welsh and Jerry F. White remind us that "a small business is not a little big business." An entrepreneur is not a multinational conglomerate but a profit-seeking individual. To survive, he must have a different outlook and must apply different principles to his endeavors than does the president of a large or even medium-sized corporation. Not only does the scale of small and big businesses differ but small businesses also suffer from what *The Harvard Business Review* article calls "resource poverty." This is a problem and opportunity that requires an entirely different approach to marketing. Where large ad budgets are not necessary or feasible, where expensive ad production squanders limited capital, where every marketing dollar must do the work of two dollars, if not five dollars or even ten, where a person's company, capital, and material well-being are all on the line—that is, where guerrilla marketing can save the day and secure the bottom line.

(Levinson, 1984, p. 9)

在这个例子中,第一句话给出了一个能引出话题的概括性的学术话题;第二句话把话题缩小到企业家身上;第三句解释为什么说企业家和他的小企业是不同的,并就研究的问题提出了建议:实施小企业管理模式的企业家如何不同于大企业的 CEO 以及大企业的管理模式;第四句又重新把企业家的话题置于学术讨论的谈论之中,主题是"资源匮乏";第五句指出讨论这个问题的意义,并指出到目前为止,这个问题可能没有得到充分的讨论或应有的重视。作者还详细说明了他的"研究空间"同本学术议题是相吻合的。最后一句较长,但它对本文的研究领域做了准确的概述,给出了主题,即"... that is, where guerrilla marketing can save the day and secure the bottom line."。

6. 引言在学术论文中的重要性

(1)使用引言来承认引文作者的知识产权,并表示谢意;这是道德规范的问题,也可以此避免被指控剽窃他人成果。

(2)使用引言来对前作者表示敬意,引述的使用表明现作者对于本研究领域中前人所取得的成就的认可。

(3)使用引言可使作者的论述更具权威性和说服力。

(4)使用引言为被引用引言的作者提供其可研究的空间,引言间接地体现了前人都

做了什么,进而引出前人没做什么,为本研究的必要性创造了空间。

第一手资料的来源:
- 本人
- 访谈
- E-Mail 联系
- 事件
- 讨论
- 辩论
- 群体集会
- 调查
- 人为
- 物体观察(有生命的和无生命的)

第二手资料的来源:
- 参考材料
- 书籍
- CD Rom
- 百科全书
- 杂志
- 报纸
- 录像磁带
- 录音磁带
- 电视

第一手或第二手资料的来源:
- 因特网站
- 曲线图、制图、图表、表格

7. 如何在引言部分引用外来资料

在引言部分引用外来资料是非常必要的,引述的外来资料用以作为论证主题的佐证。在正文中引用的方法不止一种,都可使读者据此找到参考文献中被引用的全文,同时又不会使正文的阅读被中断。下面是如何引用外来资料的例子:

"Walnut trees are known to be allelopathic (Smith 1949, Bond et al. 1955, Jones and Green 1963)".

"Smith (1983) found that N-fixing plants could be infected by several different species of *Rhizobium*."

"Although the presence of *Rhizobium* normally increases the growth of legumes (Nguyen 1987), the opposite effect has been observed (Washington 1999)".

注意:文本之中被引用的第一、二作者的姓名只写姓,不写名;如果作者人数在两个以上,只写第一人的姓,然后用表示"**等**"的拉丁语缩写 *et al.* 来代替其他人的姓名。

从上面的第二个引用中可以看出对于某一特定的论述,引用的出处不止一个。事实上,这样的引用法不但是可以被接受的,也是应受到鼓励的。因为这样的引用使论文论述更具有效性,也表明研究是全面的、彻底的。还要注意,三个引用的排列顺序依照出版时间的先后顺序而定,出版最早的排在最前面。

注意:文本中引用的所有文献都应该是在参考文献中出现过的。有关引用的详细用法,请见第四章。

8. 概括引言部分常出现的结构

(1)建立研究领域。
①给出所研究题目的重要性;
②对所研究的题目进行一般性的论述;
③全面评述一下所研究题目的研究现状。
(2)对以前的研究进行概述并进而论述你对所研究题目的情况的了解。
(3)为目前的研究做铺垫。
①提出一个相反的设想;
②揭示以前研究中存在的差距;
③确切地阐述研究问题或难题;
④探讨继续以往的研究方法/惯例的必要性。
(4)引出目前的研究。
①简述一下科研工作的意图;
②概述一下科研工作的主要特性;
③简述一下研究的重要结果;
④简单地勾画出论文的结构。

简言之,引言部分的作用是把读者引入目前的研究领域,使读者在不用参考以往出版物的前提下能看懂论文的其余部分。

9. 引言部分中不同内容的实例

(1)建立研究领域的实例。
实例1

> Since 1972, when Fujishima and Honda[1] reported the photocatalytic decomposition of water on TiO_2 electrodes, photocatalysis has been used with great success in the remediation of a wide variety of contaminants, including alkanes, alcohols, carboxylic acids, alkenes, phenols, dyes, PCBs, aromatic hydrocarbons, halogenated alkanes and alkenes,

surfactants, and pesticides[2].

自从1972年,Fujishima和Honda[1]报告用TiO$_2$电极对水中污染物进行光催化降解以来,光催化在对很多污染物的去除方面得到了应用,并取得了很大的成功。这些污染物包括烷烃、酒精、羧基酸、烯烃、苯酚、染料、多氯联苯、芳香烃、卤代烃、表面活性剂和杀虫剂[2]。

实例2

The global interest in a hydrogen economy has been stimulated by the promise of clean energy production using hydrogen in fuel cells.

氢气能够在燃料电池中产生清洁的能源,由此激发了全球对氢经济的关注。

实例3

Nitrogen (N) and phosphorus (P) are the key nutrients causing eutrophication in waterways. Therefore, they are compulsorily removed from wastewater sources in most developed countries.

氮和磷是导致废水富营养化的关键营养元素,因此多数发达国家要求废水必须去除这两种元素。

(2)下述是对以往的研究进行概述的实例,表述你对所研究题目的当前状况的了解程度。

实例1

Since the 1980's[4], the hydroxyl radical has been assigned as the reactive species in photocatalytic degradation.

自20世纪80年代[4]以来,羟基自由基一直被认为是光化降解过程中的活性物种。

实例2

A reduction in CO$_2$ emissions, however, will require sustainable hydrogen production based on renewable energy using solar, wind, and biomass sources. Currently about half of all the hydrogen produced is derived from natural gas, with the balance produced primarily using other fossil fuels, including heavy oils, naphtha, and coal. Only 4% is generated from water using electricity derived from a variety of sources (1~3).

然而,由于需要减少CO$_2$的排放,所以要求在基于太阳能、风能和生物资源这些可再生的能源基础上持续地生产氢。现今大约有一半氢气生产来自天然气,与之相对的另一半主要来源于化石燃料,包括重油、石脑油、煤。仅有4%的氢气源于在使用其他各种能源产电时的水。

实例 3

  More studies have been showing that nitrification and denitrification can occur concurrently in one reactor under aerobic conditions with low dissolved oxygen (DO), through the so-called simultaneous nitrification and denitrification (SND) process (Bertanza, 1997; Helmer and Kunst, 1998; Keller et al., 1997; von Münch et al., 1996).

  许多研究已表明,在低溶解氧(DO)的有氧条件下,硝化和反硝化作用通过一种所谓的同步硝化反硝化(SND)作用,可在同一反应器中同时发生(Bertanza, 1997; Helmer and Kunst, 1998; Keller et al., 1997; von Münch et al., 1996)。

(3) 为目前的研究做铺垫的实例。

实例 1

  Nevertheless, few research efforts have been made to assess the applicability of photocatalysis to industrial liquid effluents. This kind of work is a must if this novel process is to be used to treat wastewater as a tertiary treatment option.

  然而,在光催化处理用于工业废水的评定方面,却几乎未予以足够的研究。如果想把这一新颖的处理方式用于污水的三级处理,这方面的相关研究就是必不可少的了。

实例 2

  Microbial fuel cells(MFCs) have been discovered as a completely new path to renewable electricity production. In MFCs, microorganisms oxidize organic matter and transfer electrons directly to the anode electrode (8~9). Bacteria capable of electron transfer to an electrode, either directly or by endogenously produced mediators, include a wealth of genera, including Geobacter, Shewanella, Pseudomonas, and others (8~10, 11~13).

  现已发现,生物燃料电池(MFCs)可完全被看作是一种再生电能生产的新方法。在 MFCs 中,微生物使有机物氧化,并把电子直接传递给阳极。能够把电子传递给阳极的细菌(无论是直接地还是通过自生的中间体),它们都包含大量的菌类,如 Geobacter、Shewanella、Pseudomonas 等。

实例 3

  Ideally, if SND via nitrite could be accomplished with the DPAOs, even more COD could be saved, because the soluble COD in the domestic wastewater is typically limiting.

理想的结果是,如果反硝化聚磷菌可以实现亚硝酸盐型 SND,就可以节省更多的 COD,因为在生活废水中可溶性的 COD 是有限的。

(4) 引出目前的研究的实例。

实例1

This paper investigates the reason for the astonishing reduction in the effluent toxicity through analyses using gas chromatography (GC) and the effect of adding H_2O_2 in the photocatalytic treatment of the oil field produced water using an experimental design. The photocatalyst surface was observed in order to evaluate if corrosion was taking place during the treatment.

本文通过使用气体色谱,分析研究了废液毒性大大降低的原因,以及在实验设计中光催化处理油田产生的水中加入 H_2O_2 的影响;观察了光催化表面,以便确定在处理过程中是否出现了腐蚀现象。

实例2

We report here our preliminary findings using this system that demonstrate for the first time hydrogen produced directly from protons and electrons produced by the bacteria from the complete oxidation of organic matter with greatly reduced energy needs compared to the water electrolysis process.

我们在这里报道我们初步的发现。利用这一系统第一次证实氢气可以直接通过由细菌对有机物完全氧化而产生的质子与电子的结合而产生,这一过程所需的能量相对于电解水来说大大减少。

实例3

Experiments were designed and performed to investigate this modified process, particularly with regard to determining the N removal pathway and the organisms involved in denitrification and P removal.

本试验设计和操作的目的是研究改良该种方法,尤其要确定氮的去除途径及参与反硝化及磷去除作用的生物。

2.4 材料和方法的撰写

由于材料和方法部分直接关系到读者是否会认同研究结果的有效性,以及读者能否认真对待这些结果,因此,这一部分的写作是论文论证的一个极其重要的组成部分。写好这一部分可体现研究的每一步都是正确的:你在研究中是十分谨慎和认真的,你对问题的思考是缜密和周全的,你采用了被认同的方法,你没有犯技术上的错误。

1. 为他人重复你的研究提供依据

这一部分的写作,同时向你所在的学术界提供了可对你的工作进行重复和检验的方法和途径。因此,这部分要包含足够的细节,以便你所在研究领域里有经验的研究者能够确切地重复、再现你的研究结果。科学的本质之一就在于,其方法要求研究结果应该是可重复的,也就是说:

(1)明确指出你做研究时使用的材料是什么——反应物、酶、催化剂、生物体、实验对象(人或动物)等。你对材料的描述一定要充分具体到其他研究者能够正确地使用你所叙述的材料重复、验证你的研究结果的程度。

(2)明确指出你所从事的研究的具体条件——特殊的温度、紫外线光的照射、电流电压等。

(3)明确指出你选择材料、实验对象、实验仪器、实验方法的特殊标准是什么(如,你为什么选择了胶合材料或催化剂而不是其他的材料)。

(4)明确指出你研究时使用的具体方法。如果你遵循的是常规的步骤,在此只要提及一下就可以,但如果是新的方法,就需要对此进行详细的描述。

(5)必要的话,要对你所选择的标准、材料、方法或环境的合理性、正确性进行论证。

(6)对于基于野外的研究,通常需要对研究区域进行比引言部分更加详细的描述。一般来说,研究区域的描述在引言部分要更笼统些,在材料和方法部分对研究场地和气候的描述要更详细些。有时需要加副标题,如 Study Site、General Methods 和 Analysis 等。

(7)对现有的、不需要定制的设备和材料要详细描述(如 Licor 水下量子传感器的型号 Model LI 192SB),材料的来源也要说清楚;任何针对研究的设备或正在建造的设备的修正都要详细描述。用以制备试剂、定色剂和色素等的方法也要准确叙述(尽管在其他书籍中有大量的有关标准配方的参考文献)。

(8)方法部分通常是按时间顺序展开的,但有时由于要描述那些相关联的方法,就无法遵循常规的时间顺序。如果你的研究方法是新方法(未出版过的),就需要你提供所有后人能实现重复你的实验方法的所有细节;然而,如果你在研究中采用的方法是以前权威刊物上发表过的方法,只给出方法的名称及参考文献书目就可以了。

(9)在描述测量方法的时候要准确,也要指出测量的误差。使用普通的统计方法时不必过多解释,但如果使用的是先进的或是非常规的方法,要在文献中给出出处。

2. 描述实验结构和组织过程

为了清楚地解释你是如何完成实验的,通常采用下述的结构和组织过程(细节如下)。

(1)研究的有机体(植物、动物、人等)和实验前对它们的处理和照顾,研究是在何时、何地进行的(如果时间、地点都是要考虑的重要因素);注意术语 subject 只用于以人为研究对象的研究。

(2)如果是野外研究,要对研究场地进行描述,包括主要的物理和生物特性,以及准确的场所(经度、纬度、地图等)。

(3)实验设计或取样设计(也就是实验或研究是如何组织的,众多的取样是如何收集的、复制、测得的变量等)。

(4)数据收集的正确方式,也就是实验步骤是如何实现的,数据是如何分析的(定性分析和/或采用的统计步骤)。

这部分的写作旨在使读者很好地了解实验的全过程。合理地组织实验,要把每一个实验或步骤当作是一个单元来写。即使随着时间的流逝,它们被分开了,但每一部分都还能独立、完整地表述一个内容。有时实验设计和步骤会被有效地作为一个独立的整体提出。通常对实验的方法进行描述时,要给出足够的有关定量性细节(多少、多长、何时等),以便其他科学家重复你的实验。你也要指明用于分析你的结果的统计步骤,包括用以确定重要性的概率标准(通常的概率为 0.05)。

描述研究中使用的有机体:包括给出出处(供应者于何时、何地收集的)、大小(重量、长度等)、实验前是如何处理的、如何被培养的等;遗传学研究要包括菌种等,对有些研究,年龄也很重要。

描述野外研究的场地:对野外研究场地的描述必须包括与研究目的相关的场地的物理和生物特性,包括研究日期(如 10~15 April 1994)和研究区域的准确位置。关于场地的数据一定要尽量准确,如写成 Grover Nature Preserve, 1/2 mi SW Grover, Maine 而非 Grover Nature Preserve 或 Grover;可能的话,用经纬度标出场地的位置(如 WWW 拥有提供此类服务的场所);也可提供一幅地图来显示其位置。地图中最好再标出一个与本位置相关的一个较大的、可辨认的地理范围,以此来帮助识别研究场地。如能做到这一点就更理想了。因为这样想要重复或检验你的研究工作的人或仅仅是为了参观你的研究场地的人就能够找到你的研究的准确位置。

注:如果是实验室的研究,就不用报告研究的日期和位置了,除非这些信息与你的研究相关,多数情况下可不用。如果你做的实验是在特殊的位置或实验室进行的,而这些地方又是唯一可选的地方,那么你就应该在方法部分注明,指出是哪个实验室或哪种设备。

要对实验设计进行准确描述:记住本部分要包含试验的假设、对照标准、测得的变量、复制的数量、你实际所测得了什么、数据体现的方式等,用变量或处理的名称来区别不同的处理(如使用 2.5% NaCl 而不是试验 1)。如果你的论文中包含不止一个实验,就要使用副标题,这有助于组织对实验的陈述。现有的常规的实验设计工作表能帮助你规划基础课程中的实验。

要详细描述你的研究方案,以便使其他研究者能够重复你的工作,核实你的发现:描述中最重要的是研究的定量方面——质量、体积、孵化期、浓度等,这些是其他科学家复制你的实验所必需的。如果你使用的是标准的实验室或野外作业方式和实验仪器,就没有必要对程序(如连续稀释)或使用的设备(如自动吸量管)进行描述,因为其他的研究者很可能对这些都已十分熟悉;你可用指出商标或种类的方式来指出设备的具体类别(如用超高速离心器而不是 prep 离心器),必要时,指出使用的试剂的来源,如 poly-l-Lysine (Sigma #1309)。当使用的方法来源于另一出版物时,为节省时间和文字,只要指出这一点,提供相关引用以示来源即可。

描述一下数据是如何被概述和分析的:为了回答试验的每一个问题或假设,你要对数据进行概括和分析。在方法部分要指出这些数据的概述和分析的类型是什么。

包含的信息如下。

（1）数据是如何被概括的（是平均值，还是百分数等），以及你是如何对可变性估量的（SD、SEM 等），如：

This lets you avoid having to repeatedly indicate you are using mean ± SD.

（2）数据转换（如使差异规格化或变得均等）。

（3）针对特殊问题使用统计性的试验。如：

"A Paired t-test was used to compare mean flight duration before and after applying stablizers to the glider's wings."

"One way ANOVA was used to compare mean weight gain in weight-matched calves fed the three different rations."

（4）任何其他数字或图解等用以分析数据的方法。

3. 下面就作者常遇到的问题再提出些忠告

（1）方法部分容易出现废话连篇或过于详细的问题。如：避免使用一个简单句来连接一个简单句的行为，因为这样写出的段落必然过长，啰里啰唆。一个句子可以包含几个行为，使句子既清晰又易读。

有问题的实例：这个例子对一个很一般、非常简单的步骤进行了啰唆的描述，特点是一个句子只表明一个行为，而且其中还有很多不必要的细节。

"The petri dish was placed on the turntable. The lid was then raised slightly. An inoculating loop was used to transfer culture tothe agar surface. The turntable was rotated 90 degrees by hand. The loop was moved lightly back and forth over the agar to spread the culture. The bacteria were then incubated at 37 C for 24 hr."

改进的实例：同样的行为被并列放在了一个简单、明了的句中，重要的信息一点也没少。而且，多余的和显而易见的信息被删掉了，缺少的、重要的信息被补上了。

"Each plate was placed on a turntable and streaked at opposing angles with fresh overnight E. coli culture using an inoculating loop. The bacteria were then incubated at 37 C for 24 hr."

最好的实例：从下面这个实例中可以看出，作者首先设想读者已拥有一些生物技术方面的基本知识，因此删去了其行业内熟知的多余信息；而且由于两个行为相关，故把它们放在了一个句子中。

"Each plate was streaked with fresh overnight E. coli culture and incubated at 37 C for 24 hr."

（2）在涉及控制/对比或处理以及其他研究参数的内容时，应避免使用模糊的术语，因为这方面的内容要求有明确的标识符号，否则不易理解。这些标识符号，如 Tube 1, Tube 2 或 Site 1 和 Site 2 等，离开背景或上下文关系就不具有任何意义，很难理解。

有问题的实例：在这个例子中，如果读者要想正确地判断各种试管代表的内容，就得时时回到前面去寻找以前的信息。

"A Spec 20 was used to measure A600 of **Tubes 1, 2, and 3** immediately after chloroplasts were added (Time 0) and every 2 min. thereafter until the DCIP was completely reduced. ***Tube 4's A600*** *was measured only at Time 0 and at the end of the experiment.*"

改进的实例:注意下面斜体部分替代了处理和对照的标识符号,这样段落在有无文章上下文的情况下,意思的表达仍然十分清楚。

"A Spec 20 was used to measure A600 of **the reaction mixtures exposed to light intensities of** 1500, 750, and 350 uE/m2/sec immediately after chloroplasts were added (Time 0) and every 2 min. thereafter until the DCIP was completely reduced. The A600 of **the no-light control** was measured only at Time 0 and at the end of the experiment."

4. 材料和方法部分的文体及注意事项

材料和方法部分的文体具有什么特点呢?它应给读者的感觉就像你在口述一个实验的操作过程。尽管这部分比其他部分要求更多地使用第三人称和被动结构,但在一定程度上应尽量使用主动语态;在这一部分尽量避免使用第一人称。有的作者认为这一部分应使用**过去时**,因为报道的研究工作是已经完成了的工作,是在报道**过去**做的事,不是将来的事。但据本书作者的实际调查表明(基于多个学科的学术论文),这部分的写作也有越来越多地使用现在时的趋势(不排除使用过去时的事实)。但下面这点却得到了共识,即方法部分的写作,不同于实验手册,不要写成一步步指导的说明书或指南。

(1)避免在学术文章中使用祈使句。

命令式的祈使句在课本、指导手册、讲义、实验室等地方经常出现,如:

Analyze the results in figure 1.

Complete the following sentences.

Notice the relationship between A and B.

Prepare 5cc of distillate.

Carry this total *forward*.

但在学术文章中,祈使句的使用不是很普遍,因为它给人一种不礼貌、冒犯人的感觉;使用祈使句也不利于保持原本就已经十分脆弱的作者和读者之间的关系。

然而,有一个动词在学术文章中被广泛地使用,它的使用频率占学术论文中祈使句的50%,这个词就是 *let*,如:

Let *p* stand for the price-cost ratio.

Let *N* equal the number of consumers.

在数学论证中,会见到一些用于祈使句的动词,如 suppose、substitute 和 assume。

如果你认为祈使句会由于不礼貌而引起读者不满,可采用其他可回避的方法,如:

把祈使句改为被动句或使用条件从句,如:

祈使句:Now compare the results in tables 4 and 5.

被动句:The results in tables 4 and 5 can now be compared.

条件句:If we now compare the results in tables 4 and 5, we can see that....

可这样使用的动词还有：

Observe, Refer, Consider, Compare, Note, Imagine, Notice, Recall, Disregard, Take the case of 等。

（2）注意时态的用法。

尽管材料部分的写作中习惯使用过去时，但目前的趋势是现在时使用的频率越来越高。下面为这部分的象征性例子：

We examined. ...

Each occurrence was identified. ...

It was designated. ...

It was class interpreted. ...

We included. ...

We counted. ...

（3）体现叙述性。

本部分提供所有有关方法方面的必要细节，这部分的写作目的是便于其他研究者借以复制此研究工作。

要把实验或研究中采用的步骤加以叙述，但不应写成食谱那种指导性的书籍清单或明细表。

在这部分的写作中，可以设想其他研究者同你一样已经掌握了基本的技能，但不知晓你实验的确切细节，因此你不必写成这样：

"*We poured N-free fertilizer solution into a graduated cylinder until the bottom of the meniscus was at the 30 ml line. We poured the fertilizer onto the top of the soil in a pot and then repeated this procedure 24 times.*"

而是要设想其他研究者已经知道如何对液体进行测量，如何把它们加到罐子里，因此可以写成：

"We added 30 ml of N-free fertilizer to each of 24 pots."

写学术论文的一个重要问题是要确定你在提供细节信息时到底应该写哪些方面的细节，但绝**不能引用实验室手册**！

在这部分的最后一段，要描述使用的统计实验（**统计学就是方法**！）。一定不要加入额外信息，尽管研究者能够识别哪些是没有价值的假定、何时去除这些没用的假定。

2.5 结果的撰写

1. 基本要求

（1）在结果部分，要利用例证性的材料（表格和图形）和文字材料客观、富有逻辑地依次给出研究中的发现，给出经过整理和浓缩的数据，并从中提取和描述其展现的重要趋势。因为结果部分包含对社会做出贡献的新知识，所以对发现的陈述就要既确切又要简单明了。

（2）统计分析的概述可出现在文本之中，通常以附加说明的形式或以相关表格或图表、图例或作为表格或图表的注脚的形式出现。结果部分的组织应按表格和/或图表所反映的主要发现的重要性给出。结果部分的文本也要遵循这个顺序,突出所研究的问题/假设的答案;重要的消极/不利的结果也要如实报道。作者在写这部分的文本时通常是根据表格和图表的顺序展开的。

(3)结果部分应该简短扼要,没有空话。不要说下面的话:

"It is clearly evident from Fig. 1 that bird species richness increased with habitat complexity."

而要写作:

"Bird species richness increased with habitat complexity" (Fig. 1).

但也不要过于简练,不能期待读者从独立的数据中自己去找出重要的趋势,能做到这一点的人不多。要充分利用文本、表格和图表来浓缩数据,突出可能的趋势。关于这一点,可参看附录部分的有关表格和图表的指导方针。

(4)避免段落结构的重复,不要在此解释数据。如果变成了解释,你可能就会处于棘手的、危险的处境,看下面的两个例子。

这个例子突出了作者想要读者关注的趋势/不同。

The duration of exposure to running water had a pronounced effect on cumulative seed germination percentages (Fig. 2). Seeds exposed to the 2-day treatment had the highest cumulative germination (84%), 1.25 times that of the 12-h or 5-day groups and 4 times that of controls.

相比之下,下面这个例子有点偏向解释,涉及最优性(一个概念模型),还把观察结果和那个概念结合起来。

The results of the germination experiment (Fig. 2) suggest that the optimal time for running-water treatment is 2 days. This group showed the highest cumulative germination (84%), with longer (5 d) or shorter (12 h) exposures producing smaller gains in germination when compared to the control group.

2. 写结果部分时需要考虑的问题

(1)"关键的结果"是什么?当你提出一个通过实验可以回答的试验性的假设的时候,或当你提出一个通过收集样板就可以回答问题的时候,你实际上是在对那些有机体或现象积累观察资料,通过分析那些观察资料得出问题的答案。一般来说,答案就是"关键的结果"。

不管你使用的分析方法有多么复杂,上面的陈述都适用。因此开始的时候你的分析可能包括对图形的直观检查、平均值的计算和标准偏差,但后来你应该对各种统计试验进行应用,并加以解释。

如:假设你提出这样的问题:"Is the average height of male students the same as the female students in a pool of randomly selected Biology majors?" 你首先应该做的是对男女学生进行大量的随机抽样调查,然后要对那些抽样进行描述统计(平均值、SD、n、排列等),

还要根据这些数字进行绘图。如果没有使用统计检验,你就只是直观地对这些绘图进行检查。如果你发现学习生物的男性学生比学习生物的女性学生身高平均高出12.5 cm,这就是你得出的答案。

注意:统计分析结果并不是关键的结果,但可作为分析工具/手段来帮助我们理解关键的结果是什么。

(2)结果部分的组织结构应以出现的表格和图表的顺序为依据。一旦分析完数据,就要制作图和表,并以最能够体现你的发现的顺序来安排阐述的先后。需要了解的一个策略是:在结果部分的文本中要表述一两个基于每个图或表的关键结果。要遵循下述有关表格和图表的简单规则:

- 图和表都要按照在文本中出现的先后顺序分别标上数字号码。
- 涉及的第一个图标号为图1,下一个为图2,依次类推。
- 同样,第一个表标号为表1,下一个为表2,依次类推。
- 每一个图或表都必须包含一个简短的描述,描述的内容是给出的结果以及必要的有关符号的信息。
- 有关图符号的解释要放在**图之下**,图的阅读要从下到上。
- 有关表符号的解释要放在**表之上**,表的阅读要从上到下。
- 在涉及文本的图时,Figure 可缩写为 Fig.,如 **Fig.** 1;但 Table 从不缩写,还是 Table,如 **Table** 1。

(3)结果部分的主干应是以文本形式对主要发现的叙述,叙述的主要发现一定是与每个表格和图表的内容相关。文本要起到引导读者读懂以关键结果为重心的研究结果,使读者得到研究问题的答案。文本的一个主要功能在于提供起梳理作用的信息。你要分别地、按顺序地涉及每一个表格和/或图表,给读者明确指出每一个图和表所给出的关键结果。是不是关键结果,取决于你探讨的问题,它们可能包含明显的趋势、重大差异、相似处、相关性、最大限度以及最小限度等。

(4)需要避免的一些问题。

- 不要重申图或表中的每个数值——除非是关键结果或从中看出的趋势。
- 不要重复地在图和表中给出同样的数据——这会被看作是多余的,既浪费空间又浪费精力。确定适合说明结果的形式,并始终使用这一形式。
- 如果原始数据能够被概述为平均值、百分比等的形式,就不要报告原始数据。

(5)通常以放在括号里的方式来报告统计试验的汇总(试验名称、p-值),还包括它们所体现的结果。在报告结果的时候通常用括号的形式体现你所发现的统计结论(假设在你的研究过程中使用了统计试验)。括号中的信息应该包括使用的统计试验和具有的意义(试验统计量和 DF 是可选择的)。如,如果你发现从事某一专业的男性平均身高比从事这一专业的女性的平均身高高很多,你可以把这一结果用文字的斜体形式来报告,用文字的加粗形式(如下)来报告统计结论:

"*Males* (180.5 ±5.1 cm; n = 34) *averaged* 12.5 cm *taller than females* (168 ± 7.6 cm; n = 34) *in the AY* 1995 *pool of Computer majors* (**two-sample t-test, t = 5.78, 33 d.f., p < 0.001**)."

如果汇总的统计数据在图中表示出来了,上面的句子中就没有必要明确地对此进行报告,但必须提及一下在什么地方能看到图。

"*Males averaged* 12.5 *cm taller than females in the AY* 1995 *pool of Computer majors* (two-sample t-test, t = 5.78, 33 d.f., p < 0.001; **Fig. 1**)."

要注意报告的关键结果(用斜体表示)应该同不包含使用的统计试验的论文中的报道相一致,而粗体部分不应该出现,除非提到了图(**Fig. 1**)。

- 避免把所有的句子都用于报告统计出的结果。
- 对于词 significant(ly)的使用还要说明如下两点:

①在学术研究中,这个词的使用意味着统计试验的使用是为了判断数据,在这种情况下,试验表明的平均身高之差非常大,远远超出了单纯的偶然结果,significant 的使用应该仅限于这一目的。

②如果括号中说明的统计信息包括了表示具有**重大的**含义 p-值,就没有必要在句中再使用 significant(见上例)。

(6)给出的有关实验结果的报道应该同引言部分的论述顺序相一致,这样才能合乎逻辑地支持你的设想或给出的问题答案。如在报道有关试验性节食对老鼠的骨骼质量的影响的研究中,首先要考虑给出控制饮食喂养的老鼠骨骼质量的相关数据,然后给出实验饮食喂养的老鼠的骨骼质量的相关数据。

(7)报告负面结果很重要!如果你没能从实验中得到预期的结果,说明你的假设不正确,需要重新规划,也说明你可能遇到了不在意料之中、需要进一步研究的事。在这两种情况下,你的研究结果可能对他人是重要的,尽管这样的结果不能为你的假设提供证据。不要陷入那种误区,认为与自己预期的结果相违背的一定就是"不好的数据"。如果你的整个过程都是正确无误的,这一结果就该是你的实验结果,需要你对它进行解释,很多重大发现都可被上溯到"不好的数据"。

(8)在报告数据或汇总统计时,使用的单位名称要保持正确。

- 对于**个体价值**,要写作"the mean length was 10 m"或"the maximum time was 140 min"。
- 如果包含可变性的测量,则要把**单位**置于误差值之后,如"... was 10 ± 2.3 m"。
- 同样,**单位**要放在拥有同样单位的数列里最后那个值的后面,如,"lengths of 5, 10, 15, and 20 m"或"no differences were observed after 2, 4, 6, or 8 min. of incubation"。

结果部分和讨论部分的划分不总是十分明确的,尽管很多作者认为在结果部分你要做的只是介绍和报告你从收集的数据中得到的发现,但也有一些作者认为在这部分中加入你对数据的评价和解释性说明也是合适甚至是必要的。对此,作者本人可酌情处理。

对于如何写表格、图表、曲线图以及如何组织它们所包含的信息,关于这方面的要求是有详细而精确的惯例可供遵循的。使用的条件是,你一定确信在你使用它们时,它们能给读者提供信息,而不是带来困惑或不解。在随后的解释说明和讨论中,涉及图解时要用图解的号码,具体说明你涉及的是什么。针对图解的内容,要给出一个描述性的标题。根据经验,图解的顺序是名称、图、解释。有关更多制表、制图方面的细节,请看本书后的附录。

3. 结果部分可能涉及的评论

从读者的角度出发,作者在本部分中常常要加入一些对数据的评论。作者能预料到读者会提出一些问题,如"Why did they use this method rather than that one?"或"Isn't this result rather strange?"。出于这些考虑,作者一般不会把读者想象的问题和评论意见推迟到文章的最后再做出反应。

多数的论文中都会有一个部分专门讨论数据。通常数据是用表格、曲线图、图形以及其他非语言的形式来表示的。数据可被置于文本之中或作为附录置于文章的后一部分,这部分的写作被称为数据说明。

同写作的其他方面一样,数据说明起到帮助定位的作用,因此这既带来了机遇,又存在着一定的危险。危险之一是你可能会单纯地用文字来重复展示那些已经用非文字形式表示了的数据。换句话说,只是描写,没有说明。另一个危险是走向了反面:对数据的解读过了头,得出了不恰当的结论。问题的关键在于对数据的解读要恰到好处,说明的方法适当(如说明是从最重要的到不大重要的)。多数情况下,说明的过程是从一般到具体。

(1)要想准确说出作者在数据说明中应该做些什么是很困难的,但通常讨论数据有如下的目的:
- 突出显示研究结果;
- 依据给出的数据来评价常规的理论或一般的惯例;
- 对不同的数据组进行比较和评价;
- 依据产生数据的方法来评价数据的可靠性;
- 论述数据可能的影响。

当然,数据的评论会包含不止上述中的一项,可能同时包含几项。

(2)Swales(1993)对20份发表过的生物化学论文进行了研究,发现其中的数据说明大多涉及以下几个方面。
- 证明方法的正确性;
- 解释结果;
- 引证说明同前期研究的一致;
- 对数据进行解释;
- 承认在解释上存在的困难;
- 指出差异;
- 提出进一步研究的必要。

4. 结果部分常出现的有关数据说明的实例

(1)对数据进行说明。

实例1

The implementation of the path generation techniques and the estimation of route choice models to the two data sources enable to describe the results from the application of the methodology for testing transferability in route choice modeling and to provide insight into the transferability of existing techniques and models.

实例 2

The difference in parameter estimates translates into the non-transferability of model parameters across the two data sources as confirmed by the transferability test statistics.

When using FF algorithm, let information sharing coefficient $\lambda = 0.5$ while subsystem just uses a part of predicting information of system, so the subsystem cannot get the optimal estimation.

实例 3

Together, these three figures indicate that public administration research is conducted predominantly by those who work in public administration-related fields in universities.

实例 4

As we see in Fig. 4, 13.5% of the articles addressed issues related to the federal government.

(2) 解释结果。

实例 1

This has resulted in extensive losses (Table 1) with 98.2 percent reporting vegetative agricultural losses, and another 92.1 percent lost agricultural animals. In light of these numbers, it is not surprising that 81.6 percent of participants indicated that they had had problems related to work.

实例 2

The combined estimation shows that the Turin dataset contains less noise, as the variance of the error term is lower with respect to the Boston dataset.

实例 3

Simulation results show that simulation time of EFF algorithm is 98.36s and the FF algorithm is 103.41s. We can prove that the computing time of EFF algorithm is smaller than that of FF algorithm through theoretical analysis.

实例 4

In terms of the university authors' departmental affiliation (see Fig. 2), 36% reported that they are affiliated with stand-alone public administration departments or schools, 9.8% are from departments named both political science and public administration, and 4.9% are from departments named as public administration and management or business administration.

实例 5

The calculated data shown above were obtained in the form of curve. As shown in Figure 14, Beam Current Ratio and Thrust Factor Ratiok's distribution curve proved that the efficient parameters of the grid are the ones listed before.

实例 6

This is consistent with expectations for this generator.

实例 7

As can be seen, the maximum error is comparable to the added noise. This and other similar trials indicate that....

实例 8

We use bilinear interpolation to generate registration image. The results are as Fig. 3.5 shows. The difference between registered image and reference image is as Fig. 3.6 shows. From Fig. 3.6, we can see that the registered image is almost completely consistent with the reference image.

(3)证明方法的正确性。

实例 1

As the table shows that the difference in proportions between test and hold-out samples for the three methods are very small (less than a percentage point for all methods at all four levels of depth). Moreover, none of these differences are statistically significant. Therefore, this set of analyses suggests that for this particular file with a rather large response rate, all three methods are generally able to provide an accurate prediction of the response rate when the results of a test mailing are applied to the full file.

实例 2

The standardized paths in the structural model are shown in the first three columns in Table 4, and several model-fit indices are shown in the bottom rows. These fit indices are all above the suggested cutoff of 0.9 (Barua et al. 2004), indicating a good model fit.

实例 3

Using EFF algorithm, the subsystem makes use of all predicting information of the system, so it can get the optimal estimation. But from the global perspective, IW is the same for two methods, so two methods can obtain global optimal estimation.

实例 4

In this section the relevant parameters are compared in Table 1. It is immediately obvious that there is a wide range of possible design realization. For example, the flanges that stick out on the SUITE RMA allow one to bolt the actuator down from the perimeter.

实例 5

This is essentially identical to the data obtained from the oscilloscope expected for the residual noise and distortion products which are clearly lower, reflecting the wider dynamic range expected for the new instrument.

(4) 讨论可能的影响。

实例 1

This would provide the Air Force with an ability to operate spacecraft much as it operates aircraft. It would increase availability, flexibility, capability life span, and cost effectiveness of space assets.

实例 2

Therefore, the full coupled nonlinear model formulated here could be very useful for the detailed analysis of complex dynamic behavior, such as bifurcation and chaos, of the slender rods.

实例 3

　　Retail sales display the commonly found hump shaped response with. This response is statistically significant. . . .

实例 4

　　Proposition 8 and Corollary 7 imply that an increase in the precision of the accounting system affects voluntary disclosure and the role of external information production by the analyst in two important ways.

(5) 引证与前期研究的一致。

实例 1

　　Table 3 shows the test parameters and results for the thick TABI blankets. The results of hypervelocity impact test shots can verify the conclusion of the previous studies.

实例 2

　　Theses Figures show the comparisons between the theoretical and experimental results.

实例 3

　　As can be seen in Figure 1, our method is better than the method [7].

实例 4

　　This is consistent with the expectations for this generator.

实例 5

　　Fig. 3 shows the temperature dependence of. . . . This is in agreement with the observations made by Barret et al.

实例 6

　　On the other hand, the positive effect of relative humidity on the desulfurization activity of the sorbent was in agreement with the results reported in the literature [11-13].

(6) 与前期研究进行比较。

实例

　　Unlike previous concept, MOS does not rely on expensive and range limited astronauts, or large and complicated robotics.

(7) 提出进一步研究的必要性。
实例
　　Diagnostic and stand-off repair technologies, including sensors, effectors, and algorithms for autonomous yet intelligent operation, still need to be developed.

(8) 指出差异。
实例1
　　Of all the actuators, the VRSl and SA-10 give the best performance per unit mass and are generally "squarish" in shape. The other two, the VIS6 and the SUITE RMA's, were developed for specialized requirements and deviate from the standard form factor.

实例2
　　Compared with mock- and anti-sense-SMYD3-expressing plasmid, PCDNIA-SMYD3 induced markedly more colonies.

实例3
　　The fatigue test results are shown in Figs. 4 to 6 for comparison of the effect of discontinuities with the standard series. The welds with excessive porosity failed at a slightly lower load than the standard series (1.1 kN compared to 1.3 kN at 10cycles)....

(9) 承认在解释上存在困难。
实例1
　　The computed *ne* is more of a problem. The main difficulty here appears to be that....

实例2
　　In all cases, the multisensor classifications perform better than the single sensor by a percentage of 3.6, 1, 27.8, and 13.

5. 数据说明的结构
数据评论通常依次包含下列要素：
● 所指要素和/或及其概述；
● 对重要内容的陈述；

- 讨论其含意、问题、异常现象等。

下面是一则在表格之后兼具上述要素的数据评论的例子。

Table 1. Means of PC Virus Infection in US Businesses

Source	Percentage
Disks from home	43%
Electronic bulletin board	7%
Sales demonstration disk	6%
Repair or service disk	6%
Company, client, or consultant disk	4%
Shrink-wrapped application	3%
Other download	2%
Disk from school	1%
Local area network supervisor disk	1%
Purposely planted	1%
Came with PC	1%
Undetermined	29%

© 1992 IEEE

Table 1 shows the most common modes of infection for US businesses. As can be seen, in the majority of cases, the source of viral infection can be detected, with disks being brought to the workplace from home being by far the most significant. However, it is alarming to note that the sources of nearly 30% of viral infections cannot be determined. While it may be possible to eliminate home-to-workplace infection by requiring computer users to run antiviral software on diskettes brought from home, businesses are still vulnerable to major data loss, especially from unidentifiable sources of infection.

用 as 从句连接
亮点1

亮点2

推论

下面是对上述实例中各要素的分解说明：
（1）所指要素和/或及其概述。
①主动语态的实例。
a. Table 1 shows the most common modes of computer infection for US businesses.
b. Table 5 provides details of the fertilizer used.

    c. Figure 4.2 gives the results of the second experiment.

②被动语态的实例。
    a. The most common modes of infection are shown in Table 1.
    b. Details of the fertilizers used are provided in Table 5.
    c. The results of the second experiment are given in Figure 4.2.

不知你是否注意到,到目前为止,上述所有的主动、被动例句都属于指示性的,也就是说都没有表明通常的感染源是什么,使用的化肥是什么,或者说第二个实验的结果是什么。

其实作者也可以把它们写成信息性的概述,即作者完全可以对数据进行概述,如：
    a. Table 1 shows that home disks are the major source of computer viruses.
    b. Table 5 gives the ingredients of the chosen fertilizer-SP401.
    c. Figure 4.2 suggests that the experimental results confirm the hypothesis.

③聚焦语言点:起连接作用的 as-从句。

前面我们在涉及非语言表述的数据的时候,把这些非语言表述的数据当作了主句的主语,或是施动者。然而,用以引出信息性陈述的、更普遍使用的结构是起连接作用的 **as-从句**,下面是 4 个这样的例子：

实例 1
    As shown in Table 1, home disks are the most frequent source of infection.

实例 2
    As can be seen in Figure 8, infant mortality is still high in urban areas.

实例 3
    As revealed by the graph, the defect rate has declined.

实例 4
    As described above, the determination of pesticides in this work is based on the use of stabilized AChE within a liposome nano-biosensor.

这种起连接作用的 as-从句是英语语法中的例外(as 不等于 since),在被动语态中这些从句没有主语。比较一下下面 a、b 两个句子：
    a. As it has been proved, the theory may have practical importance.
    b. As has been proved, the theory may have practical importance.

在 a 句中,主句和从句之间存在一种因果关系:要是这一理论没被证实,它就没有实用价值;在 b 句中,as-从句只起宣告或确认的作用:正如这一理论被证实的那样,它有实用价值。

记住:在被动的起连接作用的 as-从句中千万不要使用主语!

还要提到的一点是,在使用这类需要有连接词的陈述时,介词容易用得不当,下面举一些常用的介词的标准用法。

in	As shown *in* Table 3, ...
from	As can be seen *from* the data in Table 1, ...
by	As shown *by* the data in Table 1, ...
on	As described *on* Page 24, ...

以下是 as-从句使用的范例。

实例 1

We performed successive runs of confirmatory factor analysis and refinement. We also assessed construct reliability, convergent validity, discriminant validity, and validity of the second-order construct, **as reported in Table** 3.

实例 2

As shown in Table 3, all of our constructs meet this criterion.

实例 3

As shown in Fig. 2a, a single verifier can accept a significant portion of the location space as plausible.

实例 4

The gratings then disperse X-rays in the directions given for sectors a and e, **as shown.**

实例 5

As seen in Fig. 4, for the entire test collection, we found that ILAc had a mean precision of 0.971 and a mean recall of 0.947. Of course, without the use of a symbol table, we did not expect to obtain perfect precision and recall values of 1.0 when using ILAc.

实例 6

As can be seen, the maximum error is comparable to the added noise. This and other similar trials indicate that....

（2）对重要内容的陈述。

数据评论的主要部分用来突出论述的重点。重点论述就是对得出的繁杂的数据进行归纳和概括。重点论述需要有良好的判断力,它也为你提供了展示你聪明才智的机会；尤其是给你提供了机会,使你展示你具有从数据中发现某种趋势或规律的能力,展示你能把更重要的和不大重要的发现分离开来的能力,以及你能从中得出恰到好处的主张的能力。因此,数据评论不能单纯地用文字对数据进行详细的复述,也不能试图对所有信息进行论述,更不能给出不合理的、无法辩解的主张。

那么如何限定主张使其更具力度呢?

我们说过,突出论述重点需要良好的判断力,也需要具有把这种判断力展示出来的能力或手段。对此,提出两方面的要求:一是对待数据的处理要谨慎,有时还要体现出具有批判性。O'Connor（1995）就曾经说过,学生学会如何表述一个既能体现出自信又能展示对某一问题的不确定是非常重要的("It is important for students to learn to be confidently uncertain.")。二是掌握和利用语言技巧来表达这种谨慎,即要对提出的主张加以限定或使提出的主张适度。下面是为达此目的而给出的建议:

①表概率。在英语学术写作中,有很多表达概率的方式。最简单的方式是使用情态助动词,下面三个句子的语气是逐渐减弱的。

A reduced speed limit *will result in* fewer highway injuries.

A reduced speed limit *may result in* fewer highway injuries.

A reduced speed limit *might/could result in* fewer highway injuries.

下面例子中短语所体现的语气也是逐渐减弱的。

It is *certain* that
It is *almost certain* that
It is *very probable/highly likely* that
It is *probable/likely* that } a reduced speed limit will result in fewer injuries.
It is *possible* that
It is *unlikely* that
It is *very unlikely/highly improbable* that

There is a *strong* possibility that
There is a *good* possibility that
There is a *definite* possibility that } a reduced speed limit will result in fewer injuries.
There is a *slight* possibility that
There is a *remote* possibility that

②学会如何表示保持距离,避免过多地涉入。保持距离是另一种使自己避免涉入一个强硬的、很可能是一个不合理的主张的方法。下面这四个例句的语气逐渐减弱。

Consumers *have* less confidence in the economy today than 10 years ago.

Consumers *seem to have* less confidence in the economy.

Consumers *appear to have* less confidence in the economy.

It would seem/appear that consumers have less confidence in the economy.

还有一种策略可以使你与数据间保持一定的距离,就是采用"温和"的方式,如:

On the limited data available,
In the view of some experts,
According to this preliminary study,
Based on informal observations made by highway patrol officers

a lower speed limit may reduce highway fatalities.

③归纳概括。动词 tend 是对归纳、概括起限定修饰(或辩护)作用的一个经典动词。

Consumers *tend to have* less confidence in the economy.

另一个对归纳概括起到辩护作用的方法是对主语加以限定,如:

Many consumers have less confidence in the economy.

A majority of consumers have less confidence in the economy.

In most parts of the country, consumers have less confidence in the economy.

Consumers *in most income brackets* have less confidence in the economy.

第三种可供选择的方法是将例外的内容补充上,如:

With the exception of
Apart from
Except for
a few oil-rich states, national economies in Africa are not likely to improve greatly over the next decade.

④选用语气较弱的动词。最后,可采取选用语气较弱的动词的方式来缓解你的强硬主张。

Deregulation *caused* the banking crisis. (强)

Deregulation *contributed to* the banking crisis. (弱)

⑤几种限定/修饰方式的组合应用。当然,在构建一个无懈可击的、突出重点的论述过程中,可以把几种限定/修饰方式组合起来用,下面就是这样的一个例子,在下面的两个例句中,第一个句子的语气最强。

The use of seat belts prevents physical injuries in car accidents.

现在再看加了限定修饰语之后是什么样的：
prevents → reduces　　　　　　　　　（改用语气较弱的动词）
reduces → may reduce　　　　　　　　（加情态助动词体现结论的有限性）
+ in some circumstances　　　　　　　（限定其所适用范围）
+ certain types of injury　　　　　　　（对概括性进行限定）
+ According to simulation studies　　　（增加客观性/保持一定的距离）

加上修饰语后的句子：
According to simulation studies, *in some circumstances* the use of seat belts *may reduce certain types of* physical injuries in car accidents.

这是一个既表现出自信又表明对某一问题不确定的很好的例子（当然也要意识到过分的修饰会等于你什么也没说）。

（3）结束对数据的评论。
数据讨论的结尾部分通常涉及下面的问题：
- 解释或探讨其含意（通常是要求有的）；
- 预料之外的结果或数据（如必要的话）；
- 可能需要的进一步研究或预言（如恰当的话）。

①涉及"问题"的语句。
下面的短语可能对你讨论不理想的数据有用。

实例1
　　The difference between the expected and obtained results may be due to the incorrect calibration of the instruments.

实例2
　　This discrepancy can be attributed to the small sample size.

实例3
　　The anomaly in the observations can probably be accounted for by a defect in the camera.

实例4
　　The lack of statistical significance is probably a consequence of the weaknesses in the experimental design.

实例5
　　The difficulty in dating this archeological site would seem to stem from the limited amount of organic material available.

②涉及图表的短语。
语言点：有关曲线的术语。

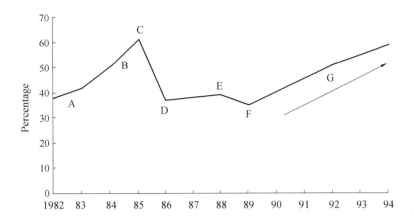

Figure 1　Qualifying examination pass rates 1982—94 for mechanical engineering at Midwestern University

描述曲线的术语:

upward trend	peak	low pint	sharp rise
steep fall	rise	leveling off	fell of
remained steady	spike	increase	decline
kink	minimum	local dip/local minimum	
maximum/peak	local maximum	linear increase	

③涉及年代的数据。

语言点:涉及时间的介词。

From 1982 *to* 1985 the pass rates rose.

During the first four years, the pass rates rose.

The pass rate fluctuated *from* 1982 *to* 1994.

The pass rate fluctuated *throughout* the period.

The pass rate remained under 50% *from* 1986 *to* 1991.

The pass rate remained under 50% *until* 1991.

6. 完整实例:结果部分

RESULTS OF INVESTIGATION

　　The stagger angle of tested large turning tip additional blades (TTAB-L) was changed from 40 to 700. It was found that the rotor performance curve was shifted to lower values of flow coefficients, with maximum value of $\Delta A = 180$ at the stagger angle of 600 (Fig. 5). However, this phenomenon was accompanied by substantial drop of the rotor peak efficiency (approximately of 30%). This was, of course, somewhat unwelcome effect.

　　Tests of short turning tip additional blades (TTAB-S) were conducted in two phases. Firstly, the stagger angle of tested TTAB-S was changed from 30 to 500 (and also 900). The rotor performance curve was shifted to lower values of flow coefficients, with maximum value of $\Delta A = 100$ at the stagger angle of 300 (Fig. 6). The relative axial clearance S_{ax} between short additional blades and succeeding elements of rotating blades was equal to 5% (of rotating blade chord). In the range of relative axial clearances from 5 to 20%, maximum effect of the change of operating range ($\Delta A = 42\%$) was found for $S_{ax} = 15\%$ and $\theta_{TATB-S} = 450$ (Fig. 7).

All above mentioned TTAB-S constructions were tested simply after machine turning of inlet edges of the succeeding elements of rotating blades without sharpening. At the second phase of tests, there were sharpened inlet edges of the succeeding elements of rotating blades. The sharpening procedure has permitted considerable recovering from losses in the tip flow field of the rotating blades. Thus in the variant of $\theta_{TATB-S} = 450$ and $Sax = 15\%$, only a 2.5% loss in rotor peak efficiency was observed (for comparison, a 19.5% loss in the variant without sharpening procedure), in common with the change in operating range $\Delta A = 32\%$ (Fig. 8).

It should be mentioned that, in all tests of additional blades, the point of maximum flow coefficient was shifted to lower values (at 13~15% for TTAB-L and at 7~13% for TTAB-S) as well as the point of stalling flow coefficient (at 15~20% for TTAB-L and at 6~24% for TTAB-S). Isentropic head coefficient was significantly decreased, with corresponding decrease of rotor peak efficiency and deformation of the efficiency curve (see Fig. 4). Radial profiles (Fig. 9) show some deformation. However, decreasing of total pressure coefficient near blade tip is significantly compensated by the pressure coefficient increasing near blade hub, so the isentropic head drop was not great.

调查结果

实验所用的大附加叶片 TTAB-L 的叶栅安装角由 40 度变化到 70 度。发现动叶流量系数的性能曲线移向低数值，在安装角为 60 度时（如图 5），ΔA 达到最大值 18%。然而这同时伴随着动叶最大效率的下降（大约 30%）。这当然是不好的效应。

首先，实验 TTAB-S 的安装角由 30 度变化到 50 度（也可变到 90 度），动叶性能曲线的流量系数降低。当安装角为 30 度时 ΔA 时达到最大值 10%（如图 6）。短顶部附加导叶和动叶的相对轴向间隙 S_{ax} 平均为动叶弦长的 5%。相对轴向间隙的范围是 5% 到 20%，运行范围的变化最大 ΔA=42%（如图 7）。

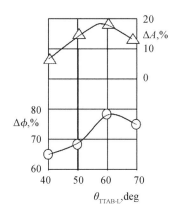
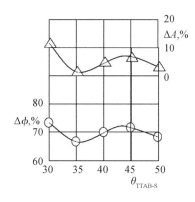

Figure 5 Results of TTAB-L tests

Figure 6 Results of TTAB-S tests ($\bar{S}_{ax} = 5\%$; without leading edge sharpening)

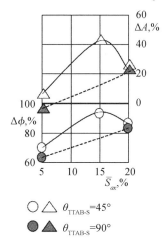

Figure 7 Results of TTAB-S tests (without leading edge sharpening)

短的顶部附加可调叶片(TTAB-S)的实验,分两个阶段进行。以上所述的 TTABS 结构是在动叶进口边旋转以后进行实验的,没有削尖。实验的第二阶段,动叶进口边被削尖。削尖的过程是为了减少动叶顶部流场的损失。当 $S_{ax} = 15\%$,$\theta_{TTAB-S} = 45$ 度时,动叶最大效率的损失只有 2.5%(没有削尖的最大效率的损失是 19.5%),运行范围的变化(如图8)。

需要强调的是,在实验中所有的附加叶片的流量系数的最高点都降低,(TTAB-L 是 13~15%,TTAB-S 是 7~13%),滞止流量系数最高点也降低,(TTAB-L 是 15~20%,TTAB-S 是 6~24%)。等熵压头系数明显降低,相应动叶最高效率也降低,其效率曲线发生变形,辐射状剖面也发生变形(如图9)靠近叶片顶部的总压系数虽然降低,但可以由叶片根部总压系数的增加来弥补,因此等熵压头下降并不大。

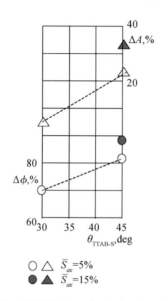

Figure 8　Results of TTAB-S tests (with leading edge sharpening)

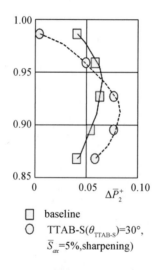

Figure 9　Radial profiles at the exit of the rotor

2.6　讨论/结论部分的撰写

讨论/结论部分与引言部分之间以某种方式相呼应。讨论/结果部分就好像是一个沙漏的下半部分,这部分的写作是由部分到整体的一个过程,先是精确的结果,然后是概括性的结论。讨论部分的作用是在借鉴已知研究的基础上,对目前从事的研究得出的结果进行解释,并在考虑了研究结果的基础上,说明就同一个问题可能出现的新的理解。

在讨论部分中,要对研究结果可能带来的影响进行解释。从理论和实验的角度把你的研究结果与他人的研究结果联系起来,从而把你的研究结果置于你所在的研究领域。

同引言一起,这部分的写作是解释并说明为何你的工作是重要的,你的研究工作是如何为学科领域的发展做出贡献的。要避免在这部分中引入新的思想,或论述那些与你的论题没有直接关系的内容。讨论部分的写作一定既要谨慎,又要精确、透彻。正如 Robert Day 指出的,很多的论文被所投的刊物编辑拒绝刊登,即使有的论文的数据可能是正确、值得关注的,究其原因,在于其讨论部分有问题;论文被拒刊的另一个原因是讨论部分没有能够表达出数据的真正含义。

1. 科学的研究方法

如果你要表达你的工作是如何为所在研究领域的发展做出了贡献,就要首先考虑所谓的"促进本领域的发展"意味着什么。或者说,你要考虑发展的条件是什么。

哲学家 John Platt 认为,有些领域之所以会比其他领域发展得更快,就在于在这些领域中已形成了缜密的、科学的研究方法。

这些迅速发展的领域之所以能迅速发展,就在于研究者们掌握了可被系统地应用和传授的科学研究的具体方法。这是一个有效的、学者们所熟悉并广泛应用的归纳推理和累积的方法。这种有说服力的推论方法在科学问题的研究中具体体现在:

(1) 设计出可供选择的假设;

(2) 设计出主要的实验,这个实验可能会产生可供选择的成果,进而可能由此排除已设计出的假设;

(3) 完成这个实验,以便得到一个确切的结果;

(4) 重复上述步骤,再设计出必要的假设或系列假设,以便通过论据或证据来证明剩余的可能是假的或错误的。

掌握这一系统方法的关键在于用严谨缜密、可供选择的假设、重要的实验、反证等来证明假设是错误的。这一过程使研究领域的科学家首先发现那些促进学术领域发展的重大问题,进而构建出解决每一个问题的合理的比较方案,并不断地排除那些无效的假设和探寻方法。这一系统方法减少了时间的浪费。因为它把大量的研究领域的理论和实验工作用到了可能会产生良好结果的假设和方法的探寻上。

从这种观点出发,在讨论部分应该讨论些什么呢?如何使人相信你的研究工作对本领域的发展是重大的、有价值的?为达此目的,你要论证你的研究工作是经过重大的实验检验的,你的研究证明了哪些假设是错误的,哪些是正确的;而且还要在这部分中如实报道和讨论负面的结果,如"Hypothesis A predicted that I would find B, but I did not. This result questions the validity of Hypothesis A or indicates its inadequacy"。这样的陈述能节省其他研究者的时间,使他们不至于再浪费几年无谓的努力,也是科学家对自然界所能做的最好的陈述。

哲学家 Karl Popper 曾经说过,科学上不存在唯一无懈可击的证据,因为而后的其他解释可能会同样,甚至于更好;因此科学是在反证的基础上发展的。假如构建出的假设一定是不可能的,或是不真实的,或是虚假的,那么,这样的假设什么也说明不了,这样的假设也就毫无意义。因为,"由经验证实的科学体系是可能反过来又被经验所驳倒的"。

2. 论证的一些基本问题

在论证说明你的工作是重要的、是基于重大实验的时候,要特别回答下面的一些或全

部的基本问题:
(1) 你的研究结果是否表明、证明或进一步说明了使用的模式、原理及其相互关系?
(2) 你的研究结果是预期的吗? 如果不是,为什么?
(3) 你能从你的研究结果中得出什么样概括性的结论或主张?
(4) 你是怎样比较你和他人的发现的? 与他人的发现有何关系? 如何与以往工作的期望值进行比较? 与以往工作的期望值的关系如何?
(5) 你的研究结果与他人给出的相一致吗? 如果不同,是否说明可从中得出另一种解释,或说明你的或他们的实验中可能存在未预料到的设计上的不足?
(6) 你的结果是证实还是反证了现有的理论?
(7) 你的结果是否说明现有的理论需要得到修正或拓展? 如果是,该如何做?
(8) 你的研究工作是否具有理论/实践上的意义?

在涉及这些问题时,重要的一点是你的讨论一定要紧紧地依赖于结果部分给出的证据,要不断地提及你的结果(但不要重复)。最重要的是你的结论不能超越你的结果所能证实的范围。讨论部分中可以有推断,但不能过多。要确定在讨论部分中探讨研究的目的,并讨论结果的意义。不要让读者处于困惑之中,如产生"那么又怎样呢""结果怎样""那有什么关系呢"等想法。讨论部分的结尾要有一个简短的概要或结论涉及你研究工作的意义。

3. 讨论部分的整体结构安排应该与实验结果出现的顺序相一致

要按照结果中给出的顺序逐渐展开讨论。你在对结果的意义的解读时要考虑你所研究问题的背景,也就是说你的研究是在什么样大的背景下展开的。在这部分中不要重复结果部分的内容。如果你认为有必要提醒读者你要对结果进行讨论,可以使用起连接作用的句式,把结果和解释联系起来。

"The slow response of the lead-exposed neurons relative to controls suggests that...."

你有必要在此提及他人的发现以便为你的解释做佐证。有必要的话,使用副标题来帮助你组织你的陈述;提防别错把对结果的重复当作是解释;在此也不能出现结果部分中没有出现过的新结果。

4. 要把你的工作与其他人的研究成果联系起来

在讨论部分,也要包括可能是你自己做的前期研究和他人所做的研究。如前所述,你可能在别人的研究中发现了有助于解释你的数据的重要信息,你也可能借助于你的发现来解释别人的发现,无论是这两种中的哪一种情况,你都该讨论为什么你的发现和他人的发现存在着相似或不同。考虑一下怎样把他人的研究结果和你的研究结果结合起来,以此更好地解释你所证实的研究问题。你在叙述从结果得出的结论时一定要考虑上述这些方面。你也可能选择简单地提一下你接下来要做的研究,以便阐明你的研究设想。不要忘记要像在引言部分那样提及引自他人的原始资料。

5. 叙述不能过于宽泛

谁也不可能仅通过一次 Rhizobium-legume 实验就得出下述这样的结论:在两种有机体中不存在互相依存的现象。你的结论只能是基于数据的结论,如"We did not find a significant effect of Rhizobium inoculate on soybean biomass in this experiment"。你也可以在此基础上,借助其他人的发现,进一步推测为什么会发生这种现象,以及这样的结果是否是你所期望发生的,或提出进一步研究的新方向、新方法、与以往公布的结果之间的差异的可能的解释等。可能的话,说一说所采用的方法中存在的问题,并解释数据中出现的反常现象。不能简单地把问题列举出来,而不从结论的角度讨论这些误差可能的含义是什么。

6. 讨论部分不能出现新的结果

尽管偶尔你会在这部分中包含那些有助于你讨论问题的表格和图表,但不能包含那些与你研究的问题有关的早期得出的数据,与本文研究的结果不相干的结果包括那些能够表明某种数据如何导致或与其他数据相联系的流程图、从文献汇集的数据等。比如说如果你在研究 membrane-bound transport channel,你发现了一些有关它的机理的新情况,你可能就会给出一个流程图来表明你的发现有助于解释 channel's 的机理。

7. 如何在讨论部分引用原始资料

为了为你提出的主张找证据,有必要在讨论部分中引用原始资料。下面用实例说明如何在文本中引证,以便读者能在论文最后的文献部分中找到详尽的参考资料,而且还不会妨碍读者对文本的阅读。

实例1

"Walnut trees are known to be allelopathic (Smith 1949, Bond etal. 1955, Jones and Green 1963)".

实例2

"Smith (1983) found that N-fixing plants could be infected by several different species of *Rhizobium*."

实例3

"Although the presence of *Rhizobium* normally increases the growth of legumes (Nguyen 1987), the opposite effect has been observed (Washington 1999)".

注意:在文本中引用的一、二作者的姓名中,引用的是姓,不是名。但如果作者超过两人,只给出第一作者的姓,然后加缩写的 **et al.**(拉丁语为"等")来代替其他作者。

上面第一个引用例句不但是合乎要求的,而且也是极力推崇的。为了阐述一个观点引用了不止一个资料,这样更增加了其论述的有效性,同时也表明你的研究是详尽、彻底的。

还要注意三个资料的引用顺序是按出版的先后顺序排列的,越早的则越排在前面。

文本中提到的所有文献一定要在文章最后部分的参考文献中详尽给出。

8. 一个完整的结论部分实例

A two-substrate, single biomass model integrating hydrolysis and acidogenesis in anaerobic digestion of cattle manure was validated using batch experimental data. The model was based on the following premises: (a) cattle manure is composed of two distinct fractions—a readily degradable fraction (hemicellulose) and a slowly degradable fraction (cellulose); (b) the hydrolysis process is according to a surface-limiting reaction; and (c) the acidogenesis process is according to a two-substrate, single biomass system. The model parameters included two yield coefficients, four hydrolysis rate constants, and four biokinetic coefficients. Predictions by the model using the parameters established in this study agreed well with the data measured under different conditions, with overall r_2 of 0.91, with p_o 0.002. Sensitivity analysis procedures indicated that the hydrolysis rate constant for cellulose fraction is the most sensitive parameter in the hydrolysis-acidogenesis of cattle manure. Since hydrolysis has been recognized as the rate-limiting step in the anaerobic digestion of complex particulate substrates, the findings of this study regarding readily degradable and slowly degradable fractions can be of value in designing, monitoring, analyzing, and optimizing the anaerobic gasification process.

一个双底物、单生物膜模型使牲畜粪肥的厌氧生物水解酸化，并由实验数据所验证。该模型建立在以下前提下：(a)牲畜粪肥是由两种不同的基质构成，一种为容易降解的物质(半纤维)，另一种是降解缓慢的物质(纤维)；(b)水解依据表面受限反应；(c)水解过程依据一个双基质单生物膜系统。该模型参数包括两个生长系数，四个水解速率系数和四个生物动力学系数。在研究中模型使用的参数与不同条件下测量的数据一致，其中 r_2 为 0.91，p_o 小于 0.002。灵敏性分析步骤得出了纤维素水解常数是牲畜粪肥水解酸化最敏感的参数。由于在厌氧生物消化复杂颗粒基质中，水解被看作是限速的步骤，本研究关于容易降解和缓慢降解值的发现可以用来设计、检测、分析、优化厌氧生物气化工艺。

2.7　致谢的撰写

如果你在对实验进行构思、设计、实现研究过程中得到了他人的很大帮助，例如为你提供了需要的财力等方面的帮助，你一定要就他们给予你的帮助、提供的服务或提供的资料表示感谢。作者总是要对给予作者初稿提出批评意见以及给予在其研究中提供资金帮助的人以感谢。在此，对使用的文体没有提出严格的规定，但致谢部分的写作要简洁，避免词藻浮华。

致谢通常出现在第一页的下方,也可能出现在讨论部分和文献部分之间。致谢部分给你提供了一个机会,借此表明你是某一学术团体的一分子并从中获益。尽管论文中的致谢部分被看作是必需的,但它确实表达的不仅仅是必要的礼节。曾经有一位著名的学者说他在阅读论文的时候,最先读的是致谢部分,他在回答为什么这样做的时候说,"我首先要了解的是谁在和谁进行交谈。"这句话表明致谢能使你的同行加深对你的了解。

1. 致谢部分通常包含的要素及例句

(1)财力上的帮助。

实例1

Financial support was provided by the University of Abertay Dundee, UK.

实例2

We are grateful to the U. K. Department of the Environment (Air Quality division) for funding the TOMPs program on Contract EPG1-3-69.

实例3

This work was financially supported by National Science Foundation grant BES-0401885, United States Department of Agriculture grant 68-3A75-3-150, the Penn State Huck Life Sciences Institute, and the Stan and Flora Kappe Endowment.

实例4

Funding for this study was provided, in part, by US Environmental Protection Agency, Grant No. SU832485, and by the National Science Foundation, Contract No. BES-0607175.

(2)研究或手稿方面的技术援助或建议/提供原始材料/手稿准备方面的帮助等。

实例1

Authors are extremely grateful to Prof. I. A. Zakharov (VIGG, Moscow, Russia) who inspired authors to proceed with this study and to Dr. V. Levitsky and Dr. M. Ponomarenko for their extremely valuable help with the biophysical aspects.

实例2

Masoumeh Sikaroodi and Mike Estep greatly helped with the proofreading of this manuscript.

实例3

Dr. J. Huppert helped a lot with quadruplex predictions.

实例4

Dr. R. Lebovitz helped a lot with filing a patent regarding findings described in this manuscript. A. B. was partially covered by NIH

实例 5

  The Authors are grateful to Mr. MartinKierans (School of Life Sciences, University of Dundee, Dundee) for his expert technical assistance in operating the transmission electron microscope.

(3) 他人不承担责任的声明(出现在上述(1)、(2)之后)。

实例 1

  The views expressed in this publication are those of the authors and do not necessarily represent/reflect those of Wessex Water, UK.

实例 2

  However, the opinions expressed here do not necessarily reflect the policy of (sponsor).

实例 3

  The interpretations in this paper remain my own.

实例 4

  None, however, is responsible for any remaining errors.

实例 5

  However, any mistakes that remain are my own.

(4) 阐明本文曾经出现在其他形式中。

实例

  An earlier/preliminary version of this paper was presented at (conference or seminar).

(5) 原始资料。

实例 1

  This article is based on the first author's doctoral dissertation.

实例 2

  This paper is based on the research completed as partial fulfillment for the Ph.D. requirements at (university name).

注意：

(1) 可能的话，致谢部分用第一人称来写，一个作者用 I，两个以上(包括两个)用 We。也可以用短语 the present authors，但这个短语的使用给人的感觉是有些过于正式。

(2) 据我们所知，财政上的协助通常最先写，而后是致谢；不承担责任的声明可有可无；(4)(5)项要是有的话可出现在最前面，也可出现在最后。

(3) 硕、博论文中，致谢部分的开头应是对导师、学术委员会等表示感谢。

2. 下面为三则完整的致谢的例子

实例1

  This work was supported by NIH (NS19806) and Biotech, Inc. A preliminary report was presented at the Pharmacology Society, May 25, 1999. We thank Jose Guera for the technical assistance and the assistance in the preparation of this manuscript. One of the authors (JD) is a paid consultant for Biotech, Inc.

实例2

  We are grateful to the many volunteers who helped with soil sampling worldwide; Sophie Parkman and Ben Dyson; our partners in the GLOBALSOC project; notably Dr. Johan Axelman, Dr. Orjan Gustafsson, and Professor Dag Broman at Stockholm University; the European Union for funding under Project ENV4 CT97 0638; and anonymous referees for helpful comments. K. C. J. is grateful to Eurochlor for funding at Lancaster University for work on HCB and to the Dow Chemical Company Foundation for financially supporting research on the global cycling of POPs. K. B. acknowledges financial support from the European Chemical Industry Council (CEFIC-LRI).

实例3

  Results are derived from POSEIDON Project "Assessment of Technologies for the Removal of Pharmaceuticals and Personal Care Products in Sewage and Drinking Water Facilities to Improve the Indirect Potable Water Reuse" supported by the European Union, Project number EVK1-CT-2000-00047 and the Project ARCEM "Austrian Research Cooperative on Endocrine Modulators" funded by Austrian Ministry of Agriculture, Forestry, Environment and Water, Kommunalkredit Austria AG and the nine Austrian Federal States.

2.8 关于参考文献

  如在前面提到的,科研论文的写作不同于其他类型的写作。科研论文不是作者自己观点的汇编,它的基础是对已发表的、与他本人研究主题相关的资料做全面、彻底的查询。因此,科研论文的关键在于研究的质量和如何在论文中准确地以专业的方式对研究发现予以陈述。一篇好的科研论文一定会在文献的提供过程中严格地遵循已确立的准则。下面就这些准则予以阐述。

  提供参考文献是对在论文写作过程中被使用的他人资料的一种肯定,所有借用的他人资料,包括引用语、解释、观点、信息、事实和统计数字等都要有所记载和体现;唯一不在其中、属于例外的是常识性的知识。

记载参考文献的地方有两处:文本之中位于参考资料之后的括号中和文章最后部分的参考文献目录中。文本之中的引用特点为:引用的文字不多;但也要指明你是在参考他人的资料,同时还要向读者说明文献目录中还会提供较充分的信息,以便读者在必要时借助文献目录准确找到所需的全文。

在撰写科研论文之前,先要确定稿件所投的刊物、会议、出版机构对稿件的格式要求,通常遵循的是两种格式:the APA (American Psychological Association)和 the MLA (Modern Language Association)。这两种相似的格式是有很大区别的,所以写作前就要确定要采用的是哪种格式。

APA 格式的文献目录(The Reference)和 MLA 格式的文献目录(Works Cited)都详细地列出了文本中提到的所有参考资料的信息。引用的格式要求是已经明确地被规定好的,十分规范,因此必须遵守,其页码是论文的延续。

文献目录属于论文的基本成分,专业化地、准确地标明原始资料的出处是必需的。因此一定要严格地按撰写文献目录的要求去做,论文的分量在很大程度上取决于这部分的撰写。下面分别介绍 APA 和 MLA 两种格式的文献目录。

2.8.1 APA 科研论文写作格式(APA Style)

1. 含圆括号式的引用

——含圆括号式的引用,用在论文文本之中,用以识别文本中引用的参考资料。圆括号是一个很短的符号标志,通常放在使用的参考资料的句子末尾,包括作者的姓、出版日期,使读者以此得知此素材是外来借用的,不属于作者自己的思想。日期在科研中意义重大,故在引用中标明作者和出版日期。

• 通常作者的姓名、出版日期要放在被参考的资料的后面,而且是放在括号里,还要放在被引用的资料所在段落、句子、从句或短语的最后的标点符号的前面。

• 作者和出版日期之间要有一个逗号。

• 只有使用了从原文中直接引用的资料才在引用中标出具体的页码。标明引用的页码时,使用表示页码的缩略形式 p. 或 pp.。缩略形式 p. 表示引用的资料在原始资料的一页内;缩略形式 pp. 表示引用了一页以上的原始资料。

例句:

"The period of Gorbachev's reforms—the so-called perestroika, or restructuring—has seen an increase in nationalistic unrest"(Roth, Warwick & Paul, 1989, p.267).

• 如果作者的姓已经在文本中出现,那么在括号中只标出出版日期,但要注意,在这种情况下,引用语要直接跟在作者的姓之后。

例如:
> Roth, Warwick, and Paul (1989) state that the lowest level of rural hierarchy is the production team.

- 如果作者的姓和出版日期都已经在文本中出现,就不要再用括号来引用了。

例如:
> In 1989, Roth, Warwick and Paul stated that the lowest level of rural hierarchy is the production team.

- 如果原始资料的作者不止一人,第一次提到时,全部列出,用逗号来分隔每一个作者,最后的作者前用 &(and 的记号名称)。在而后的引用中,只提第一作者,再加上表示"等人"的符号 et al。

例如:
第一次引用
(**Roth, Warwick & Paul**, 1989)

再次引用
(**Roth et al.**, 1989)

- 如果参考资料的作者在六个以上,只写第一位作者,其他的用 et al. 代替。
- 如果作者是集体的,第一次引用时,写出全称,接着是其缩写形式,放在方括号中;以后再次引用时只用缩写形式。

例如:
第一次引用
(**National Institute of Mental Health [NIMH]**, 2002)

再次引用
(**NIMH**, 2002)

- 如果没给出作者,就用标题的前几个单词和出版日期。
- 如果使用的是电子资料,常常会发现无法找到这方面的信息,要是没有作者或标题,就用文件名,放在括号里。

例如：
(enterprise.com, 2002)

• 如果没有出版日期，就用你提取这个信息的日期，以日、月和年为序。

例如：
(Treidler 25 Apr. 2002)

2. 参考文献专页

• 参考文献专页位于论文的最后，单独一页，其中列出论文撰写中用到的所有参考资料。
• 每一条目都要包含完整、准确的信息，提供的参考文献使用的是 APA 格式。
• 所有条目的排列顺序都是依照作者姓的字母排列；没有作者姓名的，依照标题第一个单词的字母顺序，不包括 A、An 或 The。
• 每一条目都是双倍距离，条目间也是双倍距离。
• 每一条目起始于左边的页边空白，如果一行写不下，其他行向后缩进五个间隔。
• 书和期刊的名称要用斜体字。
• 论文标题不用引号。
• 论文标题的第一个单词和专有名词要大写。
• 引用中使用作者的姓和名的词首字母大写。
• 如果两篇以上的论文或书（包括两篇）是属于同一个作者的，文献按时间先后顺序列出。
• 下面给出的是最常用的参考文献条目。不包括的，可到网上参阅 Publication Manual of the American Psychological Association（APA 手册）或网站（APA website）。

(1) 书籍。
该类型参考文献的内容包括：
• 作者；
• 用括号表示的出版年份；
• 用斜体表示的书名；
• 出版地，出版地之后是冒号；
• 发行人名称。

书籍的作者为一人的：
Sickly, A. (2001). *Analyzing health care*. New York: Association of Hospitals.

无作者姓名的书籍：
Still a mystery. (2000). Detroit: Random Press.

书籍作者为两人的：
Seer, B. & Mystic, E. (1999). *Searching for crystals*. San Francisco: Society for Enlightenment.

书籍作者多达四人的：
Clemens, S. J., Cotter, L. G., Jennings, K. A. & Kandel, S. M. (2001). *In pursuit of truth*. New York: Viking.

书籍的作者在六人以上的：
Olson, H. E. et al. (2000). *Psychology today*. Vancouver: Canadian Press.

书籍的作者为集体作者，而且作者同时还是发行者：
American Cheerleaders Association. (1999). *Cheering manual* (2nd). Jessup, MD: Author.

多卷作品：
Story, G. (2000). *The history of civilization*. (vols. 1-16). Philadelphia: University of Pittsburgh Press.

参考书的一部分：
Singleton, L. (1998). *The lone voice*. In Will Boss (Ed.), *Getting it all together* (pp. 120-122). New York: Norton.

(2) 期刊。
该类型参考文献的内容包括：
- 作者；
- 用括号表示的出版年、月；
- 论文的标题（不用引号，标题的第一个单词要大写）；
- 期刊的名称要用斜体字；
- 卷号要用下划线；
- 页码索引。

定期刊物文章：
Rebert, S. (2001). Preserving the rainforests. *Journal of Social Issues*, 4, 14-18.

杂志文章：
Hawkings, S. (1988, January). Black holes. *Science*, pp. 21-23.

(3)报纸等。

该类型参考文献包含的信息：
- 作者；
- 确切的日期(放在括号中,其中包括年、月、日)；
- 文章标题；
- 报刊名称；
- 页码。

报刊文章：

Flowers, F. (1999, March 21). Rain in the forest. *Laurel Leader*, Sec. 2, p.2.

报刊社论：

Killing the earth (editorial). (2002, May 10). *Baltimore Sun*, Sec. A, p.19.

小册子：

Abbot, C. (2000). Canning apples. Washington: Dept. of Agriculture.

访谈：

Dance, D. (1986, February 16). [Interview on the David Letterman Show.]

影片：

Artly, J. B. (producer) & Starr, B. A. (director). (1990). *The big picture* [film]. Hollywood: Metro Goldwyn Mayer.

信息源：

Kotulak, R. (1986, December 21). *Growing up at risk*. Chicago Tribune. (SIRS, VOL. 3, #19).

(4)电子宣传工具。

该类型参考文献包括的信息：
- 作者的姓,之后是第一个词首大写字母；
- 发表文件的日期放在括号中；
- 标题(其中只有第一个词和专有名词的第一个字母大写)；
- 网站的名称(其中只有第一个词和专有名词的第一个字母大写)；
- 译文或版本；
- URL 或电子地址；
- 你提取信息的日期。

网络文章:

Hafer, H. R. (2000, April). *Yoga for body and mind.* Retrieved July 8, 2002 from http://www.ivillage.com/fitness/yoga/html.

网络期刊的文章:

Janowitz, J. P. & Phizer, R. J. (2001, Jan. 24). Walking for life. *Time.* Retrieved April 26, 2002 from http://www.time.com.

(5) 电子信函、讨论表和新闻组。
该类型参考文献包括的信息:
- 作者的姓和第一个词首大写字母;
- 只大写第一个词和专有名词的主题;
- 讨论表的名称或新闻组的名称(第一个词和专有名词的第一个字母要大写,而且要用斜体);
- 名单地址;
- 日期(提取时间放在括号里)。

Kepler, J. The art of writing. *Computers and Writing discussion group.* jkepler@ulc.edu (March 5, 2001).

(6) 来自电子数据库的文章。

电子数据库的文章来源渠道多种多样,有的来自于期刊、杂志,有的来自报刊和百科全书。这些文章多数都有书面文字资料,因此,如果你在文献专页中纳入的文章来自于电子数据库,你应该补充一些信息来说明你的文章是来自于网络,而不是印刷本。

期刊和报刊的文章引用的格式同出版物格式一样,之后是你提取文章的日期和资料库名称。

定期期刊文章:

Furlong, M., and Morrison, G. (2000). The school in school violence: Definitions and facts. *Journal of Emotional and Behavioral Disorders* 8.2, 71. Retrieved 2001, November 2, from InfoTrac database (Expanded Academic ASAP).

杂志文章:

Peele, S. (1996, September/October). Recovering from an all-or-nothing approach to alcohol. *Psychology Today*, 29, 35–36. Retrieved 2001, November 2, from InfoTrac database (Expanded Academic ASAP).

报刊文章:

Dilllin, J. (2000, November 2). Independent voters are helping Bush to pull ahead. *The Christian Science Monitor*, p. 2. Retrieved 2001 November 2, from LexisNexis database (Academic Universe.)

百科全书和字典数据库:

APA 对从百科全书或字典数据库引用文章的格式要求略不同于已出版的百科全书或字典。

如果知道作者的姓,首先是作者的姓;如果没有作者的信息,开始就是条目的名称(也就是你在网上找到的东西),用它作为标题;之后是提取方面的注释,同上面的例子相同。

Robinson, L. J. (2000). Hubble space telescope. Retrieved 2001 November 2, from *Encyclopedia Americana* database.

(7)参考文献专页的实例。

REFERENCE LIST

Beck, A. (1999). *Cognitive therapy and emotional disorders*. New York: International Universities Press.

The fight to conquer fear. (2002, April 23). *Newsweek*. Retrieved June 24, 2002 from http://www.newsweek.com.

Goodwin, D. W. (1996). *Phobia: the facts*. New York: Oxford University Press.

Lehman, B. (2001, June 3). Holding fear of fear at bay. *Boston Globe*. Retrieved February 4, 2002, from http://www.bostonglobe.com.

Melville, J., Tearnan, B. H. & Taylor, C. (1977). *Phobias and obsessions*. New York: Scribner's.

Wolpe, J. (1985). *Psychotherapy by reciprocal inhibition*. Palo Alto: Standford University Press.

Wolpe, J. (1987). *Our useless fears*. Boston: Houghton Mifflin.

2.8.2 MLA 科研论文写作格式(MLA Style)

1. 含圆括号式的引用

- 引用时要明确地指明引用文献的出处和日期。
- 通常作者的姓名、出版日期要放在被参考的资料后面,而且是在括号里,还要放在被引用的资料所在段落、句子、从句或短语的最后那个标点符号的前面。

例如：

"Human rights! Respect as human beings! That's what America's black masses want" (Haley 272).

- 被引用的作者和页码在引用语之后，两者之间不用标点符号。

例如：

(Haley 272)

- 如果作者姓名已经出现在了文本的句子之中，括号内只写页码。

例如：

Haley states that believing in peaceful coexistence is not enough (368).

- 再次连续引用时只写页码。

例如：

(Haley 272) (376)

- 如果作品的作者没有出现，就用标题中第一个有意义的词，而且要把它放在引号内。

例如：

("Power" 30)

- 如果你参考了同一位作者的一篇以上的文章，引用中要写作者姓名，标题中第一个有意义的词和引用的页码。

例如：

(Smith "Power" 30) (Smith "Energy" 13)

- 如果参考资料的作者是两三位，引用中应写上所有作者的姓。

例如：

(Cohen, Cotter, Jennings 257)

- 如果参考资料的作者在三个以上，只写第一位作者的姓，接着写表示"等人"的拉丁语 et al. 。

例如：

(Robert et al. 224)

2. 参考文献专页

- 在参考文献目录中规范地列出你在论文写作中参考过的所有原始资料。
- 参考文献中包含的只能是论文中引用过的资料。
- 每一条目都要包含完整、准确的信息，严格按照 MLA 格式来引用参考过的文献。
- 参考文献位于论文的最后，单独一页，其中列出所有在论文撰写中用到的参考资料。
- **参考文献**这几个字要居中，英文为 **Works Cited**。
- 参考文献专页的页码号是论文前部分页码的接续。
- 所有条目的排列依照作者姓的字母顺序；没有作者姓名的，取标题中第一个重要的单词，把它按作者姓的字母顺序排列。
- 每一条目的起始都从左侧的页边空白处开始。
- 参考文献专页的每一条目都是双倍间距，条目间也是双倍距离。
- 如引用同一作者的多部作品或文章，只需在第一条中列出作者的名字。此后，用——代替作者的名字即可。
- 超过一行的条目从下一行起向里缩入五个空格。
- 每一条目包括三个主要部分：作者、标题和出版资料；每一部分之后是句号，留有两个空格。
- 书籍、期刊、报刊、电视节目、电影、比赛等的名称之下要加下划线，或者是用斜体字。
- 在写作者的姓名时先写姓，然后是名。
- 如果作者人数为两个或两个以上，第一个作者先写姓，之后是名；后面的作者先写名，然后是姓；其间用逗号。
- 如果两本或两本以上的书籍、两篇或两篇以上的文章同属同一作者，只在第一条目中列出作者的姓名，而后用符号——代替作者的姓名。
- 如果要引用的页码是连续的，列出被引用范围内的前后两页的页码。

例如：

4-8.

- 如果被引用的几页页码不是挨在一起的，注明文章的第一个页码，之后是符号+。
- 下面给出的是最常用的几种参考文献条目。不包括的，可到网上参阅《MLA 科研论文写作规范》(The MLA Handbook for Writers of Research Papers)。

(1) 书籍。
该类型参考文献包括的信息：作者姓名、标题、出版地、出版商和出版日期。

一个作者的书籍：
  Sikly, Al. Analyzing Health Care. New York: Association of Hospitals, 1986.

没有作者姓名的书籍：
  Still a Mystery. Detroit: Random Press, 1989.

两本书籍属同一作者：
  Smith, Harry. The First Page. Chicago: Houghton Mifflin, 1980.
  ——. Second Thoughts. Chicago: Houghton Mifflin, 1985.

两位作者的书籍：
  Seer Bertha, and Emma Mystic. Searching for Crystals. San Francisco: Society for Enlightenment, 1990.

三位以上作者的书籍：
  Joiner, Ed, et al. Becoming Part of the Group. New York: Scribner's, 1985.

多卷作品中的一卷：
  Story, Grant. The History of Civilization. vol. 1. Philadelphia: University of Pittsburgh, 1980. 10 vols.

文选或参考书的一部分：
  Singleton, Leslie. "The Lone Voice." Getting It All Together. Ed. Willy Boss. New York: Norton, 1992. 250–255.

(2) 期刊。
该类型参考文献的信息包括：作者、文章标题、期刊名称、日期、整个文章的页码。

标有连续页码的文章：
  Hawking, Stephen. "Black Holes." Science Jan. 1988: 21–23.

页码不连续的匿名文章：
  "Blowing Bubbles." Kids Weekly 24 Jan. 1986: 14+.

(3)报刊等。

该类型参考文献的信息包括:作者、文章标题、报刊名称、日期(日、月、年)、页码。

一篇报刊上的文章:

Jennings, Veronica. "Plea Set in Cheating Case in Maryland." Washington Post 21 July 2001: D5-D7.

社论:

"Develop a Date Rape Policy." Editorial. Breeze 3 Oct. 2000: 14.

给编者的信:

Curiouss, Carl. Letter. *New York Times* 2 Sep. 1999: B2.

小册子:

Abbott, Corless. *Canning Apples*. Washington: Dept Agriculture 2001.

访谈:

Dance, Dianna. Interview. David Letterman Show. *NBC*. 16 Feb. 1998.

电影:

The Big Picture. Dir. B. A. Starr. Metro Goldwyn Mayer. 1990.

电视和广播节目:

The First Americans. Narr. Hugh Downs. Writ. And Prod. Craig Fisher. *NBC News. KNBC, Los Angeles*. 21 Mar. 1988.

新闻部门:

Kotulak, Ronald. "Growing Up at Risk." *Chicago Tribune*. 21 Dec. 1986, Sec: 1+. SIRS, Youth, vol. 3, art. 19.

Washington Post. 18 June 1982. Editorials on File. 1982. Illegal Aliens 703.

(4)电子宣传工具。

该类型参考文献的信息包括:

• 作者姓名(姓,之后是名);

- 放在引号中的文章标题,所有主词的第一个字母都要大写;
- 网站的名称下加下划线;
- 文章张贴的日期;
- 文章被提取的日期;
- URL(电子地址)放在< >中。

因特网上的文章:

  Hafer, Helen. "Yoga for Body and Mind." *Ivillage*. 25 Apr. 2000. 8 July 2002 <http://www.ivillage.com/fitness/yoga/html>.

因特网期刊文章:

  Janowitz, Paul, Rachael Phizer. "Walking for Life." *Time*. 24 Jan. 2001. 26 Apr. 2002 <http://www.time.com>.

(5)电子信函、讨论表和新闻组。

  Kepler, Jana. "The Art of Writing." Online posting. 5 Mar. 2001. Computers and Writing Discussion Group. 7 Apr. 2001 <jkepler@ulc.edu.>

(6)来自电子数据库的文章。

  电子数据库的文章来源是多渠道的,例如期刊和百科全书。这些文章多数都有书面文字资料,因此,如果你的文献专页中纳入的文章来自于电子数据库,你该补充一些信息来说明你的文章是来自于网络,而不是印刷本。

  期刊、杂志和报刊的文章引用的格式同出版物格式是一样,之后是你提取文章的所在资料库名称、位置、提取信息的日期和 URL。

期刊文章:

  Peele, Stanton. "Recovering from an All-or-nothing Approach to Alcohol." *Psychology Today* Sep.—Oct. 1996: 35. InfoTrac Expanded Academic ASAP. Howard Community College Library, Columbia, MD. 2 Nov. 2001 <http://www.galegroup.com>.

杂志文章:

  Getz, Arlene. "Out in the Cold: Travel Nightmare: Far from Home with a Frozen Credit-Card Account." *Newsweek*. 30 Oct. 2000: 102. InfoTrac Expanded Academic ASAP. Howard Community College Library, Columbia, MD. 2 Nov. 2001 <http://www.galegroup.com>.

报刊文章:

  Dillon, John. "Independent Voters are Helping Bush to Pull Ahead." *The Christian Science Monitor*. 2 Nov. 2000: 2. LexisNexis Academic Universe. Howard Community College Library, Columbia MD. 2 Nov. 2001 <http://web.lexis-nexis.com/universe>.

百科全书和字典数据库:

  "Hubble Space Telescope." Encyclopedia Britannica Online. Howard Community College Library, Columbia MD. 31 Oct. 2001 <http://eb.com>.

CD-ROM:

  Williams, Denise and Francis Robinson. "Whites and the Entertainment Industry." *Tennessee Tribune*. 25 Dec. 2000: 28. Ethnic Newswatch. CD-ROM. Data Technologies. 4 Mar. 2002.

(7)参考文献专页实例。

WORKS CITED

Akins, Joanna, and Laurie Ellen. *Birth Control in the Classroom*. New York: McGraw Hill, 1998.

Berger, Joseph. "Desperation and Anger in Debate on Condoms." *New York Times* 7 Feb. 1999: B1-2. LexisNexis Academic Universe. Howard Community College Library. 4 Mar. 2001 <http://web.lexisnexis.com/universe>.

——. "5 of Boards 7 for Condoms in the Schools." *New York Times* 27 Sept. 1990: B3+. LexisNexis Academic Universe. Howard Community College Library. 4 Mar. 2001 <http://web.lexisnexis.com/universe>.

"The Facts of Life about Teenage Sex." Editorial. *Washington Post* 27 Sept. 1990: A22+.

"Strong Medicine for AIDS." Editorial. *New York Times* 5 Dec. 1990: A26. Tifft, Susan. "Better Safe Than Sorry." *Time* 21 Jan. 1991: 66-69.

2.9 关于附录

  就对论文的理解而言,附录中包含的信息不是必不可少的,但其作用却是不可小觑的,在不增加文章主干部分的前提下,它能使所阐述的观点更加清晰。附录就全文而言,是可有可无的部分,用在论文中的情况也不是很多。

  每个附录都要用罗马数字排序,如附录一为 Appendix Ⅰ,附录二为 Appendix Ⅱ等;每个附录所包含的材料是不同的。

1. 附录中常见的内容有(不是唯一的):

- 原始数据;
- 图(特别是插页);
- 特别的照片;
- 公式说明(特别是那种你"发明"的一些用于数据分析的统计或数学应用程序);
- 针对某一特定程序编制的专门计算计划;
- 文本中提过的、简化的或以普通名称使用过的化学品或合成物的完整属名;
- 专门仪器示意图。

2. 附录中的图形和表格

附表中常会出现一些图形和表格,而且都是有一定格式的,但页码是单独排列的,不和文章的主要部分相连,因此,附录中的第一个图标应该写为 Figure 1,表格一应为 Table 1,以此类推。如果使用了不止一个附录的话,除了图表和表格需要编号码,附录同样也要编号码。

第三章
标点符号的用法

3.1 标点符号概述

我们在讲话时,可用停顿、变换语调等方式来突出重点;而在写作中,句子意义和重点内容的表达则需借助标点符号来实现。因此,掌握标点符号的正确使用十分必要。英文的标点符号与中文的大同小异。英文中也有句号(period)、冒号(colon)、逗号(comma)、分号(semicolon)、感叹号(exclamation mark)、引号(quotation mark)、省略号(ellipsis)等。中英文标点符号也有不同的地方,如英文**句号**不是一个圈(a tiny circle)"。",而是一个点(a dot)".";省略号在英文中是3个点"...",在句尾用4个点"....";而中文里则为6个点"……";英文里只有逗号",",没有顿号"、",但中文里没有表示所有格的撇号"'"(即's);中文里有书名号"《》",如《英汉字典》,英文则没有。英文中的书名常采用把每一个单词的首字母大写的形式,如 An English-Chinese Dictionary,或用斜体字如 *Gone with the Wind* 的方式来表示。下面只简单介绍常用标点符号的使用方法。

两个术语:独立分句和从属子句。
独立分句:有主语和动词,并能单独使用的分句叫作独立分句。
从属分句:有主语和动词,但并不能单独使用的分句叫作从属分句。

1. 逗号(,)

逗号(**comma**)在写作中使用最多,正确使用逗号对于句子分析、语义表达都非常重要。逗号通常预示着停顿。

(1)逗号同并列连词一起用于连接两个独立/并列分句,或用于复合句中。逗号要放在连词(*and*、*but*、*or*、*for*、*so*、*nor*、*yet*、*or not only... but also*)之前。

实例1

Road construction can be inconvenient, *but* it is necessary.
修路会带来不便,但却是必要的。

实例2

The new house has a large fenced backyard, *so* I am sure our dog will enjoke it.

新房子后院很大，还被篱笆围着，我相信我们家的狗一定喜欢。

实例 3

The sun is shining, *and* everything looks very bright.

阳光照耀，万物看上去闪烁着光芒。

实例 4

No dielectric constants are available for concentrated acids, *so* it is difficult to give a quantitative explanation for the results.

因为在浓酸中不存在电容率，因而很难对结果做出定量性的解释。

实例 5

He is an eccentric boy, *yet* you can't help liking him.

他很古怪，然而你却会情不自禁地去喜欢他。

注意：如果两个句子都很短，可以省去两句之间的逗号。

实例：

He was ill and he was absent.

他生病了，没来。

（2）在介绍性短语、介词短语、从属子句后使用逗号。

实例 1

To get a good grade, you must complete all your assignments.

要想得高分，你必须完成所有的作业。

实例 2

Because Dad caught the chicken pox, we canceled our vacation.

由于爸爸出水痘，我们不得不取消了度假。

实例 3

After the wedding, the guests attended the reception.

结婚典礼后，客人们参加了婚宴。

实例 4

The products, which were produced at high temperature, were unstable.（非限定从句）

这些高温下生产的产品性能不稳定。

实例 5

The action of direct current, which is a current flowing always in one direction, was dealt with.（非限定从句）

探讨了始终沿着一个方向流动的直流电的事。

实例 6

To climb the pole, cold and wet with snow, was no easy task.（形容词短语做非限制性后置定语）

爬上那沾着雪且又冷又湿的极点很不容易。

实例 7

Drawn up in front was a sofa, covered with red rep.（过去分词短语做非限制性后置定语）

前面摆着一张套着红棱纹平布套的沙发。

实例 8

At the center of each atom there is a nucleus, in which are found protons, possessing a positive electric charge, and neutrons, possessing nocharge.（现在分词短语做非限制性后置定语）

每个原子的中心有一个原子核,核内有带正电的质子与不带电的中子。

实例 9

Our forces, now in control of all the bridgeheads, were ready to take the city.（介词短语做非限制性后置定语）

我们的部队已控制了所有的桥头堡,正准备拿下这座城市。

（3）逗号用以分割系列中的要素,尽管没有明确的规定要求在系列的最后一项前用逗号,但学术惯例是在系列的最后一项前用逗号。

实例 1

On her vacation, Lisa visited Greece, Spain, and Italy.

丽莎在度假期间参观了希腊、西班牙和意大利。

实例 2

In their speeches, many of the candidates promised to help protect the environment, bring about world peace, and end world hunger.

许多候选人在讲话中都承诺要为环保、促进世界和平和解决世界性饥饿问题做出贡献。

实例 3

water(H_2O), sodium hydroxide (NaOH), and ammonia(NH_3)

水(H_2O)、氢氧化钠(NaOH)和氨水(NH_3)

实例 4

The red needles were collected, washed with toluene, and dried in a vacuum desiccator.

红色针状物被收集起来,用甲苯清洗并在真空干燥器里烘干。

实例 5

Electrical energy may be converted to mechanical motion, heat, light, chemical energy, sound, or radiation.

电能可转变为机械运动、热、光、化学能、声或辐射能。

(4) 用逗号把非基本的成分同句子分开。具体地说,当句子中包含的某些信息相对于句子的意图而言不是至关重要的时候,用逗号把这部分的内容分割开来。

实例 1
  John's truck, a red Chevrolet, needs new tires.
  约翰的红雪佛兰卡车该换新轮胎了。

实例 2
  When he realized he had overslept, Matt rushed to his car and hurried to work.
  发现自己睡过头后,马特急匆匆地钻进他的车,赶去上班。

实例 3
  Beijing, the capital of China, is situated in the East Asia.
  中国首都北京位于东亚。

实例 4
  The boiling temperature, or boiling point, is the temperature at which a liquid boils under ordinary pressure.
  沸腾温度,即沸点,是液体在常压下沸腾的温度。

实例 5
  They met Mr. Wang, an oil engineer, yesterday.
  昨天他们遇见了石油工程师王先生。

实例 6
  There are two kinds of charges, namely, positive and negative (charges).
  电荷有两种,即正电荷与负电荷。

实例 7
  There are many cities, for examples (e.g.), Beijing, Shanghai, Tianjin, and Chongqing in China.
  中国有许多城市,如北京、上海、天津和重庆。

实例 8
  Weight is directly related to the mass of a body, that is, to the amount of matter in it.
  重量与物体质量,即物体内物质的数量有直接关系。

(5) 在两个并列形容词之间用逗号。

实例 1
  The irritable, fidgety crowd waited impatiently for the rally speeches to begin.
  烦躁不安的人群焦急地等待着集会演说的开始。

实例 2
  The sturdy, compact suitcase made a perfect gift.

这个小巧、结实的手提箱是个不错的礼物。

（6）在过渡词或短语（however、therefore、nonetheless、also、otherwise、finally、instead、thus、of course、above all、for example、in other words、as a result、on the other hand、in conclusion、in addition）后使用逗号。

实例 1

For example, the Red Sox, Yankees, and Indians are popular baseball teams.

例如，红袜队、洋基队以及印第安人队都是深受欢迎的棒球队。

实例 2

If you really want to get a good grade this semester, however, you must complete all assignments, attend class, and study your notes.

然而如果你这学期想要得高分，就必须完成所有作业，上好课，弄懂笔记。

实例 3

In my opinion, physical changes have nothing in common with chemical changes.

在我看来，物理变化与化学变化无共同之处。

实例 4

Generally speaking, iron is apt to rust.

一般说来，铁易生锈。

实例 5

This instrument, I think, is useful, not to say important.

我认为，此仪器虽谈不上多么重要，但还是有用的。

（7）用逗号引出直接引语，但如果引语是句子的主语或宾语，则不用逗号。

实例 1

"Yes," she promised. Todd replied, saying, "I will be back this afternoon."

"是的。"她承诺道。托德答道："我今天下午返回。"

实例 2

In the words of Pasteur, "Chance favors the prepared mind."

用巴斯德的话说，"机会偏爱于有心人。"

实例 3

Pasteur said "Chance favors the prepared mind."

巴斯德说过"机会偏爱于有心人"。

实例 4

"Chance favors the prepared mind" is a translation from the French.

"机会偏爱于有心人"是从法语译过来的。

(8) 在日期、数字、个人头衔中使用逗号,或用逗号来分隔城市与州/国家。

实例1
  October 25, 1999

实例2
  Monday, October 25, 1999

实例3
  25 October, 1999

实例4
  15,000,000

实例5
  Mike Rose, Chief Financial Officer for Operations, reported the quarter's earnings. West Lafayette, Indiana.

(9) 注意 when、while、although、though 等位于主句之后,并且其前面有逗号时做并列连接词用。

实例1
  There is another formula for finding the power in watts, **when** we must know only the current (I) and resistance(R).
  有另一种求功率瓦数的公式,这时我们只需知道电流(I)和电阻(R)。

实例2
  Air is very light, **while** lead is quite heavy.
  空气很轻,而铅则十分重。

实例3
  Mercury is also a metal, **although/though** it is in the liquid state.
  水银也是金属,尽管它处于液体状态之中。

实例4
  Air has weight, **though** it is very light.
  空气有重量,虽然它很轻。

(10) 句中较长的从句之后或介词短语之后需加一逗号。

实例1
  Because of the known reactor period of the super-critical reactor, it is easy to calculate the reactivity.
  由于超界反应堆的反应堆周期是已知的,因此很容易计算出反应性。

实例2
  Because the reactor period of the super-critical reactor is known, it is easy to calculate the reactivity.
  由于超界反应堆的反应堆周期是已知的,因此很容易计算出反应性。

(11) 注意:下列诸情况不需加逗号。

① 用 et al. 表示众多人等时,一个人时其前不加逗号,但两人以上时,则加逗号。例如:

  Jones et al.　　Brown, Smith, et al.

② 不用逗号来分隔句中的主语和谓语动词,或谓语动词和宾语。

实例 1

  把 X-糖添加到 Y-溶剂已得到广泛研究。

  [误] The addition of X-sugar to Y-solvent, has been studied widely.

  [正] The addition of X-sugar to Y-solvent has been studied widely.

实例 2

  此项研究中所使用的溶剂是环戊烷、甲醇和甲苯。

  [误] The solvents employed in this study were, cyclohexane, methanol, and toluene.

  [正] The solvents employed in this study were cyclohexane, methanol, and toluene.

注意:避免用逗号连接两个独立的分句。可用句号把两个独立的分句分开;或先用逗号,然后紧跟着是并列连词;最后还可选择用分号连接。

2. 分号(;)

(1) 当两个或多个分句在没有连接词(and、but、or、nor、for、so、yet)相连的情况下,可用分号(semicolon)来分隔这些独立的分句。

实例 1

  Road construction in Dallas has hindered travel around town; streets have become covered with bulldozers, trucks, and cones.

  达拉斯道路的建设已阻碍了城镇的交通;街道上到处都是推土机、卡车和施工段用的路标。

实例 2

  所有溶剂都是从一种适宜的干燥剂中蒸馏出来的;四氢呋喃和二乙醚也用活度 I 的铝帆土预处理过。

  [误] All solvents were distilled from an appropriate drying agent, tetrahydrofuran and diethyl ether were also pretreated with activity I alumina.

  [正] All solvents were distilled from an appropriate drying agent; tetrahydrofuran and diethyl ether were also pretreated with activity I alumina.

实例 3

  No one is born with knowledge; knowledge must be taught and

learned.

知识不是先天就有的;知识必须经过后天的学习和教育才能获得。

(2)分号可用于由连接副词或转换词(that is(i.e.)also、furthermore、nevertheless、therefore、besides、however、otherwise(副词/连词)、thus、consequently、then、moreover、still、in fact、for example、that is、for instance、in addition、in other words、on the other hand、even so)连接的两个独立分句之间。

实例 1

所给出的中间体是不易被察觉的,所以最终的产物是开始观察到的那个。

[误]*The proposed intermediate is not easily accessible, therefore, the final product is observed initially.*

[正]The proposed intermediate is not easily accessible; therefore, the final product is observed initially.

实例 2

Mr. Smith is an amateur athlete; moreover, he's a first-rate teacher.
史密斯先生是一名业余选手;而且他还是一名一流的教师。

实例 3

My mother is a nurse; my father works in a factory.(这两个句子句意关系密切,结构又相近,因此用分号连接。)
我妈妈是护士;我爸爸是工人。

实例 4

Your composition is good; still, there is room for improvement.
你的作文写得不错;但还有需进一步改进的地方。

实例 5

The soldier was badly wounded; nevertheless, he kept on fighting.
士兵伤得很重;然而他还在坚持战斗。

实例 6

He is not poor; on the contrary, he is one of the richest men in our neighborhood.
他不穷;相反,他属于我们社区内最富有的人。

实例 7

John goes to school regularly and studies very hard; therefore/thus, he is making good progress.
约翰按时上学,学习又努力,因而他的进步很快。

实例 8

This city has too many people and too little land; consequently/accordingly, housing is limited in space and difficult to obtain.
这个城市人多地少,因此可建住房的空间有限,一房难求。

实例 9
  The driver was drunk; as a result, he made a car crash.
  司机喝醉了,结果发生了撞车事故。
(3)假如一个或多个条目已经包含逗号了,则分号可用于系列条目之间。
实例 1
  Persons in attendance were James Taven, University of Maryland; Anne Schmidt, University of London; Robert Berren, The Ohio State University;and Zhang Wei, Tsinghua University.
  出席的人有马里兰大学的 James Taven、伦敦大学的 Anne Schmidt、俄亥俄州立大学的 Robert Berren 和清华大学的张维。
实例 2
  If she married that man, her parents would be unhappy; if she left him, she herself would be unhappy.
  如果她嫁给那个人,她父母会不高兴;如果她离开那个人,她自己会不开心。
实例 3
  Recent sites of the Olympic Games include Athens, Greece; Salt Lake City, Utah; Sydney, Australia; and Nagano, Japan.
  最近举办过奥运会的有希腊的雅典、犹他州的盐湖城、澳大利亚的悉尼以及日本的长野。

3. 冒号(:)

(1)当你想要强调的是两个独立的子句中的第二个时,用冒号连接这两个独立的子句。例如:
  Road construction in Dallas has hindered travel around town: parts of Main, Fifth, and West Street are closed during the construction.
  达拉斯道路的修建已经影响到城镇的交通:在修路期间,部分主路、第五大街以及西街等部分封闭了。

(2)当独立子句后跟着出现了序列、引用语、同位语,以及能说明、阐述或扩展前述信息的若干完整句子时,使用冒号(colon)。

实例 1
  The electron density was studied for the ground state of three groups of molecules:(1) methane-methanol-carbondioxide,(2) water-hydrogen peroxide, and (3)ferrous oxide-ferric oxide.
  研究了三组分子基态的电子密度,它们是:(1)甲烷-甲醇-CO_2;(2)过氧化氢(H_2O_2);(3)氧化亚铁(FeO)-三氧化二铁(Fe_2O_3)。

实例 2
  We now report a preliminary finding: No chemical shift changes were

detected in the concentration range 0.1 ~ 10 m.

现在我们报告初步的发现:在浓度为 0.1 ~ 10 m 的范围里,并未检测出化学位移变化。

实例 3

The following are our conclusions: Large-angle X-ray scattering studies give us an accurate picture of structures up to 9A. They do not allow the specification of defects, such as random strongly supported by magnetic measurements.

以下是我们的结论:大角 X-射线散射研究使我们获得一个多达 9A 个的准确的结构图。但它们给不出缺陷的说明,特别是由磁测随机产生的缺陷。

实例 4

Julie went to the store for some groceries: milk, bread, coffee, and cheese.

朱莉去食杂店买了牛奶、面包、咖啡和奶酪等食品。

实例 5

I know the perfect job for her: a politician.

我知道什么工作最适合她:政客。

实例 6

In his Gettysburg Address, Abraham Lincoln urges Americans to rededicate themselves to the unfinished work of the deceased soldiers: "It is for us the living rather to be dedicated here to the unfinished work which they who fought here have thus far so nobly advanced. It is rather for us to be here dedicated to the great task remaining before us—that from these honored dead we take increased devotion to that cause for which they gave the last full measure of devotion—that we here highly resolve that these dead shall not have died in vain, that this nation shall have a new birth of freedom, and that government of the people, by the people, for the people shall not perish from the earth."

在葛底斯堡演讲中,阿伯罕姆·林肯敦促美国人献身于已死难的战士未完成的事业。他说:"我们今天活着的人要去继续那些由死难的战士曾在此为之英勇奋斗、但还未完成的使命。是我们该去为我们面前未尽的伟大事业献身的时候了。这些令人尊敬的死者,为了这一伟大的事业付出了他们最后的热血,这使我们下定决心,不让烈士的鲜血白流,我们定将在我们这个国家实现新的民主,使由人民领导、为人民服务的人民政府永远屹立在这片土地上。"

(3)在商务信函问候语之后用冒号。

例如:To Whom It May Concern:

(4)小时和分钟之间用冒号。

例如:12:00 p.m.

(5)冒号不可用于动词与其宾语之间,也不能用于介词与其宾语之间。

在增加氢氧化钠浓度的情况下,反应速率常数是3.9、4.1、4.4、4.6和4.9。

[误]*The rate constants for the reaction in increasing concentrations of sodium hydroxide are:3.9, 4.1, 4.4, 4.6, and 4.9.*

[正]*The rate constants for the reaction in increasing concentrations of sodium hydroxide are 3.9, 4.1, 4.4, 4.6, and 4.9.*

4. 圆括号(( ))

用圆括号来强调所述的内容。圆括号比逗号更能起到对括入的内容进行强调的作用。用圆括号来把非重要的材料与句子分割开,如日期、起澄清作用的信息或资料。

Muhammed Ali (1942—present), the greatest athlete of the time, claimed he would "float like a butterfly."

穆罕默德·阿里(1942—)是我们这个时代最优秀的运动员。他说他游泳"会像蝶泳一样自如"。

5. 破折号(—)

破折号用于分隔或强调破折号之间或破折号之后的内容,就强调作用而言,破折号比圆括号的强调作用更大。

实例1

Perhaps one reason why the term has been so problematic—so resistant to definition, and yet so transitory in those definitions—is because of its multitude of applications.

这个术语之所以如此棘手——很不容易对其下定义,而且即使给出了定义,其定义也是短暂的——这很可能是因为它广泛的适用范围所致。

实例2

To some of you, my proposals may seem radical—even revolutionary.

对你们中的一些人来说,我的建议似乎有些激进——甚至是革命性的。

破折号可用来分隔已经包含了逗号的同位语短语。一个词的同位语起到对其前面的名词说明、解释的作用。

The cousins—Tina, Todd, and Sam—arrived at the party together.

表兄妹们——蒂娜、托德和萨姆——一起来参加晚会了。

6. 引号（""或''）

（1）在对话引语、简短的介绍性短语、从属子句等之后，用逗号引出引语。

实例1

  The detective said, "I am sure who performed the murder."
  侦探说："我能确定谁是凶手。"

实例2

  As D. H. Nachas explains, "The gestures used for greeting others differ greatly from one culture to another."
  正如 D. H. 内可斯所说的："用于打招呼的手势语因文化的不同而有所不同。"

（2）逗号和句号要放在引号内，除非之后有用圆括号形式出现的文献参考。

实例1

  He said, "I may forget your name, but I never forget a face."
  他说："我可能忘了你叫什么名字，但我不会忘记你的脸。"

实例2

  History is stained with blood spilled in the name of "civilization".
  历史被冠以"文明"之美名的血腥所玷污。

实例3

  Mullen, criticizing the apparent inaction, writes, "Donahue's policy was to do nothing" (24).
  在批判显而易见地不作为时，Mullen 写到，"Donahue 的政策是什么也不做"(24)。

（3）冒号和分号要放在引号之外。

实例1

  Williams described the experiment as "a definitive step forward"; other scientists disagreed.
  威廉斯将实验描述为"前进中的决定性一步"；其他科学家不这样想。

实例2

  Benedetto emphasizes three elements of what she calls her "Olympic journey": family support, personal commitment, and great coaching.
  Benedetto 强调了她称之为"奥运之旅"的三要素：家庭的支持、个人的全身心投入以及教练的英明指导。

（4）如果问号或感叹号是针对引文本身的，把问号或感叹号置于引文内；如果是针对全句的，则放在引文之外。

例1

  Phillip asked, "Do you need this book?"
  菲利普问道："你需要这本书吗？"

例2

  Does Dr. Lim always say to her students, "You must work harder"?
  利姆博士常这样对她的学生说"你们必须更加努力学习"吗?

例3

  He asked, "When will you be arriving?" I answered, "Sometime after 6:30."
  他问我:"你会什么时间到?"我答道:"6:30以后。"

(5)当一个词被异常地、具有讽刺性地或有所保留地使用的时候,使用引号来指出这个词。

  History is stained with blood spilled in the name of "justice."
  历史被冠以"正义"之美名的血腥所玷污。

(6)短诗、歌曲、小说、杂志、报刊文章、短文、演讲等的标题通常用引号。

实例1

  "Self-Reliance," by Ralph Waldo Emerson
  R. W. 拉尔夫(所著)的《自立》

实例2

  "Just Like a Woman," by Bob Dylan
  鲍勃·迪伦的《就好像女人》

注:引号不用于间接引语或一段引语。

7. 斜体字

下划线和斜体字常被互换地使用。在有计算机文字处理以前,作者通常在某些特定的词下画一条线,以此来告知出版方把下方画线的词变成斜体字。尽管现在的趋势是使用斜体字而非下划线,但你应确定在全文中选择使用哪一种,以保持前后一致。

(1)杂志的标题、书名、报刊、学术期刊、电影、电视节目、长诗、歌剧、艺术作品、网站、飞机或船只等的名称通常用斜体字。

实例1

  Time
  《时代周刊》

实例2

  Romeo and Juliet by William Shakespeare
  莎士比亚的《罗密欧与朱丽叶》

实例3

  Amazon.com
  亚马逊网站

实例4

  Titanic
  《泰坦尼克》

(2)外来语用于斜体字。

实例

  Semper fi, the motto of the U. S. Marine Corps, means "always faithful."

  美国海军的座右铭,*Semper fi*,意思是"永远的忠诚"。

(3)起强调作用的词或短语要用斜体。

实例

  The *truth* is of utmost concern!

  真相最令人关注!

(4)谈论中专指的**那个**词使用斜体。

实例

  The word *justice* is often misunderstood and therefore misused.

  Justice 一词常被理解错误,也就常被用错。

8. 斜线分隔符(/)

(1)当句子中有分数的时候,斜线分隔符(slash)可用于分隔分子与分母。

实例1

  Alilometre is 31/50 of a mile.

实例2

  a/b $(x+y)/(2x-y)$ $x^{1/2}$

(2)斜线分隔符在测量单位时相当于"每"(per)的意思。

实例1

  10 kg/cm^2 即每平方厘米 10 千克

实例2

  100 m/s 即每秒 100 米

(3)斜线分隔符可用于日期表示。

例如:5/8/1986→1986 年 8 月 5 日,但这种表示不规范,在英国,它表示 1986 年 8 月 5 日,而在美国则为 1986 年 5 月 8 日了。所以现今正式著作、文件里一律采用 August 5, 1986。August 可以缩写为 Aug.,但 May、June、July 三个表月份的词尽量不缩写。

(4)斜线分隔符不用于正文中词与词之间。

注:句中有时含 and/or 的情况是允许的。

9. 不同句型的标点符号

掌握如何、何时给句子加标点不是一件容易的事,特别是当你想到不同类型的句子要求加不同的标点符号的时候更是如此。下面提供的不仅是句子的种类,而且还有在何种情况下使用何种标点符号。

句子的种类如下:

(1)独立分句:有主语和动词,并能单独使用的分句叫作独立分句。

(2)从属分句:有主语和动词,但并不能单独使用的分句叫作从属分句。

(3) 简单句：由一个独立分句构成；没有标准的标点符号。

(4) 复合句：由两个或两个以上的独立分句构成。

两个独立的分句由逗号和并列连接词连接（并列连接词有 and、but、or、for、nor、so）。

  Road construction can be inconvenient, but it is necessary.

  道路建设会带来不便，但却是必要的。

当你想强调第二个分句的时候，用冒号连接这两个独立分句。

  Road construction in Dallas has hindered travel around town: parts of Main, Fifth, and West Street are closed during the construction.

  达拉斯的道路建设已阻碍了周边城镇的交通：部分的主要街道、第五街和西街的街道在建设期间被封闭了。

当两个独立分句中的第二个分句是对第一个分句的重新叙述或是两个分句所强调的内容同样重要的时候，用分号连接两个分句。

  Road construction in Dallas has hindered travel around town; streets have become covered with bulldozers, trucks, and cones.

  达拉斯的道路建设已阻碍了周边城镇的交通；街道上到处都是推土机、卡车和施工段用的路标。

(5) 复杂句：包含一个或一个以上的独立分句和一个或一个以上的从属分句。用逗号连接一个介绍性的从属分句和独立分句。

实例1

  Because road construction has hindered travel around town, many people have opted to ride bicycles or walk to work.

  由于修路影响了城镇周边的交通，许多人开始骑自行车或步行上班。

实例2

  Many people have opted to ride bicycles or walk to work because road construction has hindered travel around town.

  许多人开始骑自行车或步行上班，是修路影响了城镇周边的交通。

(6) 复合-复杂句：包含一个或一个以上的从属分句和两个或两个以上的独立分句。

①用逗号连接一个介绍性的从属分句和独立分句，用逗号和并列连接词（and、but、or、for、nor、so）连接两个独立分句。

  When it is filtered, water is cleaner, and it tastes better.

  水经过滤后更纯净，口感更好。

②用逗号连接一个介绍性的从属分句和独立分句；当你想就两个独立分句中的第二个加以强调的时候，用冒号分割两个独立分句。

  Whenever it is possible, you should filter your water: filtered water is cleaner and tastes better.

  如有可能，应该将水过滤一下：过滤过的水更洁净，口感更好。

③用逗号连接一个介绍性的从属分句和独立分句；当两个独立分句中的第二个分句

是对第一个分句的重新叙述或是两个分句所强调的内容同等重要的时候,用分号分割两个独立分句。

实例1

When it is filtered, water is cleaner and tastes better; all things considered, it is better for you.

水经过滤后更洁净,口感更好;总的来说,喝过滤水更有益。

实例2

No one is born with knowledge; knowledge must be taught and learned.

知识不是天生就有的,知识一定是经过传授后天习得的。

3.2 句子标点符号的模式

概要:本小节用实例讲述八种句子标点符号的模式。

在给句子加标点符号时,你可单独使用或结合着使用这些句子标点符号的模式。

模式1:简单句

此模式是一个简单句的实例:

独立分句[.]

Doctors are concerned about the rising death rate from asthma.

医生们对由哮喘病引起的、不断攀升的死亡率感到担忧。

模式2:并列复合句

此模式是一个带有一个并列连接词的并列复合句的实例:

独立分句[,]含并列连接词独立分句[.]

并列连接词有七个:and、but、for、or、nor、so和yet。

Doctors are concerned about the rising death rate from asthma, but they don't know the reasons for it.

医生们对由哮喘病引起的、不断攀升的死亡率感到担忧,然而他们尚不清楚哮喘病的致病原因。

模式3:并列复合句

此模式是一个带有一个分号的并列复合句的实例:

独立分句[;]独立分句[.]

Doctors are concerned about the rising death rate from asthma; they are unsure of its cause.

医生们对由哮喘病引起的、不断攀升的死亡率感到担忧;他们无法确知其产生的原因。

模式4:并列复合句

此模式是一个带有一个独立标记的并列复合句的实例:

独立分句[;]独立标记[,]独立分句[.]

独立标记包括:therefore、moreover、thus、consequently、however、also。

  Doctors are concerned about the rising death rate from asthma; therefore, they have called for more research into its causes.
  医生们对由哮喘病引起的、不断攀升的死亡率感到担忧;因此他们呼吁对其病因进行深入的研究。

模式5:复杂句

此模式是一个带有一个从属标记的复杂句的实例:

从属标记+从属分句[,]独立分句[.]

从属标记包括:because、before、since、while、although、if、until、when、after、as、as if。

  Because doctors are concerned about the rising death rate from asthma, they have called for more research into its causes.
  因为医生们对由哮喘病引起的、不断攀升的死亡率感到担忧,因此他们呼吁对其病因进行深入的研究。

模式6:复杂句

此模式是一个带有一个从属标记的复杂句的实例:

独立分句+从属标记+从属分句[.]

从属标记包括:because、before、since、while、although、if、until、when、after、as、as if。

  实例:Doctors are concerned about the rising death rate from asthma because it is a common, treatable illness.
  因为哮喘病是一种常见的、可治疗的疾病,因此医生们对其引起的、不断攀升的死亡率感到担忧。

模式7:复杂句

此模式包括一个独立分句,这个独立分句被嵌入了一个非基本的子句或短语。

独立分句的一部分[,] 非基本子句或短语 独立分句的其他部分 [.]

非基本子句或短语是指在其被去除之后,句子的意义不发生变化,或句子的语法仍然是正确的。换句话说,非基本子句或短语给出的是附加的信息,句子本身在缺少这部分的情况下意义仍然完整。

  Many doctors, including both pediatricians and family practice physicians, are concerned about the rising death rate from asthma.
  许多医生,包括儿科医生和家庭医生,都对由哮喘病引起的、不断攀升的死亡率感到担忧。

模式8:复杂句

此模式是被嵌入了一个必不可少的分句或短语的独立分句。

独立分句的第一部分或独立分句的其他部分[.]

必不可少的分句或短语是指那种不可去除,否则将会改变整体句意的分句或短语。

  Many doctors who are concerned about the rising death rate from asthma have called for more research into its causes.
  那些对由哮喘病引起的、不断攀升的死亡率感到担忧的医生呼吁对哮喘病产生的原因进行深入的研究。

3.3 逗号衔接的错误

1. 什么是逗号衔接的错误?

(1)逗号衔接的错误,是指在两个完整的句子之间,在没有使用连接词的情况下使用了逗号。逗号是无法单独把两个完整的句子组成一个合乎语法要求的句子的。

下面就是一个逗号衔接错误的实例。

错误的实例:

  I completed my essay, I have not submitted it.

  我的文章写完了,我还没交。

(2)连写句也是与这类错误非常相近的句子,也就是在不使用任何标点符号的情况下把两个完整的句子连在了一起。

错误的实例:

  I completed my essay I have not submitted it.

  我的文章写完了,我还没交。

修改连写句的方法和修改逗号衔接错误的方法是一样的。

2. 如何修改逗号衔接有错误的句子

有四种方法可直接解决逗号衔接的错误。要对这几种方法的微妙差别有所了解,不应养成只用一种方法的习惯。把你写的文章中的这方面的错误找出来,利用这个机会来练习,掌握如何写出复杂句。

解决方案 1:用句号

修改逗号衔接错误的最简单的方法是把连接不当的两个句子分开,用句号代替逗号。一前一后两个句子读上去有些生硬,但总比出现语法错误要好。

  I completed my essay. I have not submitted it.

  我的文章写完了。我还没交。

在下列情况下最好选用句号来解决逗号衔接错误:(1)两个独立分句之间的逻辑关系是不证自明的;(2)两个分句中的一个或两个分句都过长;(3)两个分句表述的内容是截然不同的。

  I completed my English essay. Now I must go to the library and begin research at once on my fifteen-page History term paper.

  我的英语文章写完了,现在我得去图书馆,立即着手研究写本学期15页的历史作业。

解决方案 2:用分号

如果你要寻找的方法是既简单又不至于把两个分句分成两个独立的句子,那么就使用分号。

  I completed my essay; I have not submitted it.

我的文章写完了;我还没交。

在下面的两种情况下,分号是修改逗号衔接错误的最佳选择:(1)两个独立分句间的逻辑关系已经很清楚;(2)两个分句表述的思想关系密切。特别是当两个分句之间是属于序列的关系时(时间序列或逻辑序列),更适合使用分号。

I completed my English essay; next, I will tackle my History essay.

我的英语文章写完了;接下来,我要着手写历史作业。

解决方案 3:使用并列连词

同分号一样,连词能使两个分句合并为一个句子,而且它还有一个长处,就是能表明两个观念的逻辑关系。逗号衔接错误的例子,体现的是一种对照的关系:

I completed the essay, but I haven't submitted it even though that would have been the *expected* thing to do.

我的文章写完了,尽管是该交作业的时间了,可我还没交。

并列连词 but 就能很好地表达这种意想不到或相矛盾的含义。

I completed my essay, but I have not submitted it.

我的文章写完了,但还没有交。

并列连词总共有七个:and、but、or、nor、for、so 和 yet。这些连词的使用有助于表达最基本的、存在于两个独立概念之间的逻辑关系。

解决方案 4:使用从属连词

和并列连词一样,从属连词也表明两个独立分句之间的逻辑关系;但同并列连词又有所不同,从属连词对句子的两个部分的强调分量是不同的。我们可以用从属连词 although 来解决逗号衔接问题,但采用的方法却可以是两种截然不同的。

例 1

I completed my essay, although I have not submitted it.

我的文章写完了,尽管我还没有交。

例 2

Although I completed my essay, I have not submitted it.

尽管我的文章写完了,但我还没有交。

由从属连接词引出的分句的强调力度不如另一个分句。在上述的第一个例句中我没有交作业这个事实是事后想起来的;第二个例句中没交作业这个事实是讲话的要点。

英语语言中有很多从属连接词,下面给出的只是较常用的一些:while、although、because、if、since、unless、whether、when、why、as、before、after、if、whether、that、once。

3. 如何才能避免逗号衔接错误

永远不要用逗号再加上连接副词来连接两个句子,这种错误最常见于 however 连接的两个句子中:

错误的例句:

I completed my essay, however I have not submitted it.

这个句子仍然还是一个有逗号衔接错误的句子。要学会区别什么是连接副词,什么是从属连接词,二者的语法作用是不同的。连接副词可以用于引出一独立分句,但不是连接独立分句。

下面是一些常见的连接副词,注意连接副词既可以由短语构成,也可由单个词构成:however、nevertheless、furthermore、moreover、hence、therefore、similarly、certainly、by contrast、in other words、in addition。

注意:你可以用连接副词来修改逗号衔接的错误,但要记住在第二个独立分句前要用句号或者分号。

实例 1

  I completed my essay. However, I have not submitted it.
  我写完了短文。但我还没交上去。

实例 2

  I completed my essay; however, I have not submitted it.
  我写完了短文,但我还没交上去。

同连接词 but 和 although 相比,分句之间使用连接副词 however 更正式,语势更强。如果过多地依赖于连接副词,写出的句子会显得呆板。尽量少用 however,留着确实需要的时候再用。很多文体学家不赞成在句子的开头使用 however。下列情况可考虑使用:(1)论述中的关键时刻——转折时使用;(2)发出信号来表明要在既长又复杂的句子之间进行比较时使用。

  I completed my essay in just one draft, a process that took me only three hours. This last essay, however, was a mere two pages long, and I have learned the hard way that neglecting to revise my papers inevitably results in a weaker paper and a lower grade.

  我一蹴而就地写完了作文,整个过程只用了 3 个小时。然而这最后一次作业,虽然只有两页长,却给了我惨痛的教训:不认真对文章进行修改,肯定写不出高质量的文章,也不会得高分。

3.4 标点符号练习(逗号、冒号、分号、破折号)

请找出下列句子中标点符号用得不当的地方。错误包括缺少标点符号,标点符号多余或错放了的冒号、分号、括号和引号。注意:每个句子中标点符号的错误不超过一个。

练习 1

  The new material, which will be available next week is composed of plastic and iodine.

  改为:The new material, which will be available next **week, is** composed of plastic and iodine.

  下周就会有了的新型材料其材质为塑胶和碘。

讨论:缺少用于 which 分句起说明作用的另一个逗号。

练习 2

  As World War II escalated the United States became locked into a race with Germany to develop the first atomic bomb.

改为: As World War Ⅱ **escalated, the** United States became locked into a race with Germany to develop the first atomic bomb.

随着第二次世界大战的逐步升级,美国陷入了与德国展开开发第一颗原子弹的竞争之中。

讨论:介绍性分句之后缺少一个逗号,没有这个逗号,读者不易确定介绍性分句何处结束。

练习 3

The three largest earthquakes occurred in San Francisco, Tokyo and Lima.

改为: The three largest earthquakes occurred in San Francisco, **Tokyo, and** Lima.

三大地震发生在旧金山、东京和利马。

讨论:Tokyo 之后缺少一个逗号,如果有三个以上(包括三个)的成分属于并行结构,连接最后一个成分的 and 前要有逗号。

练习 4

On February 5, 1990 Mount St. Helens had another eruption, this one smaller than the eruption 10 years before.

改为: On February 5, 1990, **Mount** St. Helens had another eruption, this one smaller than the eruption 10 years before.

1990 年 2 月 5 号,圣·海伦斯山又一次喷发了,此次喷发程度小于十年前的那次。

讨论:1990 之后缺一个逗号。

练习 5

Every year, an earthquake of magnitude between 8.0 and 8.9 on the Richter scale, will be experienced somewhere in the world [Haughton, 1989].

改为:Every year, an earthquake of magnitude between 8.0 and 8.9 on the Richter **scale will** be experienced somewhere in the world [Haughton, 1989].

世界上每年都会发生震级为里氏 8.0~8.9 级之间的地震。

讨论: scale 之后不需要逗号。

练习 6

As the flame front propagates hot combustion products expand, resulting in a rapid pressure increase.

改为: As the flame front **propagates, hot** combustion products expand, resulting in a rapid pressure increase.

随着火头的蔓延,易燃品开始膨胀,导致压力迅速增加。

讨论：介绍性分句之后缺少一个逗号；否则，读者分不清分句到哪里结束。

练习 7

  The concentrations of these gases, which are called greenhouse gases control how much infrared radiation escapes.

  改为：The concentrations of these gases, which are called greenhouse **gases, control** how much infrared radiation escapes.

  这些被称为温室气体的气体浓度控制着红外线漏出的程度。

讨论：起说明作用的 which 分句之后缺一个逗号。

练习 8

  After 1987 parachuting accidents decreased significantly because instructors started teaching novices with tandem jumps rather than static lines.

  改为：After 1987**,** **parachuting** accidents decreased significantly because instructors started teaching novices with tandem jumps rather than static lines.

  自 1987 年之后，跳伞事故明显减少，其原因是教练采用了 tandem jumps 方式训练新手跳伞，而不是 static lines 方式。

讨论：介绍性短语 After 1987 之后缺一个逗号；否则，读者会在理解上遇到困难。

练习 9

  On May 18, 1980, a cloud of hot rock and gas surged northward from Mount St. Helens.

  在 1980 年 5 月 18 日，从圣·海伦斯山向北喷出一团熔岩和气体烟云。

讨论：本句没有标点符号错误。

练习 10

  The synergistic reactor contains a chamber in which the exhaust from the burning coal mixes with limestone, see Appendix A.

  改为：The synergistic reactor contains a chamber in which the exhaust from the burning coal mixes with **limestone, as discussed / can be seen in** Appendix A.

  此种增效反应器内有一小室，其间燃煤后产生的废气与石灰岩混合，详见附录 A。

讨论：这个句子的问题是有两个动词（contains 和 see）。解决的方法有三个，一是把 see Appendix A 改为动词短语，二是把这部分改为另一个分句，三是把这部分放在括号里。

练习 11

  The local economy should benefit from the operation. Local property taxes would decrease for area residents and the Nicolet Minerals Company, formerly the Crandon Mining Company, is expected to spend more than $40 million on local goods and services.

改为:The local economy should benefit from the operation. Local property taxes would decrease for area **residents, and** the Nicolet Minerals Company, formerly the Crandon Mining Company, is expected to spend more than $40 million on local goods and services.

地方经济会从此项举措中获益。地方居民的财产税将降低,尼克莱矿业公司(即前身为格莱顿矿业公司)有望在地方产品和服务方面支出超过四千万。

讨论:如 and 前不加逗号,读者不易知道第一个独立分句在哪里结束,第二个分句从哪开始。

练习 12

The three largest earthquakes occurred in: San Francisco, Tokyo, and Lima.

改为:The three largest earthquakes occurred **in San** Francisco, Tokyo, and Lima.

三大地震发生在旧金山、东京和利马。

讨论:去掉 San Francisco 前的冒号。

练习 13

According to Dr. D. Simpson [1986], **a** biologist at the Harvard Medical **School, "Only** 30,000 rads are needed for interphase death to occur in yeast **cells".**

改为:According to Dr. D. Simpson [1986], a biologist at the Harvard Medical School, "Only 30,000 rads are needed for interphase death to occur in yeast **cells."**

按照哈佛大学医学院的生物学家 D. 辛普森博士的说法:"在酵母细胞中的细胞分裂间期死亡只需 30,000 拉德。"

讨论:MLA 和 APA 格式都要求把引号放在 **cells** 之后的句号外。

练习 14

The synergistic reactor contains a **chamber in** which the exhaust from the burning coal mixes with **limestone—see** Appendix A.

改为:The synergistic reactor contains a chamber in which the exhaust from the burning coal mixes with **limestone--see** Appendix A.

此种增效反应器内有一小室,其间燃煤后产生的废气与石灰岩混合,详见附录 A。

讨论:用两个连字号代替长破折号,而不是原句中的一个连字号。

练习 15

The synergistic reactor contains a **chamber in** which the exhaust from the burning coal mixes with **limestone**(See Appendix A.)

改为：The synergistic reactor contains a chamber in which the exhaust from the burning coal mixes with **limestone（see Appendix A）.**

此种增效反应器内有一小室，其间燃煤后产生的废气与石灰岩混合，详见附录 A。

讨论：与括号相关的标点符号用得不正确。首先，括号前应该有空格；第二，因为括号内的内容属于句子的一部分，因此不该用大写；最后，因为括号属于句子的一部分，因此句号不该只属于括号内，而应该属于全句，即应该放在括号外。

练习 16

The absorption A is calculated **by**：

$A = 1 - kR,$

Where k is the correction **factor and** R is the measured reflectance.

改为：The absorption A is calculated **by**

$A = 1 - kR,$

where k is the correction factor and R is the measured reflectance.

通过公式 $A = 1 - kR$ 可计算出 A 的吸收性，其中 k 为修正系数，R 为测到的反射系数。

讨论：by 后不用冒号。

练习 17

下面哪项应以斜体出现？

书名和期刊文章的题目

书名和期刊标题

章节标题和期刊标题

章节标题和期刊文章的标题

讨论：斜体字用于名称较大的文献：书名、期刊名、期刊、报刊、超过 75 页的报告的名称、大部头电影名称、网站名称等。因此，书名和期刊标题用斜体。

练习 18

下面哪项应使用引号？

书名和期刊文章的题目

书名和期刊标题

章节标题和期刊标题

章节标题和期刊文章的标题

讨论：引号用于短的文献：书籍章节的名称、定期期刊、期刊和报刊的文章名称、少于 75 页的报告的名称、小部头电影的名称、歌曲名称、个人网站名等。因此，章节标题和期刊文章的标题用引号。

3.5　综合练习：语法、标点符号和惯用语

在下面提供的每一段中，分别有四个有关语法、标点符号或用法上的错误，如连写句、

不完整的句子、主谓不一致、用词错误、缺逗号、逗号多余、冒号用错、代词所指不清或所属关系上的错误等,请把这些错误找出来。

段落 1

A greenhouse is a glass building <u>used</u> to grow plants. A greenhouse has transparent glass <u>that</u> allows the sunlight to pass <u>through</u>, <u>but</u> does not allow the heat inside to escape. The same <u>affect</u> occurs on the earth. The <u>suns</u> radiation passes through the atmosphere to heat the earth's surface. When <u>heated</u>, the earth's surface produces infrared <u>radiation</u>, <u>which</u> has a longer wavelength than that of sunlight. This infrared radiation rises into the atmosphere where <u>gases</u>, <u>such</u> as carbon dioxide, <u>prevents</u> the infrared radiation from escaping into space. The concentrations of these <u>gases which</u> are called greenhouse gases, control how much infrared radiation escapes. The retained radiation heats the earth's <u>atmosphere</u>, thus keeping the planet <u>warm</u>.

参考答案

A greenhouse is a glass building used to grow plants. A greenhouse has transparent glass that allows the sunlight to pass through, but does not allow the heat inside to escape. The same **effect** occurs on the earth. The **sun's** radiation passes through the atmosphere to heat the earth's surface. When heated, the earth's surface produces infrared radiation, which has a longer wavelength than that of sunlight. This infrared radiation rises into the atmosphere where gases, such as carbon dioxide, **prevent** the infrared radiation from escaping into space. The concentrations of these **gases**, **which** are called greenhouse gases, control how much infrared radiation escapes. The retained radiation heats the earth's atmosphere, thus keeping the planet warm.

温室是一种用来种植植物的玻璃建筑。温室的玻璃是透明的,以便阳光射入,又确保了室内的热量不至于散发到室外。地球也具有与温室相同的效应。太阳射线穿过大气,温暖了地球表面。受热的地球表面会产生红外线辐射,其波长长于阳光的波长。此种红外线辐射到大气,而大气中的气体,如二氧化碳等,会阻止红外线辐射逃逸到太空中。这些被称为温室气体的气体浓度决定了红外线辐射逃逸的程度。剩下的辐射使地球大气变暖,从而使我们的地球保持温暖。

段落 2

During the last century, the concentrations of greenhouse gases <u>have increased</u> substantially [Holman, 1985]. Scientists believe that further increases could cause excess warming of the <u>earth's</u> climate. Moreover, many *scientists believe this warming could produce side effects. For example, the changing of the earth's wind patterns. These wind patterns control the amount of rain received in a particular area. If the greenhouse gases warm the earth's climate too much, areas that now receive plenty of rainfall could become deserts, moreover, some scientists speculate that additional increases in warming could cause another effect, a rise in the ocean levels ["Greenhouse," 1990]. How would this rise occur? An increase in global temperature would melt the polar ice caps, thus emptying more water into the oceans. They also predict that this ocean rise, which may be as high as 1 meter could flood port cities and coastal lands.*

参考答案

During the last century, the concentrations of greenhouse gases have increased substantially [Holman, 1985]. Scientists believe that further increases could cause excess warming of the earth's climate. Moreover, many scientists believe that this warming could produce side effects. **An example** would be the changing of the earth's wind patterns. These wind patterns control the amount of rain received in a particular area. If the greenhouse gases warm the earth's climate too much, areas that now receive plenty of rainfall could become **deserts. Moreover**, some scientists speculate that additional increases in warming could cause another effect, a rise in the ocean levels ["Greenhouse," 1990]. How would this rise occur? An increase in global temperature would melt the polar ice caps, thus emptying more water into the oceans. **Scientists** also predict that this ocean rise, which may be as high as 1 **meter**, **could** flood port cities and coastal lands.

近一个世纪以来,温室气体的浓度增加很显著[Holman,1985]。科学家们认为浓度的进一步增加会导致全球气候的过度变暖。而且,许多科学家相信变暖会产生负效应。地球季风风型的变化就是一个实例。这些季风风型控制某一地区的降水量。如果温室气体使全球的气候过于温暖,降水丰沛的地区就有可能变成沙漠。一些科学家还预测加剧变暖会产生另一负效应,即海平面的上升["Greenhouse,"1990]。为什么海平面会上升?全球升温将会使极地的冰盖融化,使更多的水注入海洋。科学家们也预测,海平面可能会被升高高达1米,港口城市和沿海国家就有可能被淹没。

段落3

The gas that contributes most to the greenhouse effect, is carbon dioxide [Houghton, 1990]. Carbon dioxide cannot be seen, smelled, or tasted. In fact, *its* not even considered a pollutant. Plants use carbon dioxide in combination with chlorophyll, water, and sunshine for *photosynthesis*, which is a process essential to life. Besides aiding in *photosynthesis*, *it* also absorbs the earth's radiation. This gas occurs naturally in the *atmosphere*, *however*, man has dramatically increased the concentration of carbon dioxide over the last twenty years.

参考答案

The gas that contributes most to the greenhouse **effect is** carbon dioxide [Houghton, 1990]. Carbon dioxide cannot be seen, smelled, or tasted. In fact, it is not even considered a pollutant. Plants use carbon dioxide in combination with chlorophyll, water, and sunshine for photosynthesis, which is a process essential to life. Besides aiding in photosynthesis, **carbon dioxide** also absorbs the earth's radiation. This gas occurs naturally in the **atmosphere. However**, man has dramatically increased the concentration of carbon dioxide over the last twenty years.

导致温室效应的主要气体是二氧化碳[Houghton, 1990]。二氧化碳无色、无臭、无味。实际上，人们并未将其视为污染物。植物通过二氧化碳与叶绿素、水和阳光进行光合作用，这是维系生命所必需的过程。除了辅助光合作用，二氧化碳也吸收了地球的辐射。二氧化碳天然产生于大气中。然而在过去的20年间，人类在很大程度上加大了二氧化碳的含量。

第四章
有效引用的方法

引用语的使用非常不容易。误用的形式非常多，如过多强调、过多引用、引错了段/节、观点和引用的原始资料相混淆、引用语的使用破坏了论述的流畅等。本章就如何有效地引用提出了一些基本的建议。最好将本章与第二章中的参考文献一节一起阅读。本章遵循的是 MLA 文体。

1. 与引号使用相关的标点符号的使用规则

(1) 在对话之后使用逗号来引出引用语、简短的介绍性短语或从属分句。

实例1

"Get your bundles and follow me," he told them, leading the eight men and two women toward the river.

"拿好包裹跟我走，"他一边吩咐他们，一边领着这八男二女朝河边走去。

实例2

As D. H. Nachas explains, "The gestures used for greeting others differ greatly from one culture to another."

正如 D. H. 内卡斯所说，"用来问候他人的手势因文化不同而有所不同。"

(2) 逗号和句号要放在引号之内，除非在引号之后又出现了标示参考文献的括号，如：

实例1

He said, "I may forget your name, but I never forget a face."

他说，"我可能会记不住你的名字，但我不会忘记你的样子。"

实例2

History is stained with blood spilled in the name of "civilization."

他说，历史被冠以"文明"的美誉玷污了。

实例3

Mullen, criticizing the apparent inaction, writes, "Donahue's policy was to do nothing" (24).

Mullen 在批判显而易见的无作为时说,"Donahue 的政策就是什么也不做(24)。"

(3) 把冒号和分号放在引号的外面。

实例 1

Williams described the experiment as "a definitive step forward"; other scientists disagreed.

Williams 把此次实验描述为"向前迈出的决定性一步,"而其他科学家不这样认为。

实例 2

Benedetto emphasizes three elements of what she calls her "Olympic journey": family support, personal commitment, and great coaching.

Benedetto 在谈到她称之为的"奥运之旅"时,强调了三大要素:家庭的支持、个人的努力和优秀教练的指导。

(4) 如果问号或感叹号是与引用语本身相关,要把它们放在引号之内;如果它们与整个句子相关,要把它们放在引号之外。

实例 1

Phillip asked, "Do you need this book?"

菲利普问道:"你需要这本书吗?"

实例 2

Does Dr. Lim always say to her students, "You must work harder"?

兰姆博士总是对学生们说,"你们必须更加努力学习"吗?

实例 3

"Have you felt so proud to get at the meaning of poem?" Whitman asks.

惠特曼问道:"你们在领悟到了诗的含义之后,是否感到非常自豪?"

下面给出一些比动词 prove 更具说服力的动词,如表建议、结果、争论的动词:

suggests	indicates	demonstrates
implies	argues (that, for)	supports
testifies to	shows	underscores

假如你在写一篇有关车间妇女的文章,其间你又引用了一句描写女性职场压力的引语。对这句引语该如何评论呢?

原评论:

This quotation proves that women encounter rampant discrimination in the workplace.

此段引文证实了在职场所对女性的歧视仍然十分猖獗。

修改过的评论：

> Smith's comment suggests how much resistance women still face in the workplace.
>
> 史密斯的评论表明，女性在职场所遇到的阻力还是相当大的。

原评论的不足之处在于过多地依赖了引用语，尽管其出发点是为了使作者的观点更具说服力。但评论就是评论，终究不是数据，没有那么强大的说服力。

2. 准确的含义

(1) 如果原引用语本身中有错误怎么办？照原样写下拼错的词，然后在原拼错的词的后面加上[*sic*]这个符号，以此来提醒读者此处有拼写错误(方括号中的词是拉丁语，同英文的 *thus* 或 *so*)。

> Halder does his argument no credit when he opines, "History shows that men are more intelligent then [*sic*] women" (34).
>
> Halder 的论点没有根据，他怎么能认为"历史表明男性比女性更聪明"(34)。

(2) 如果你想对引用语做修改，或在其中加些评论，要用方括号[ ]来标示改变或者增加了什么内容，不要用圆括号( )。

有时逐字的、不加任何添加的引用反而会导致对引用语理解上的困难，下面是原句，其中代词 *them* 和 *themselves* 的所指就不大清楚：

原句：I do not wish them to have power over men; but over themselves.

在这个句子中不难辨认出 them 指 *Women*，但如果你不解释一下这个词的意思，读者会感到如同汽车在行驶中突然遇到了障碍一样，读上去不是很顺畅，用方括号中的解释就避免了类似问题的出现：

> Mary Wollstonecraft does not wish to reverse the sexual balance of power, but to move from domination to autonomy: "I do not wish them [women] to have power over men; but over themselves" (156).
>
> Mary Wollstonecraft 无意要翻转目前性别造成的权利的不平衡，只是希望使其由统治权转向自治权，"我不是想让妇女的权利压过男性，而是希望妇女拥有她们自己的权力"(156)。

不要沉醉于使用方括号，要尽量少用；更好的方法是在引用语之后解释括号中的术语：

> Mary Wollstonecraft wants women to strive for autonomy, not domination: "I do not wish them to have power over men; but over themselves" (156).
>
> Mary Wollstonecraft 是要妇女为获得自主权而奋斗，而不是为了获得统治权："我不是想让妇女的权利压过男性，而是希望妇女拥有她们自己的权力"(156)。

3. 清晰问题

使用引用语时,是在你的讨论过程中给别人讲话的机会,当然这是有其目的,也是有作用的,但这也同时会给读者带来很大的困惑,不知道在讲话的人是谁,或不知道引用语和你本人的论述之间是什么关系。有些新手由于不习惯从读者的角度来看问题,因此常常会忘掉这一点。尽可能从读者可能会遇到什么问题这一角度来考虑问题。引用语对读者来说,有如下的作用:支持或加强作者的某一观点、由此引出一个新观点或给出一个相反的观点等。不要理所当然地认为你的读者会知道你为什么在使用引用语。

为了使读者清晰地了解你的观点,在使用引用语时,要注意下面两个涉及清晰的问题。

(1) 区分哪儿是你的论述,哪儿是引用语的论述

常常你会用引用语来对你在某种程度上不同意或非常不赞同的观点进行概括,特别是当你对过去的研究或观点进行审视,进而为你的论述奠定基础的时候更是如此。

下面是著名的评论家 Stephen Greenblatt 对以往研究莎士比亚戏剧的方法的论及:

> Those plays have been described with impeccable intelligence as deeply conservative and with equally impeccable intelligence as deeply radical. Shakespeare, in Northrop Frye's words, is "a born courtier," the dramatist who organizes his representation of English history around the hegemonic mysticism of the Tudor myth; Shakespeare is also a relentless demystifier, an interrogator of ideology, "the only dramatist," as Franco Moretti puts it, "who rises to the level of Machiavelli in elaborating all the consequences of the separation of political praxis from moral evaluation." The conflict glimpsed here could be investigated on a performance-by-performance basis....

> 那些剧本被巧夺天工地描绘为保守的,同时又为激进的。用 Northrop Frye 的话来说,莎士比亚是一位"天生的朝臣"和剧作家,他用都铎式神话中的霸权神秘主义再现了英国历史。正如 Franco Moretti 所说,莎士比亚也是一位始终如一的非神秘主义者和意识形态审讯者:"他在阐述把政治实践同道德评价相分离产生的后果方面达到了 Machiavelli 的观点的程度"。在此看到的分歧可以在依照性能执行的基础上进行研究……

Greenblatt 希望人们关注莎士比亚的两个被他称为"分歧"的观点(保守的和激进的),但 Greenblatt 在论述中努力不表现出他个人站在这两种观点的哪一边,因此他在论述中对两种观点持中立态度。这一摘录取自 Greenblatt 一篇文章,展示了 Greenblatt 的观点,我们可以把他游离于两种观点之间的手法看作是一个很好的典范,它采取了"磋商"和"暧昧"的方式,而不是用强硬和明朗的方式表达自己的观点。

有时可能要使用有争议的素材,这时最好采用下述的引用方式,这样能表明你是知道这一争论事实的。

原句：

  Many Germans participated in genocide: "an enormous number of ordinary, representative Germans became—and most of their fellow Germans were fit to be—Hitler's willing executioners" (Goldhagen 454).

修改句：

  Scholars have long debated what degree of responsibility ordinary Germans bore for the Holocaust. For Daniel Goldhagen the answer is clear: "an enormous number of ordinary, representative Germans became—and most of their fellow Germans were fit to be—Hitler's willing executioners" (454).

原引用语在给出 Goldhagen 的话时没能标记出围绕他的论述所出现的争论，而修改过的引用语注意到了这一争论，在此基础上进一步表明是赞同还是不赞同 Goldhagen 的观点，或采取一个倾向性不大的态度。这样做的好处在于这样为作者发表自己的观点创造了空间，而不是把自己的观点和引用语的观点掺杂在一起。

（2）解释引用语的观点或意义。

与引用语使用中出现的清晰问题相关的另一个问题是如何解释引文的观点。如果原文献中的观点本身就表述得不十分清楚，这一点就更为重要。如下面出自于莎士比亚悲剧《奥赛罗》的引文，其中就没有标示出原文的讥讽风格。

原句：

  Iago says to Othello, "Who steals my purse steals trash;.../.../ But he that filches from me my good name / Robs me of that which not enriches him / And makes me poor indeed" (3.3.157–61).

修改句：

  Drawing Othello further into his web, Iago suggests that public embarrassment would be intolerable: "Who steals my purse steals trash;.../.../ But he that filches from me my good name / Robs me of that which not enriches him / And makes me poor indeed" (3.3.157–61). Iago, of course, is utterly contradicting his earlier declamation to Cassio on the folly of reputation (2.3.256–61).

读者能从修改后的引用语中更好地理解引用语的意思，以及它在原剧中的地位和它在此论述文中的作用。

4. 要把引用语和原文融为一体

引用语通常是被嵌入到原文中的，但有时嵌入的引文很容易破坏原文的流畅。为解决这一问题，有的人认为，使用引用语时一定要用 He states 开头：

原句：

  The tension builds when Brutus accuses Cassius of accepting bribes. He states, "Let me tell you, Cassius, you yourself are much condemned to have an itching palm, to sell and mart your offices for gold..." (4.3.9–

11).

修改句：

> The tension builds when Brutus accuses Cassius of accepting bribes: "Let me tell you, Cassius, you yourself are much condemned to have an itching palm, to sell and mart your offices for gold..." (4.3.9—11).
>
> 当 Brutus 因 Cassius 接受贿赂而谴责 Cassius 时，两人之间的关系变紧张了：Brutus 对 Cassius 说，"Cassius，你贪财就该受到谴责，你是在出卖公职换取钱财"(4.3.9—11)。

去掉 He states 会使引用语的衔接更有力、更真实自然。

同样，有的作者常常会认为，必须声明他们把引用语或解释当作了例句，但他们这种出于谨慎所做的声明实际上只会使文章变得乏味(如在行文中使用这样的语句"*You have just read an example of what I'm talking about.*")。

原句：

> The Duke, disguised as a friar, gets a woman named Mariana to take Isabel's place. This is one example of how the Duke plans just as a director would do.

修改句：

> The Duke, disguised as a friar, gets Mariana to take Isabel's place. Here the Duke acts like a skilled director.
>
> 伪装为男修士的公爵让 Mariana 取代了 Isabel 的位置。公爵的行为就像是一个熟练的导演。

修改的引用语用一个词(Here)代替了最初所使用短语的措辞方式(This is one example of how)；而且你会注意到，在修改的引用语中作者使用了更有力度的动词和更简洁的措辞方式(acts like a skilled director)。

在考虑如何才能使引用语与原文融为一体的时候，也要寻找方式，使引用语的使用更加简洁、更加真实自然。

原句：

> In *The Prince* Machiavelli states that the general requirement of a prince is to "endeavor to avoid those things which would make him the object of hatred and contempt" (64).

修改句：

> In *The Prince* Machiavelli states that a prince should "endeavor to avoid those things which would make him the object of hatred and contempt" (64).

要确定你使用的引用语在语法上与文章相吻合，并不是随便就可以嵌入到一个地方。同其他写作要点一样，引用语的介入要符合语法要求，例如，独立分句的引用语就必须与另一个独立分句相接合。

错句:

Hawking is at heart a rational empiricist,"*I think there is a universe out there waiting to be investigated and understood*"（44）.

修改句:

Hawking is at heart a rational empiricist:"I think there is a universe out there waiting to be investigated and understood"（44）.

Hawking本质上是一个理性的经验论者："我认为外面的宇宙在等着我们去探索和认识"（44）。

通常,如果引用语包含一个或一个以上的完整句子,并且介绍性的句子也作为一个完整的句子出现,那么就使用冒号来引出引用语。

如果引用语不是一个完整的句子,那么你要像把其他的词、短语或从句组合到你的句子中那样,把引用语组合到句子中。

实例1

In medieval Europe love "was not the normal basis of marriage" (Trevelyan 64).

在中世纪欧洲,"爱情通常并未被看作是婚姻的基础"(Trevelyan 64)。

实例2

Fortinbras recasts Hamlet in his own image, as a "soldier" (5.2.385).

Fortinbras按照自己的意向把哈姆雷特塑造成了一个"士兵"(5.2.385)。

实例3

In Chapter 2 of the *Second Treatise*, Locke defines the state of nature as "a state of perfect freedom..." (8).

在第二部著作的第二章中,洛克把自然状态释为"一种完美的自由的状态……"(8)。

5. 进一步介绍如何引入引用语:巧用示意短语和陈述

示意短语和陈述有助于你在尽量不使读者感到困惑的情况下引出引用语,或提供足够的信息来帮助读者理解引用语的意思。有时你要对作者和文本做出详细的说明,还有的时候你要提供一些其他的背景知识或上下文信息,因此不存在可适用于一切场合的普遍规则。你只有问自己:读者需要借助什么手段才能理解引用语,以及它与你的论述之间的联系是什么。

实例1

The Founders understood the new Constitution as "a republican remedy for the diseases most incident to republican government" (Madison 343).

创始人将新宪法理解为"它是对共和党政府认为的最严重的、如同疾病一样的事件的一种党内补救措施"(Madison 343)。

实例 2

In Federalist 51 Madison observes, "Different interests necessarily exist in different classes of citizens" (345).

在《联邦党人文集》第五十一篇中麦迪逊看到,"不同阶层的公民必然有着不同的兴趣"(345)。

你常常会使用那种没有力度或含混的示意短语,如:

原句:

Another point about sexual difference is made by Rubin. She says, "The human subject... is always either male or female" (171).

修改后:

Rubin questions whether unbiased kinship diagrams are even possible: "The human subject... is always either male or female" (171).

Rubin 对是否能真有无偏亲缘关系图解提出了质疑:"人类的主体……不是男性就是女性"(171)。

原句开头用的句子对主题进行了详细的说明,但不是论点,因此没有什么意义;接着用了既不连贯又不和谐的短语 She says 来引出引用语;而修改句简要地引出了 Rubin 的论点,而且恰到好处,明确地把本句同正在讨论的话题结合了起来。修改句还避开使用 She says 这样的短语,采用了冒号的形式,既经济又快捷地把原文与引用语相衔接。

最常用的示意短语是 According to x 结构:

实例 1

According to W. C. Jordan, there were about 100,000 Jews in France in the middle of the 11th century (202).

按照 W. C. Jordan 的统计,11 世纪中期法国有大约十万犹太人(202)。

实例 2

According to Rich, we need to be careful about the risk of "presentism," of projecting present meanings on past events (3).

Rich 认为,我们要小心不要冒"现代主义"风险,把现在意义赋予过去事件(3)。

实例 3

According to the Polish critic Jan Kott, the play is best understood as a "great staircase," an endless procession of falling and rising kings (10).

按波兰批评家 Jan Kott 的观点,可把这部剧看作是一部"大楼梯",一部无休止的国王兴衰的过程(10)。

还有一个技巧,即在写作中使用行为动词,把引用语的作者当作主语,由示意动词引出引用语。在学术写作中,示意短语(或分句)有助于强动词的使用。*author + verb*(+ *that*)属于基本的示意短语结构中的一种。

实例1
> Rich warns us that we need to be careful about the risk of "presentism," of projecting present meanings on past events (3).
>
> Rich 提醒我们,我们要小心不要冒"现代主义"风险,把现在意义赋予过去事件(3)。

实例2
> Patterson reviews the legal limits placed on the murder of slaves (190–93).
>
> Patterson 就法律对谋杀奴隶方面的限制进行了评论(190–93)。

从你想要你的读者知道什么的角度考虑,你也可以在示意短语中提供各种说明性的材料,下面就是这样的一个例子。作者给出了他所引用的作者的学术观点,从而使引用语更具说服力。

> The economic historians Nathan Rosenberg and L. E. Birdsell note that in the early capitalist period (from the late fifteenth century on) people had to outgrow firms based on kinship and separate their personal finances from their firm's finances...[后面是长引文]
>
> 经济历史学家 Nathan Rosenberg 和 L. E. Birdsell 指出,在资本主义早期阶段(从 15 世纪末期开始),人民不得不跨越基于亲属关系的公司,把他们个人的财务和公司的财务分开……[后面是长引文]

是否需要这样的解释取决于你的读者。上面这个例子中作者 Fukuyama 的写作对象是普通的读者,而这些读者很可能对被引用的引用语的作者不熟悉,因此 Fukuyama 首先对引用语的作者予以解释。

6. 分开的引用语

无论你采用哪种引用方式,如果引语超过四行,就该把它放在分开的格式中。分开的引用语左端缩进(通常是 1/2 英寸),引用语是用以冒号结尾的示意叙述引出的。

实例1
> Privacy, one observer suggests, is the cardinal virtue of the Dutch:
> Dutch citizens are proud of their country; they think well of it, and they want you to think well of it, but they do not necessarily want to unpack it, know all the details.... Never have I been bamboozled as in The Netherlands, where they all tell you different things; no one want to make a full disclosure and they will pick holes in any generalization you care to profess... (Peter Lawrence, in Lawrence and Edwards 167).
>
> 保护隐私,一位观察者提出,是荷兰人的主要美德:
> 荷兰公民为他们的国家而自豪,他们认为这个国家好,他们希望你也这样想。但他们并不一定希望你对此进行剖析,或者去了解它所有的细节……我还从未像在荷兰那样困惑过,荷兰人跟你说着不同的事,他们不会什么都披露给你;却会在你想要做的概述中挑毛病……(Peter Lawrence, in Lawrence and Edwards 167)。

实例2

    In his study of the budgeting practices of more than 400 U.S. firms, Unapathy found budget games and manipulation were widespread:

        Deferring a needed expenditure [was the budget game] used with the highest frequency.... Getting approvals after money was spent, shifting funds between accounts to avoid budget overruns, and employment of contract labor to avoid exceeding headcount limits are the other relatively popular games... (90).

    在对400多家公司预算业务的研究中，Unapathy发现预算游戏和操纵是普遍存在的：

        其他使用相对普遍的预算游戏包括：推迟使用频率很高的所需支出……在未获得批准之前就把钱花掉，账目间转移资金来回避预算超支，以及雇佣合同工来规避超过人数限制……(90)。

注：好的示意叙述常常是对引用语的一个恰到好处的概括。

(1) 分开引用语的注意事项。

• 在示意引用语时要用完整的句子，不能使用只言片语。

• 示意叙述要用冒号标出(:)。

• 引用语的左端缩进(缩进多少最终取决于刊物的要求)。

• 不要用引号把分开的引用语引上。

• 在引用语最后的标点符号之后要有间隔，然后用圆括号给出文献出处(见上面的例子，注意它与在文本之中使用的标点符号有所不同)。

(2) 用错的引用语。

    Fombrum says,

    "A name essentially describes how a company is perceived on the outside. It signals to outside observers what a company stands for; the quality of its products. When the value-priced cosmetics maker Avon tried to improve its reputation by purchasing the prestige retailer Tiffany's in 1979, most doubted the wisdom of the move. That's why it came as no surprise when five years later Avon sold off the operation. Not only did owning Tiffany's fail to add luster to Avon, but negative publicity about Avon ownership was rapidly tarnishing Tiffany's reputation" (Fombrum 42).

(3) 修改后的引用语。

    Names can be highly valuable business assets:

    A name essentially describes how a company is perceived on the outside. It signals to outside observers what a company stands for; the quality of its products. When the value-priced cosmetics maker Avon tried to improve its reputation by purchasing the prestige retailer Tiffany's in

1979, most doubted the wisdom of the move. That's why it came as no surprise when five years later Avon sold off the operation. Not only did owning Tiffany's fail to add luster to Avon, but negative publicity about Avon ownership was rapidly tarnishing Tiffany's reputation. (Fombrum 42)

7. 引用语中的强调

当读者在引用语中看到强调成分时,他们就会想要知道这部分的强调是原来就有的,还是引用者后加的。下面教你如何应对这种情况:

实例1

> Locke argues that every individual in the state of nature has a right to enforce the laws of nature: "the *execution*$_9$ of the law of nature is, in that state, put into every man's hands..." (9, emphasis in the original).

实例2

> For Wollstonecraft, universal education is critical: "my main argument is built on this simple principle, that if she [woman] be not prepared by education to become the companion of man, she will stop the progress of knowledge and virtue; for *truth must be common to all*$_{86}$, or it will be inefficacious with respect to its influence on general practice" (86, emphasis added).

8. 省略

省略是一个让人产生想象的词,它的意思是省略了引用语中的部分词语。省略的使用方法不是容易掌握的,当然你也不想由于去掉重要的词语而改变原文的意思。但正如我们前面说过的,修剪引用语是使引用语更具影响力的有效方法之一。但是,也要注意让读者知道你对原文做了什么修改,虽然你也不会对原文做出实质性的修改。如果你省略了引用语中的某些词语,要用省略号标出:3~4个圆点,圆点之间及前后要有间隔。

(1)三个圆点的省略号。

当你删去的词语是引用语的开头或引用语的中间(但不超过整个句子的一半),使用三个点的省略号。

> "Most of the world's Muslims today... are not Arabs and cannot read Arabic" (Lippman 58).

注:点与点之间要有一个间隔,很多作者对此不十分清楚,故在此提醒作者。

(2)四个点的省略号。

如果引用语的删除部分包括了句子末尾的标点符号,或如果你在用引用语来结束你文章中的句子,那么你需要使用第四个实心的圆点来代表句号。如果你省去了引文的一个或一个以上的句子,你必须使用省略号的第四个点。第一个点是句号,其余三个点是省略号。你引用的成分一定由省略号之前和省略号之后的语法正确的完整句子组成。

实例1

> Frederick Douglass bores into his listeners' hearts, insisting that no

one can truly believe in the justice of slavery: "There is not a man beneath the canopy of heaven that does not know that slavery is wrong *for him*. . . . At a time like this, scorching irony, not convincing argument, is needed" (Douglass 34).

实例 2

Ann Hall perceives the difficulty in evaluating O'Neill's *Anna Christie*: "For feminist scholars, the conclusion for Anna is ambivalent at best. On the one hand, she is domesticated; she has relinquished all her ambition and now stands behind 'her man' in order that he may attain his dreams... On the other hand, Anna gains a certain degree of independence, ironically through her relationship with Andersen" (174).

引证来源放在引用语之后,当然是在第四个点省略号之前(前面提到的分开引用语除外)。下面给出几种用错省略号的例子(如间隔的地方不对),以及修改后正确的例子:

用错省略号的例子:

"*Punctuation standards have changed over time*. . ." (*Walters* 178)

"*Punctuation standards have changed over time*..." (*Walters* 178).

"*Punctuation standards have changed over time*. . . ." (*Walters* 178)

"*Punctuation standards have changed over time*. . . ." (*Walters* 178)

修改后正确的例子:

"*Punctuation standards have changed over time* . . ." (Walters 178).

对于分开的引用语,附加说明的括号要放在最后的圆点之后,即句号之后(见上述的例子)。

最后,在你删除词语的时候也不一定总是要使用省略号。使用省略号的理由是你想让读者知道引用语之后还有词语被漏掉了。如果从上下文可以看出这一点,就没有必要使用省略号。

用错省略号的例子:

Walton oversaw ". . . a massive overhaul of Wal-Mart's inventory system" (147).

修改后正确的例子:

Walton oversaw "a massive overhaul of Wal-Mart's inventory system" (147).

(3) 引用语中的引用语。

有时你要引用的引文本身就含有引号。

原始资料:

But though I was initially disappointed at being categorized as an extremist, as I continued to think about the matter I gradually gained a measure of satisfaction from the label. Was not Jesus an extremist for love: "Love your enemies, bless them that curse you, do good to them that hate

you, and pray for them which despitefully use you, and persecute you."
Was not Amos an extremist for justice: "Let justice roll down like waters and righteousness like an ever-flowing stream."

Martin Luther King, Jr., "Letter from Birmingham Jail." 1963. *What Country Have I? Political Writings by Black Americans*, ed. Herbert J. Storing (New York: St. Martin's Press, 1970), 125–26.

这时你要看主要的引用语是否长到需要把它与正文分开单独成立。如果是短的引文（不超过四行），属于放在文本中的,那么,对主要引用语使用双引号,对其中的引用语使用单引号：

Instead of denying the accusation that he is an extremist, King embraces it: "As I continued to think about the matter I gradually gained a measure of satisfaction from the label. Was not Jesus an extremist for love: 'Love your enemies, bless them that curse you, do good to them that hate you'..." (125–6).

如果是分开的引用语,就把双引号用在原来的单引号的位置(因为分开的引用语不需要引号)。

第五章
如何避免被指控剽窃

5.1 什么是剽窃?

剽窃这个词来自于拉丁语,意思是"绑匪",因此剽窃他人的观点就如同偷窃他人的财物。在学术写作中,剽窃就是把别人的劳动成果窃为己有,也就是自己的写作中借用了他人的观点或成果,却没有在文章中标明它们的出处。他人的成果可以是出版了的材料(如书籍、文章、网页、电影、视频、光盘等),也可以是未经出版的材料(如访谈、讲稿等)。

无论是有意的还是无意的,如果一个人因利用了别人的成果而受到赞誉,就是破坏了职业的或者是学术的信任。

但也不要为此而走向另一个极端,以至于不敢用。要知道,利用好原始资料是大有益处的。利用好他人的资料会增加你写作的权威性,会为你的写作提供证据。在学术写作中,常会出现的一个严重错误是文章中缺少充足的证据,而原始资料提供的正是证据。文章的可贵之处,部分在于是否正确地使用了原始资料。我们需要有能力来判断该引用哪些作者,如何把他们的成果结合到自己的写作中,以及何时引用。同样重要的是,如果你能对不同出处的资料加以综述的话,你的读者会更被你的努力所感动,也就是说,你在从不同的视角对他人的观点进行概括的同时提出了自己的新观点。

1. 自测一下你是否在剽窃

下面是一段出版的材料和一位学生的作品,看看这位学生作者是否适当地处理了他人的文献。

出版的资料:

> Anyone who is skilled at making pancakes will have the griddle very hot so that the batter solidifies quickly after being poured. Not having a thermostat on the griddle, one tests the griddle's temperature by sprinkling water on it. If the griddle is hot but not hot enough, the water drops spread out, wet the surface, and evaporate within about two seconds. If the griddle is ready for the batter, the sprinkled drops dance, vibrate, and skim over the surface for from 30 to 100 seconds. How can drops last

longer on a hotter griddle?

学生写的范文：

> If you have ever made pancakes, you might have noticed that if the griddle is hot but not quite ready for the batter, a drop of water sprinkled on the griddle will thin out and disappear in about two seconds. When the surface becomes hot enough, however, the droplets will bounce, wriggle, and skip above the griddle for anywhere from half a minute to over a minute and a half. How can this be?

学生的这个写作可接受吗？

不可以，因为学生没有在这一段中恰当地给出原始文献的出处。

2. 如何避免剽窃事件的发生

在学术界，下列事件的任何一件如果发生在你身上，都会被视为剽窃：

- 在没有承认和标明原始资料出处的情况下，把可确认为是他人所写的段落、短语、思想纳入到你的文章中；
- 使用了完全同他人一样的论述结构或观点展开的方式；
- 未能把他人的原话或信息内容放在引号内；
- 大段地使用了由朋友或指导教师改写过的东西；
- 购买、找到或接收别人的文章，并把它们当作是自己的东西使用。

3. 应在何时表达对他人的工作的赞赏

有效避免被指控剽窃的方法是在合适的时候及时表达你对他人成果的赞赏，表达对他人说的、写的、电子邮递的、画的、已经暗示的等形式的帮助表示赞赏。很多专业组织（包括 MLA 和 APA）都对如何引用原始资料给出了指导。但由于作者没有充足的时间来掌握这些规则，因此他们有时忘记在何时、何种情况下需要对他人的工作或成果表示赞赏。下面就何种情况下表达致谢给予简单的指导：

（1）当借用了杂志、书籍、报刊、歌曲、电视节目、电影、网页、电脑程序、信件、广告或其他媒体的词语或观点的时候；

（2）当你通过面对面、电话或书信同他人访谈或交流获得了信息的时候；

（3）当你准确无误地抄用了他人的言辞或独特的表达式的时候；

（4）当你翻印了他人的图表、图解、图画或其他视觉材料的时候；

（5）当你重新使用或重新投寄任何已有的电子资料包括图像、大众传播媒介（声频的、视频的等）的时候。

当然也有不需要表达出处或致谢时候，如：

（1）当你写出的是自己的生活经历、自己的观察和感受、自己的思想和自己就某个主题的结论的时候；

（2）当你写出的是基于自己通过实验研究得出的结果的时候；

（3）当你使用的是你自己的艺术品、数码照片、录像、录音等；

（4）当你使用的是大家熟知的事物的时候，如民间传说、常识性的观察材料、神话、传

说以及历史事件(但不是历史文献);

(5)当你使用的是普遍接受的事实的时候,如污染对环境有害等。

下面举例说明什么是"常识":

(1)比尔·克林顿是 1992 年被选为美国总统的。

(2)法国大革命始于 1789 年。

(3)2002 年居住在得克萨斯州的人有 21 779 893。

(4)约翰·F.肯尼迪最著名的格言之一是"不要问国家为你做了些什么,问一问你能为国家做什么"。

5.2 引证的技巧

引证的时候,一定把有关参考资料的出处放在引文的后面。如果你把参考资料的出处放在了引文的前面,读者会把随后出现的话语当作是你的东西,你由此可能被指控剽窃了他人的成果。例如:

> "By studying the cerebral cortex of rats, Diamond identified that improving the learning environments of students fosters growth in areas of the brain responsible for higher-order thinking" (Slavkin 3).

如果引用的是较长的段落(超过四行),引用语的左端缩进(通常缩进 1/2 英寸),而且引文同文本分开,还要有个以冒号结尾的论述来示意下面是关于什么内容的引文:

> Privacy, one observer suggests, is the cardinal virtue of the Dutch:
> Dutch citizens are proud of their country; they think well of it, and they want you to think well of it, but they do not necessarily want to unpack it, know all the details, sometimes tear the paper from the cracks, and reach independent judgments.... Never in the line of duty have I been bamboozled as in The Netherlands, where they all tell you different things; no one wants to make a full disclosure and they will pick holes in any generalization you care to profess... (Peter Lawrence, in Lawrence and Edwards 167).

当开始的句子中很快出现引文时,一定要清晰地表明紧跟着出现的不是你的话语,是他人的话语。可以使用下面的短语如"According to Michelle Simmons...",或"In his book *Crevice Corners*, Michael McDougal states..."等形式来引出引文,涉及的参考资料的出处要标示在引文之后。例如:

> According to Michael Slavkin, "Teachers and parents are likely to see the implications of authentic learning when it has been absent during the early years of a student's life" (5).

如果省略了引文中的材料,要用三个点的省略号(...)标出。例如:

> "Most of the world's Muslims today... are not Arabs and cannot read Arabic" (Lippman 58).

如果省略的内容是引文的末尾之后的内容,要用四个点的省略号(....)标出,第一个是句子的句号,其余的是省略的内容。

实例 1

"Educators strive to create environments that are meaningful and interesting to students...."

实例 2

In surveying various responses to plagues in the Middle Ages, Barbara W. Tuchman writes, "Medical thinking, trapped in the theory of astral influences, stressed air as the communicator of disease..." (102-02).

如果出于使读者便于理解引文的考虑,给引文加上了原引文没有的内容,要把加入的词或短语放在方括号[ ]中。

例如:

"Such a system [standards-based movement] would require that students reveal these skills through a system that demonstrates their ability to apply the information, and oftentimes implications abound that such behaviors occur in real-world contexts" (Slavkin 171).

如果引用的文本中有拼写或语法错误,你要在你的文本中准确无误地转录出现的错误,但可插入斜体的词 sic,用括号括上。sic 是拉丁语,意思是 thus、so 或 just as that 等,这样读者就会知道,错误是你发现的,不是你犯的。

例如:Mr. Johnson says of the experience, "it's made me reconsider the existence of extraterestials [*sic*].

引号的练习:

在需要的地方给下面的句子加上引号,把需要用其他符号的词语用该用的符号表示出(如斜体、括号等)。

(1) Mary is trying hard in school this semester, her father said.

(2) No, the taxi driver said curtly, I cannot get you to the airport in fifteen minutes.

(3) I believe, Jack remarked, that the best time of a year to visit Europe is in the spring. At least that's what I read in a book entitled Guide to Europe.

(4) My French professor told me that my accent is abominable.

(5) She asked, Is Time a magazine you read regularly?

(6) Flannery O'Connor probably got the title of one of her stories from the words of the old popular song, A Good Man Is Hard to Find.

(7) When did Roosevelt say, We have nothing to fear but fear itself?

(8) It seems to me that hip and cool are words that are going out of style.

(9) Yesterday, John said, This afternoon I'll bring back your book Conflict in the Middle East; however, he did not return it.

(10) Can you believe, Dot asked me, that it has been almost five years since we've seen

each other?

(11) A Perfect Day for Bananafish is, I believe, J. D. Salinger's best short story.

(12) Certainly, Mr. Martin said, I shall explain the whole situation to him. I know that he will understand.

引号的练习的答案：

(1) "Mary is trying hard in school this semester," her father said.

(2) "No," the taxi driver said curtly, "I cannot get you to the airport in fifteen minutes."

(3) "I believe," Jack remarked, "that the best time of a year to visit Europe is in the spring. At least that's what I read in a book entitled *Guide to Europe*."

(4) My French professor told me that my accent is abominable.

(5) She asked, "Is *Time* a magazine you read regularly?"

(6) Flannery O'Connor probably got the title of one of her stories from the words of the old popular song, "A Good Man Is Hard to Find."

(7) When did Roosevelt say, "We have nothing to fear but fear itself"?

(8) It seems to me that hip and cool are words that are going out of style.

(9) Yesterday, John said, "This afternoon I'll bring back your book *Conflict in the Middle East*"; however, he did not return it.

(10) "Can you believe," Dot asked me, "that it has been almost five years since we've seen each other?"

(11) "A Perfect Day for Bananafish" is, I believe, J. D. Salinger's best short story.

(12) "Certainly," Mr. Martin said, "I shall explain the whole situation to him. I know that he will understand."

5.3 意译的技巧

由于对原始资料的不正确的意译也被看作是剽窃，下面就如何意译给出一些技巧：

在意译时使用自己的话语，在读你要意译的原文的时候要格外小心，因为你要向读者传递原文的意思和观点，但你要用自己的话。

为了表明你在使用他人的观点，在意译的开头你要把它表示出来，如使用 Hanson felt that... 或 According to Hanson 等短语。

你也可以在意译后使用括号表明你在表述他人的观点，或意译之后使用尾注或脚注的形式来表示。

例如：

原始资料：

> All children learn and respond to settings differently; for this reason, many teachers consider the DAP approach beneficial for most children. DAP is gaining supporters in education due to its emphasis on meeting the needs of individual students. At a time when educators are working with more and

more divergent populations of students, differentiating practices based on each individual student's needs is critical (Slavkin 65).

意译：

Because students have learning styles that differ from one student to the next, the DAP [Developmentally Appropriate Practice] approach is considered a highly practical and useful form of teaching. The DAP is also quickly becoming a widely accepted method of reaching to all student's individual needs and not just a few (Slavkin 65).

如果在意译的时候需要在意译中加入属于原始资料的某一短语或词语，把这个短语或词语放在括号中。

例如：

原始资料：

Students involved with DAP are positively affected socially, emotionally, and cognitively. They enjoy learning more, because they can grasp the concepts through experimentation and learning activities. Also, the activities they learn directly correspond with their developmental levels; therefore, they are not expected to learn information they are not developmentally ready for.

意译：

Due to the use of DAP in the classroom, students now enjoy learning new things. Because these students are working at their developmental level they are expected only to learn what they are "developmentally ready for," and nothing more (Slavkin 67).

意译实例分析

为了帮助正确区分什么是正确的意译，什么是抄袭，请看下面的例子：

原始材料：

Teachers are required to be both educators and parental figures, filling in for too many students who arrive in schools unprepared for learning or interacting with others. Oftentimes, these learning-challenged students lack parental support, have had limited experience with literacy or problem solving, and don't know how to socialize with other children their age. These students not only have had limited experience with learning, thinking about difficult situations, and solving problems, but also have limited experience in environments that require them to work through problems. Yet, teachers are expected to prepare all of their students for achieving at grade-appropriate levels, while working on basic skills that are required for standard learning to occur, skills that should have been taught years before they arrived at the schoolhouse doors.

抄袭译本：

> These days, teachers are required to be both parent and educator, replacing any gap in social skills for students arriving to school unprepared. In too many cases, these learning-challenged students do not have the parental support they need at home and have little to no experience with reading or math, and not able to socialize with other students of their same age bracket. These children have had very little experience not only with learning, dealing with difficult situations, and problem solving, but also with their understanding of various environments they are placed in to work through their problems. Nevertheless, teachers are expected to fully prepare every one of their students not only to achieve at grade-appropriate levels, but also at everyday skills for customary learning. The everyday skills, at least, should have been taught before arriving at school (Slavkin, 3).

问题所在：

尽管其中的有些词和句子已有所变化，但此意译只改变了一些句子，使其看上去同原文有些不同，但同最初的句子结构没有区别。

正确的意译应该是：

> In this day and age, teachers have been burdened with the job of playing the role of both parent and teacher to many students entering school. These students, who come from homes with little to no support, are entering school lacking both social and problem solving skills that allow them to function and effectively interact with their peers and teachers. This has left teachers with the added burden to teach not only subjects and material appropriate for the student's grade level, but also with skills that will allow the students to be able to successfully interact with the environment around them (Slavkin, 3).

如果需要在意译中使用引用语，把需要引用的句子、短语或词放在括号中，然后标出出处。

意译练习

（说明：在另一张纸上写下你对下述段落的意译，尽量不要看原文。）

(1) "The Antarctic is the vast source of cold on our planet, just as the sun is the source of our heat, and it exerts tremendous control on our climate," [Jacques] Cousteau told the camera. "The cold ocean water around Antarctica flows north to mix with warmer water from the tropics, and its upwellings help to cool both the surface water and our atmosphere. Yet the fragility of this regulating system is now threatened by human activity." From "Captain Cousteau," Audubon (May 1990):17.

(2) The twenties were the years when drinking was against the law, and the law was a bad joke because everyone knew of a local bar where liquor could be had. They were the years when organized crime ruled the cities, and the police seemed powerless to do anything against it. Classical music was forgotten while jazz spread throughout the land, and men like Bix Beiderbecke, Louis Armstrong, and Count Basie became the heroes of the young. The flapper was born in the twenties, and with her bobbed hair and short skirts, she symbolized, perhaps more than anyone or anything else, America's break with the past. From Kathleen Yancey, English 102 Supplemental Guide (1989): 25.

(3) Of the more than 1,000 bicycling deaths each year, three-fourths are caused by head injuries. Half of those killed are school-age children. One study concluded that wearing a bike helmet can reduce the risk of head injury by 85 percent. In an accident, a bike helmet absorbs the shock and cushions the head. From "Bike Helmets: Unused Lifesavers," Consumer Reports (May 1990): 348.

(4) Matisse is the best painter ever at putting the viewer at the scene. He's the most realistic of all modern artists, if you admit the feel of the breeze as necessary to a landscape and the smell of oranges as essential to a still life. "The Casbah Gate" depicts the well-known gateway Babel Aassa, which pierces the southern wall of the city near the sultan's palace. With scrubby coats of ivory, aqua, blue, and rose delicately fenced by the liveliest gray outline in art history, Matisse gets the essence of a Tangier afternoon, including the subtle presence of the bowaab, the sentry who sits and surveys those who pass through the gate. From Peter Plagens, "Bright Lights." Newsweek (26 March 1990): 50.

(5) While the Sears Tower is arguably the greatest achievement in skyscraper engineering so far, it's unlikely that architects and engineers have abandoned the quest for the world's tallest building. The question is: Just how high can a building go? Structural engineer William LeMessurier has designed a skyscraper nearly one-half mile high, twice as tall as the Sears Tower. And architect Robert Sobel claims that existing technology could produce a 500-story building. From Ron Bachman, "Reaching for the Sky." Dial (May 1990): 15.

意译参考答案

(1) According to Jacques Cousteau, the activity of people in Antarctica is jeopardizing a delicate natural mechanism that controls the earth's climate. He fears that human activity could interfere with the

balance between the sun, the source of the earth's heat, and the important source of cold from Antarctic waters that flow north and cool the oceans and atmosphere ("Captain Cousteau" 17).

(2) During the twenties lawlessness and social nonconformity prevailed. In cities organized crime flourished without police interference, and in spite of nationwide prohibition of liquor sales, anyone who wished to buy a drink knew where to get one. Musicians like Louis Armstrong become favorites, particularly among young people, as many turned away from highly respectable classical music to jazz. One of the best examples of the anti-traditional trend was the proliferation of young "flappers," women who rebelled against custom by cutting off their hair and shortening their skirts (Yancey 25).

(3) The use of a helmet is the key to reducing bicycling fatalities, which are due to head injuries 75% of the time. By cushioning the head upon impact, a helmet can reduce accidental injury by as much as 85%, saving the lives of hundreds of victims annually, half of whom are school children ("Bike Helmets" 348).

(4) Matisse paintings are remarkable in giving the viewer the distinct sensory impressions of one experiencing the scene first hand. For instance, "The Casbah Gate" takes one to the walled city of Tangier and the Babel Aassa gateway near the Sultan's palace, where one can imagine standing on an afternoon, absorbing the splash of colors and the fine outlines. Even the sentry, the bowaab vaguely eyeing those who come and go through the gate, blends into the scene as though real (Plagens 50).

(5) How much higher skyscrapers of the future will rise than the present world marvel, the Sear Tower, is unknown. However, the design of one twice as tall is already on the boards, and an architect, Robert Sobel, thinks we currently have sufficient know-how to build a skyscraper with over 500 stories (Bachman 15).

5.4 原始资料记录

所有来自于他人原始资料的引证、意译和观点都要在文本中或文章末尾的参考文献中有所体现。文本中的引用必须是读者在文章末尾的参考文献中能够找到的。

就如何记录原始资料，请参阅附录Ⅱ。附录Ⅱ给出了能帮助你解决记录原始资料中遇到的问题的手册或指南，你可通过网络或其他渠道得到和利用这些资源，它们会为你的学术写作提供很大帮助。

第六章 项目/基金申请

本章的目的在于帮助你撰写和修改用以申请研究基金的项目申请报告(自然科学以及社会科学等),对象是研究生、教师和研究员等,概括地讲,包括所有科研基金的申请者。

6.1 项目申请的写作过程

不同的学科,项目申请的写作会有很大的不同。以认识论为目的的研究(哲学或文科)要比以实际应用为目的(医学或有关社会方针政策的研究领域)的研究更加依赖于各种不同的假设。然而,本章试图给出一个跨学科的具有概括性的指导。

尽管人文学科的学者可能不会以研究方案、假设、研究问题或结果的形式来思考申请方案,但项目评审人员和提供基金的机构却希望学者们能够用这样的申请方式来申请。你会发现用在学习如何写项目申请上的尝试和努力是值得的。你也会发现按此方式来规划你的项目会有助于从全新的视角来看待研究项目。

项目申请的写作是一个漫长的过程,首先要有一个想法。很多人认为基金申请是一个线性的过程(从开始有想法到申请成功),事实上它是一个循环的过程,图6.1概括性地给出了项目申请写作这一过程,帮助你规划如何进行项目申请的写作。

申请人必须经历写申请、提交申请、得到告知申请被接受或被拒绝的通知,然后还要经历修改项目申请这一过程。申请失败的,还要对现有的申请进行修改,以便在下一轮的申请中再次提交;申请成功的,在取得研究成果的基础上,还会萌生进一步研究、进一步再申请的想法。

同基金机构建立良好的关系会为以后的再次成功申请铺平道路,因此一定要按时地、以专业的方式汇报项目进展、完成情况。有些得到过基金资助的人担心提供基金的机构会因为上次已经给了"足够的"基金而拒绝再次提供基金资助,而事实上是财源会接踵而至,越是在过去成功申请过的申请人,越具竞争力,因此也越可能在未来得到资助。

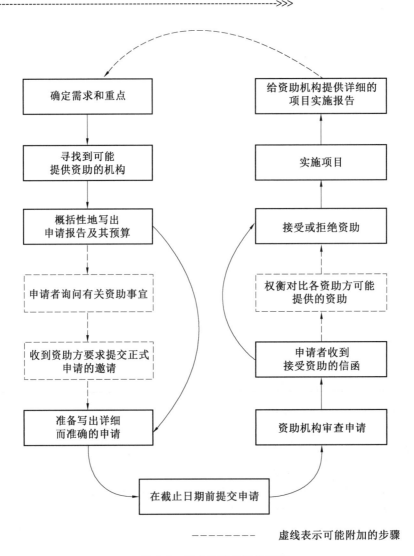

图 6.1　基金申请的写作过程

一些普遍使用的技巧

（1）早动手；

（2）早申请、常申请；

（3）申请时不要忘记附上一封说明信；

（4）回答所有的问题（主动回答所有必要的但未阐明的问题）；

（5）提供所需要的材料，准确地按照申请指南去做；

（6）阐述要有力、准确而又清楚、具体；

（7）在方案规划过程中要力求现实研究目的；

（8）要明确表明你所研究的问题和目的的关系、研究目的和方法之间的关系、研究方法和结果之间的关系以及研究结果和向公众传播信息的计划之间的关系；

（9）如申请失败了，重新修改你的提议，再次申请；

(10)准确地按照申请指南去做(之所以在这重复这一点,是因为这一点是非常非常重要的)。

1. 写项目申请前

要确定你的需求和问题的焦点

首先,确定你的需求。下面的问题可能会对你确定自己的需求有帮助:

(1)你在实施一项全面的、具有或显示出应有的完善特征的项目之前,是否已经在承担着前期的或试验性等相关的研究?

(2)你申请基金资助的目的是什么:获得博士学位的研究?博士论文的前期研究?博士后研究?实验性研究?还是野外工作?

(3)你是在申请生活津贴以便完成博士论文或书,还是为了完善手稿?

(4)你是否在申请研究资助以便能留在给予你科研帮助或提供资源的研究机构?

(5)你申请的基金是否是一个需要几年才能完成、有很多人参与的研究项目?

在考虑了上述问题之后,进一步聚焦到你的研究项目。回答下面的问题会有助于你确定你的研究范围:

(1)研究的主题是什么:它的研究为什么是重要的?

(2)你在试图回答的研究问题是什么?你所研究的问题的相关性是什么?

(3)你的假设是什么?

(4)你的研究方法是什么?

(5)为什么你的研究/项目是重要的?它的意义何在?

(6)你是打算使用定量的方法,还是定性的方法,还是两者兼而有之?

(7)你是选用实验性研究,还是临床研究?

一旦确定了你的需求和研究焦点,你就可以寻找预期的资金和资金机构。

2. 寻找预期的资金和资金机构

你的基金申请能否得到资助在很大程度上取决于你的科研目的和目标是否贴近于出资机构优先考虑的事。找出谁可能会给你提供资金是一件费时的事,但从长远的角度来看,它将给你带来不小的回报。即使你的科研项目是世界上最好的,如果你找不到合适的机构,就不可能得到基金资助。

有很多渠道可以使你了解资助机构和资助项目。几乎所有的大学和大学的学院都有专门负责科研事务的行政部门。这些行政部门主要帮助员工和学生寻找基金资助,且都配有信息中心,用以帮助教职员工和学生找到预期的资助。

3. 如何撰写项目提议

(1)读者(专家、评审人员)。

大部分的基金项目提议都要经过具有某一学科知识的学术评审人员来评审,因此在写项目提议的时候,就要设想你是在和具有专业知识但不一定是十分了解你的研究问题的同行人在说话。

要记住,多数的评审人员并不想花力气去解读你那条理不清、书写糟糕、不易理解的研究项目提议的。一定要给他提供他所需了解的内容,严格遵守你所申请的专项基金的申请指南,这可能要求你以一种不同的角度或语言来重新组织你的项目提议。修改你的研究规划以便使你的项目提议符合基金申请的要求,这是申请过程中合理、必要的一部分,除非这样做会从根本上改变你的研究项目的目标或成果,否则就要这样去做。

能否得到资助最终取决于你的项目提议是否能使评审人员确信你的项目是缜密规划和可行的,还取决于你的项目提议是否会使评审人员确信提议的研究人员有能力使项目付诸实现。在整个提议中,要尽量地使表述完全、清楚;要设身处地地思考问题,设想你的问题是评审人员的问题,也是他们所能回答的问题。

有学者认为,评审人员在评审项目提议的时候通常会思考以下三个问题:
①如果提议的项目能够被实施,将会从中获悉什么?(目的、目标和成果)
②了解它的价值所在?(意义)
③怎么能知道结论是有效的?(成功的标准)

在申请中你一定要回答这些问题。要知道评审人员是不会去读你申请中的每一个词的。可能被读的只有摘要、研究方案和方法、个人简历和预算部分。这几部分的写作一定要尽可能地清晰、直截了当。

(2)文体。

你写申请的方式本身已经在很大程度上把你的情况介绍给了评审人员,从阅读你的申请,他们就会了解到你是一位怎样的学者、研究者或一个什么样的人;他们会从中确定你是否具有创造性、逻辑性、分析性,是否洞悉相关领域的发展动态;最重要的是,他们会从中了解到你是否具有完成项目提议的能力。你的写作风格应遵循你所在学科的要求及其惯例,但你的声音和个性也要贯穿其中。一定要阐述清楚你的研究项目的理论导向。

(3)首先写一般性的提议和预算。

因为多数的申请者都是从不同的机构或基金项目申请资助,因此不妨先从写一般性的资金申请和预算开始。这种申请有时叫作"白皮书",它的对象不属于专业化极强的读者,先向他们解释你的项目。在你把提议提交给不同的基金项目之前,你要根据他们的指南和先决条件等要求来具体修改你的提议,以便使其符合特定的申请指南和先决条件等要求。

(4)组成一个有秩序的、发挥作用的、有结构的申请。

尽管每个基金部门都有其自己的(通常是非常具体的)要求,但基金申请还是有一些共有的、相当规范的要素,如下面给出的:

- 标题页;
- 摘要;
- 序言(问题的综述、研究的目的或目标以及研究的意义);
- 文献回顾;
- 设计方案(方法、程序、目标、成果或可交付的结果、评价、以及成果发布);
- 人员;
- 预算和预算说明。

提议要写得规范,以便于阅读;用小标题的形式把提议分成几个部分,如果提议太长,可以加上标有页码的内容目录。

① 标题页。

标题页通常包括代表科研项目的一个简洁明了的标题、主要研究者的姓名、申请者的所在单位(大学、院和系)、出资单位的名称和地址、申请项目日期、申请的基金数额以及申请者所在大学相关部门的签名或盖章(如必要)。多数出资单位对标题页有特殊要求，一定要按照要求去做。

② 摘要。

读者(专家、评审人员)是首先通过你的摘要了解你的项目的，因此摘要给了他们有关你的项目的第一印象；同时，专家、评审人员在就你的项目写推荐或建议的时候，也会看你的摘要，以便不时地提醒他们自己你的项目内容是什么。因此，他们对你的项目的最后印象也可能是通过阅读摘要获得的。摘要应该对你未来的研究项目的主要内容加以说明：总的目的、具体的目标、研究计划、方法和意义(贡献等)。摘要的写作要尽量有力、准确而又清楚。

③ 序言。

序言应该包括项目的主要内容，包括问题的综述、研究的目的、研究的目标和研究的意义。问题的综述要有一个背景，给出研究项目所依据的基本原理，说明研究的必要性及相关性；你的研究主题与以往的相同的主题有什么不同？你是否会采用新的方法或涉猎新的理论领域？研究目标或目的应该同研究的预期结果相一致，也要同问题的综述中所论述的必要性相一致。在引言中只列出研究的主要目的或目标，次要的目标留在对项目的叙述时再讲。

④ 文献回顾。

很多基金申请都要求有文献回顾。评审人员要知道你对你要从事的项目是否已做了前期的初步研究。文献回顾应该是有选择、评论性的，不该是面面俱到的；评审人员想知道你是如何评价相关文献的。

⑤ 项目叙述。

项目叙述给出了提议的具体内容，要求对申请项目分段叙述。项目叙述要把有关项目的所有细节都加以叙述，包括问题的详细论述、研究目标或目的、研究设想、方法、步骤、研究结果或可交付的东西、评价和研究后的成果发布方式等。

在项目叙述中，要先发制人地回答所有评审人员可能提出的所有问题，不要让评审人员有任何疑惑。比如，如果你想做一个非正式的访谈，提出一些自由回答的问题，你一定要解释为什么这种方法是你申请研究的问题的最好方法；再比如，如果你使用了项目反映理论来检验你的测量仪器的有效性，而不是用经典的测试理论，这时你要解释一下这一革新方法的优势所在。

清晰而明确地论述你的研究目标、研究问题、设想、方法以及结果之间的关系。由于各学科对项目申请的叙述的要求会有很大的差别，一定要参考具体的基金项目申请写作指南，以便了解一些附加的信息。

⑥ 人员。

要详细说明所需的研究人员，人员组成一定要合理。明确说明已有的人员的技术组成(你可以把他们的简历用作申请的一部分)；说明你需要补充的人员的技术组成，以及他们的作用。为了减少开支,把与项目研究后期无关的人员从后期所需研究人员中去掉。

⑦预算。

预算中要详细说明项目的成本,通常包括详细地给出了排列项的数据表,还包括预算叙述(也被叫作预算理由),来解释各种支出费用。即使申请指南没有具体要求对预算做说明,你也要用一、二页来说明预算。6.3 实例 1 就是预算和预算说明的实例。

为你的项目做一个详尽的预算,即使是这样会超出某一特定基金组织所能提供资助的正常范围;讲清楚你在寻求其他渠道的资金帮助,这种方法有助于你有幸得到多方的资助。

要确保列出的所有预算项目都符合出资机构的要求。如果哪一项不符合要求(如有的机构不提供设备购买或其他的资金费用),要在预算说明部分指出此项会得到其他的基金渠道的资助,以此来表明在此列出此项的理由。

许多大学要求在提供的基金中包括大学负担的管理费用,要同相关的部门相协商以便确定标准的管理比率是多少。要由学校的负责管理基金的部门审查通过一个非直接费用的和与研究没有直接关系的预算草案(如设备使用费用)。

⑧期限。

较详细地解释研究项目的期限。什么时间开始?每一步的结束时间如何?你最好是给评审人员提供一个可视的时间明细表;如果研究项目不太复杂,给出一个能概括研究时间明细的表格即可,以便评审人员了解和评估你的申请的规划和可行性。见 6.3 实例 2。

对于需要多年、程序较大、人员较多的科研项目,最好是给出一个时间分配图表,因为图表有助于阐明研究的可行性和规划。实例可见 6.3 实例 3。

6.2 修改科研基金申请

写出一份好的科研基金申请不是短时间内能完成的。要及早开始,给读者留出足够的时间,以便他们对你的草稿提出反馈意见;要选择不同的读者,既要有本行业的专家,也要有非专业的同事;你还可以从你所申请基金领域的有识之士处获得帮助,如可以安排一个与统计专家会面的机会,请他帮助你修改申请中的方法部分;如果需要学校相关科研部门的专业帮助,不要犹豫,去寻求他们的援助。

在你做修改和编辑的时候,请读者认真考虑并提出他们的观点,看看你是否已经明确地解释清楚了你的研究目标和方法的关系。

(1)你给出的申请理由令人信服吗?

(2)你是否完全、清楚地阐述了你提出的假设?

(3)你的项目提议看上去切实可行吗?它是否过于雄心勃勃?它是否存在其他方面的不足?

(4)你是否论述了一种可供出资者在你完成项目之后用来对你的项目是否成功进行评估的方式?

如果出资单位列出了用以打分和评价申请的标准,你在给你的评审人员做预审的时候,要采用同一标准。

最后的忠告

我们有些人对于申请基金资助会感到羞愧或不好意思。这些感觉与其说是与我们写作中的问题相关,还不如说是由于我们自身缺少安全感。如果你的问题是由这类障碍造成的,重要的是要记住提出申请是永远不会给你带来任何伤害的。如果你从不申请基金资助,出资单位将永远不会给你资助。

6.3 基金申请中预算和期限样本

实例1:预算

项 目	数 量	花 费	小 计	总 计
飞机旅行				
RDU-Kigali 往返旅行	1		$6 100	$6 100
生活津贴				
卢旺达	12 个月	$1 899	$22 788	$22 788
工程津贴				
研究助理/翻译	12 个月	$400	$4 800	
国内车费				
——阶段1	4 个月	$300	$1 200	
——阶段2	8 个月	$1 500	$12 000	
电子信函	12 个月	$60	$720	
MP3			$200	
摄影机			$500	
手提电脑	1		$2 895	
NUD * IST 4.0 软件			$373	
其他				
总的项目津贴				$51 576
管理费				$100
总计				$51 676
其他来源的资助				($15 000)
总基金额				$36 676

(1)飞机旅行$6 100。

此估价是基于商业旺季Sabena Belgian航空公司的价格给出的,没有飞往Kigali,Rwanda的美国航空公司,Sabena公司有学生票,学生票的价格略便宜些(大约是$2 000)。

(2)生活津贴$22 788。

生活津贴是根据富布莱特法案基金公布的基金申请指南给出的。

(3) 研究助理/翻译 $4 800。

研究助理/翻译人员是经历过至少四年学习的大学毕业生,在主要研究者做生活访谈期间陪伴并提供语言沟通方面的帮助;此外,研究助理在主要研究员观察期间提供解说,给主要研究员的观察提供便利。在国外从事项目的最初阶段,研究助理的工作时间将会是每周 40 小时,必要的时候还会超过这个时间。在项目的二期和三期阶段,助理将同主要研究员一起在必要时住在野外。每月四百元的薪水的确定基于相关规定,即参考为 Rwanda 工作人员制定的相关限定划定的。

(4) 第一期国内的交通费 $1 200。

主要研究员和助理研究员在 Kigali 期间需要有乘公交车和出租车的交通费。在 Kigali 出租车的平均费用是 $6~8,公交车的费用是 $15,第一阶段的交通费是按平均每天 $10 确定的。

(5) 第二期和第三期国内的交通费 $12 000。

项目人员还需要乡间往返的交通,如果无法在野外过夜,就需要每日的通勤费,在 Rwanda,每天租车的费用是 $130,上述交通费的计算是按照第二和第三阶段的交通费每天 $50 确定的。如果政府部门或国际援助机构提供帮助的话,可降低这部分的费用。

(6) 电子信函费 $720。

RwandaTel 提供的电子信函费用是每月 $60,获得电子信函路径关系到我们是否能收到有关 Rwanda 等地发来的最新报告,也是我们同在美国的论文评委和顾问保持联系的途径。

(7) MP3 费 $200。

需要用 MP3 来对生活访谈、音乐演奏、社团活动、讲故事和其他相关数据进行录音。

(8) 摄影机 $500。

需要摄影机来记录可视资料,如地形/风景、环境、婚礼、葬礼、社团活动等。

(9) 手提电脑 $2 895。

需要一台电脑来记录有关研究项目的观察、想法和分析,给出的价格是 Carolina Computing Initiative 针对 UNC 学生的报价。

(10) NUD*IST 4.0 软件 $373。

在野外研究期间和之后,需要 NUD*IST 4.0 软件来编目录、编索引以及管理野外记录。程序将有助于把在人生访谈过程中出现的主题编成目录。

(11) 管理费 $100。

参见富布莱特法案基金对赞助机构的规定。

实例 2:用表格格式表示项目期限

探索性研究	完成
项目提议的设计	完成
Ph.D 资格考试	完成
科研申请答辩	完成

续表

探索性研究	完成
在 Rwanda 的野外工作	Oct. 1999—Dec. 2000
数据分析和抄写	Jan. 2001—March 2001
撰写各章初稿	March 2001—Sept. 2001
修改	Oct. 2001—Feb. 2002
论文答辩	April 2002
最后批准和完成	May 2002

实例3：图表形式的项目期限

Activity	GY1				GY2			
	Q1	Q2	Q3	Q4	Q5	Q6	Q7	Q8
• Develop items for survey								
• Review and revise items with experts' panel.								
• Pre-test items with representative sample of target population.								
• Program software to administer suvey.								
• Prepare suvey sites for study. Recruit and train Study Reps.								
• Recruit 1,000 subjects and administer survey at 5 sites.								
• Statistical analysis of data.								
• Preparation and submission of manuscripts to peer-reviewed joumals.								

6.4 撰写基金申请的资源

下面是帮你撰写基金申请的资源，也是本章编写过程中参考的文献，但不是有关这一题目的所有资料，我们鼓励读者在研究过程中找出有关这一主题的最新出版资料。

Grantwriting Tips from the Donors Forum of Wisconsin

http://www.dfwonline.org/page9123.cfm

Guide for Writing a Funding Proposal by S. Joseph Levine

http://www.learnerassociates.net/proposal/

Holloway, Brian R. 2003. Proposal Writing Across the Disciplines. Upper Saddle River, New Jersey: Prentice Hall.

Locke, Lawrence F., Spirduso; Waneen Wyrick; and Silverman, Stephen J. 2000. Proposals that Work. (Fourth Edition) Thousand Oaks, CA: Sage, Publications.

Office of Sponsored Programs. Proposal Development and Preparation. N. d. State University of New York College at Cortland. 2 Feb. 2004. http://www.cortland.edu/osp/proposals.html.

Proposal Writing Online Short Course from the Foundation Center
http://fdncenter. org/learn/shortcourse/prop1. html

Przeworski, Adam, and Salomon, Frank. 1995. Some Candid Suggestions for Applicants to Social Science Research Council Competitions. In The Art of Writing Proposals. New York: Social Science Research Council. 2 Feb. 2004. http://www. psu. ac. th/PresidentOffice/EduService/research/umass/artprop. htm; http://www. psu. ac. th/PresidentOffice/EduService/research/umass/artprop. htm&.

Reif-Lehrer, Liane. 1989. Writing a Successful Grant Application. Boston: Jones and Bartlett Publishers.

Wiggins, Beverly. 2002. Funding and Proposal Writing for Social Science Faculty and Graduate Student Research. Chapel Hill: Howard W. Odum Institute for Research in Social Science. 2 Feb. 2004.

http://www2. irss. unc. edu/irss/shortcourses/wigginshandouts/granthandout. pdf

http://www2. irss. unc. edu/irss/shortcourses/wigginshandouts/granthandout. pdf

6.5 基金申请案例实例(英文版)

MINISTRY OF SCIENCE AND TECHNOLOGY OF P. R. CHINA

MINISTRY OF SCIENCE, CULTURE AND SPORT STATE OF ISRAEL

CHINA-ISRAEL JOINT RESEARCH PROGRAM
Call for Project Proposals
2009—2011

The application form consists of the following:

Part Ⅰ: General information
Part Ⅱ: Abstract (for ongoing projects – progress report only)
Part Ⅲ: a. Description of the research project
　　　　b. Time schedule and work plan
Part Ⅳ: Budget details

Instructions:

1. Ten copies in English, including an original, must be submitted by the Israeli

researchers to the Ministry of Science, Culture & Sport (Israel – MOS). One copy in English and Ten in Chinese must be submitted by the Chinese researchers to the Ministry of Science and Technology (China).

2. Proposals must be signed by the Principal Investigators and the Research Authorities, respectivlely. [Only two copies are required for renewal requests.]

3. To facilitate prompt evaluation of your application, please complete all parts of the form in full detail.

4. Applicants may attach any additional relevant documents to support their application.

5. Part Ⅱ of the application must include the following details:

   a. In a new proposal—research goals, methodology, and potential use of the results.

   b. In a renewal request—summary report of research progress.

6. Part Ⅲ of the application must be presented for both new proposals and renewal requests (see instructions).

7. If applicable, the following authorizations must be attached to the application form:

   a. Helsinki committee authorization—for research proposals involving clinical experiments in human beings.

   b. Application form submitted and authorization issued by the institutional oversight committee for experiments in animals—for research proposals involving experiments in animals.

   c. Ministry of Education authorization—for research proposals involving experiments, surveys or other activities to be carried out in schools.

8. Applications should be sent to the following addresses:

ISRAEL	CHINA
×××	×××
Deputy Director General for Planning & Control	Director of Asia andAfrica
Ministry of Science, Culture and Sports	Department of International Cooperatioin
P. O. Box 49100	15B,Fu Xing Road, Beijing, China
Jerusalem 91490, Israel	100862
Tel: 972-2-5411170/3	Tel: 86-10-58881346
Fax: 972-2-5823030	Fax: 86-10-58881344
E-mail: avi@ most. gov. il	E-mail: hzs_yfc@ most. cn

The application forms and accompanying material (in "pdf" or "doc" format) should be submitted together on CD

APPLICATION FOR JOINT CHINA-ISRAEL RESEARCH GRANT

PART I GENERAL INFORMATION

Title (in English): Fan Impeller hydraulic locking device for wind generator	
Title (in the local language): 风力发电机叶轮锁紧液压装置研究 **Hebrew**:	
Research topic (cite paragraph number/s from Call for Proposals): Direct Drive Volume Control Hydraulic servo System	

Application Type: New: The field of wind power Renewal: _____	Budget Requested: Total: $ 139,920 Year 1: $ 69,960 Year 2: $ 69,960	**Area of research** (according to the categories mentioned in the Call for Proposals)

Names, institutional affiliation, and contact information of Co-Principal Investigators

Name: Last, first + degree	Position	Department, Faculty, Institution	Telephone	Fax	email
ISRAELI Co-Principal Investigator					
Dr. ×××	Associate Professor	Ben-Gurion University Engineering Sciences Mechanical Engineering	+972-8-6477092	+972-8-6477090	avi@bgu.ac.il
Chinese Co-Principal Investigator					
Dr. Ing. ×××	Professor	Harbin Institute of Technology Mechatronic Engineering Fluid Control & Automation	+86-451-86415272	+86-451-86402724	jjh@hit.edu.cn

Addresses of submitting institutions

ISRAELI institution
Ben-Gurion University, Beer Sheva, Israel
CHINA institution
Director of Asia and Africa Department of International Cooperatioin 15B, Fu Xing Road, Beijing, China100862

Institutional authorization

Signatures of the Principal Investigators from China and Israel:
Name(China)　×××　　signature　　date: Feb. 1st , 2009 Name(Israel)　×××　　signature　　date: Feb. 14th, 2009
Signatures of the authorizing official from China and Israel:
Name(China)　　position　　signature　　date: Name(Israel)　　position　　signature　　date:

Background Information Regarding the Chinese Co-Principal Investigators

Family name:	×××		
First name:	×××		
Passport Details:	G28845965		
Birth year:	1957.02.03	Gender:	M
Title:	Prof. Dr. Engr.	Other:	Professor Dr. Ing.
Academic Rank (Lecturer, etc.):	Professor		
1. Main Institution (Name):	Harbin Institute of Technology		
Faculty:	School of Mechatronic Engineering		
Department:	Department of Fluid Control & Automation		
Street No.	YiKuang Street, Nangang, HIT Distri		
P.O.B. City:	3040,Harbin, P.R.C.	Zip Code:	150080
2. Other inst. Affiliation:			
Faculty:			
Department:			
Street No.			
P.O.B. City:		Zip Code:	
Work Tel. No. :	+86-451-86405272		
Fax No. :	+86-451-86412724		
Email:	jjh@ hit. edu. cn		
Internet site:	yyqd@ hit. edu. cn		
Home Address:	802, Xiaowai Street 11, Nangang	Street No.	
P.O.B City:	Harbin, P.R.C.	Zip Code:	150001
Tel. No. :	+86-451-86415372		
Fields of specialization (key words):	Fluid Power Transmission & Control, Mechatronic Engineering, Hydraulic Transmission, Hydraulic Control		

PART II ABSTRACT

> **INSTRUCTIONS**
> An abstract of <u>20 lines</u> should be written in <u>third person</u> and describe the work plan of both the Chinese and Israeli research teams and how their work is to be integrated.
> <u>In a new application, the abstract should present</u>:
> 1. Objectives
> 2. Methodology
> 3. Potential scientific contribution of the proposed research
> 4. Mode of cooperation
> 5. Potential social and economic contribution of the proposed research
>
> <u>An updated abstract, including a description of the project implementation, should be submitted with requests for renewal.</u>

Abstract (in English):

  Since the 70s of the 20th century, with the development of economy and the increasing awareness of the issues of environmental protection, shortage of energy, energy saving, and wind energy as a clean, rich and renewable resource receive greater concern in the world. At present, global wind energy is developing on a large scale. In recent two years, the speed of wind power production of electricity has reached over 100%. Under this circumstance, the application of DDVC system to wind power production of electricity promotes the development of AC servo technology and hydraulic technology on the one hand, and also the development of wind power enterprise on the other hand, leading to the relief and solution of energy shortage in China as well as in the world.

  The aim of the research is to apply the direct drive volume control (DDVC) electro-hydraulic servo system to the fan impeller locking device for the wind power generator. The research method adopted for the project is a combination of investigation, theoretical study, simulation and experimental studies, a combination of theory and practice. Practical work is guided by theory; theory is verified by the experimental study, a research method that follows the cognitive principle.

  At present, electro-hydraulic servo system controlled by electro-hydraulic servo valve is applied to the fan impeller locking device for the wind power generator. Due to the high precision requirements for electro-hydraulic servo valve, the cost of the whole system in turn becomes higher; this electro-hydraulic valve requires high quality for system oil so as to avoid jam failure of electro-hydraulic valves, thus increasing the cost of the locking system; and the constant use of oil increases the aging and jam failure of the system even under good sealing and filtering conditions. Since the system not only is sensitive to the change of temperature and consumes much energy but also causes large cutting fever, it is necessary to improve cooling system by adding a cooling device and a set of pumping station for constant pressure oil, thus increasing the system's size and complexity. The project developed a direct drive volume control (DDVC) electro-hydraulic servo system to replace the traditional electro-hydraulic control system, so as to increase the ratio of energy utilization of the fan impeller locking device and the reliability of the system. It can also decrease the frequencies of breakdowns of the system.

During the project cooperation, C-IJRG would share the use of scientific research facilities, materials, equipment, and services and communicate existing materials and research results. Research team of China should analyze the principles of DDVC electro-hydraulic servo system, the main structural design of this system, and production and commissioning while the team of Israel should be responsible for product parameter calculation and verification, noise and hydraulic shock reduction, simulation analysis of the dynamic characteristics of direct drive electro-hydraulic servo system, and its mathematical model.

PART Ⅲ RESEARCH TOPIC AND PLAN OF WORK

1. Detailed Description of the Joint Project

The project description should be submitted on separate pages.

In a new application, the project description should include:

Detailed description of the research topic

Discussion of the scientific and technological background of each element of the project

Explanation of the conformity of the project to the priority research fields and type of research, as detailed in the call for proposals.

Expected scientific, social, and economic contribution of the project.

Detailed research program, including specific goals, methodology, and work plan. Key scientific issues should be emphasized. The roles of the Chinese and Israeli partners in carrying out the proposed research plan should be indicated, and the mode of integrating the work of the teams should be described.

Statement describing the state of the art in the research field, the approximate number of research groups working in the field, and the special strengths of the Israeli-Chinese research team.

Report on preliminary results relevant to the proposal (not yet published).

Detailed description of available research resources, including CV's of research team members and inventory of relevant equipment.

Bibliography of relevant literature.

Notes:

Please number the sections of the project description according to the items in the list above.

Items are limited to a total of 10 pages.

Applications for project renewal must include:

Abstract (as described in Part Ⅱ above).

A summary joint progress report including results up to the application date.

Future work program: On the basis of progress already achieved, describe in detail the different steps of the planned work program for the coming year, making use of the time table (see page 6) and with reference to the original goals of the project.

2. Time Schedule and Work Plan

During the project cooperation, C-IJRG would share the use of scientific research facilities, materials, equipment, and services and communicate existing materials and research results. Research team of China should analyze the principles of DDVC electro-hydraulic servo system, the main structural design of this system, and production and commissioning. Research team of Israel should research on product parameter calculation and verification and, simulation analysis of the dynamic characteristics of the direct drive electro-hydraulic servo system, and its mathematical model. C-IJRG should assess research results.

No.	Stage	Month				
		0	6	12	18	24
1	Literature review and project scheming by both teams	1—6				
2	Parameter design and verification by Israel team, as well as noise and hydraulic shock reduction	1—6				
3	Principle analyses of DDVC electro-hydraulic servo system and structural design of fan impeller locking device for winder power byChina team		7—	—15		
4	Mathematical modeling of DDVC electro-hydraulic servo system and simulation of its dynamic characteristic byIsrael team		7—	—15		
5	Revising the whole system and setting up its final designing plan by both teams			13—	—24	
6	Producing prototype product by China team			16—	—21	
7	Trial run period of the whole system inChina by both teams and model validation				22—24	

Keys:

Stage 1: Review of literature and project scheming by both teams
    Output: Report

Stage 2: Parameter design and verification, study on noise and hydraulic shock reduction by Israel team;
    Output: Report on parameter data of the system

Stage 3: Principle analyses of DDVC electro-hydraulic servo system and structural design of fan impeller locking device for winder power by China team

Output: Analytical report and blueprint for overall structural design

Stage 4: Mathematical modeling of DDVC electro-hydraulic servo system and simulation of its dynamic characteristic by Israel team

Output: Data report on simulation

Stage 5: Revising the whole system and then setting up its final designing plan by both teams

Output: Report on the final designing plan for the system and designing blueprint

Stage 6: Producing prototype product by China team

Output: Prototype product

Stage 7: Trial period of the whole system in China by both teams and models validations

Output: Report on the trial run

Part IV. Budget Description

Separate budgets should be prepared for the Chinese and Israeli teams.

INSTRUCTIONS

Manpower (Salaries)

List all staff participating directly in the project, including principal researchers whose salaries may not be included in the project budget.

In case a specific staff member has not yet been recruited to the project team, name the designated position to be filled or provide a short description of the position in the space reserved for the name of person: forexample "programmer," "laboratory technician," "research assistant," etc.

Man-months should be calculated as follows: months of work on the project during the contract period multiplied by the fraction of work time allocated to the research project.

Gross salary includes the following components: basic salary, cost of living increment, seniority increment, family increment, academic qualifications and "on-call" increments, including social benefits. Dollar professional advancement fund and sabbatical fund payments may not be included.

Do not include secretarial services, bookkeeping and other such items which are included in overheads.

A principal investigator planning to suspend his/her participation in the project for a period exceeding 3 months, including sabbatical leave, must note this intention.

Research Equipment, Supplies, and Overheads

The Ministry of Science, Culture, and Sport (Israel) will provide 50% of the cost of equipment, provided the equipment is purchased during the first year of the project. For equipment purchased in the second year, the Ministry's contribution will not exceed 40%.

The Ministry of Science, Culture, and Sport (Israel) will provide over 50% of the cost of equipment, when the equipment is of a special character directly related to the implementation of the research project.

Durable equipment whose cost does not exceed $575 should be listed in Table 3, "Consumable Supplies and Materials."

Overhead costs shall not exceed 15% of the total budget.

Other Sources of Funding

With regard to continuing projects, please update if any changes have occurred.

Ⅳ(A). Budget Details in US Dollars—Israeli Team

1. Salaries*

Total time devoted by each researcher, including those whose salaries are not included in the project budgets, must be indicated by man months they invest in the project.

Full Name & Title	Position in the Project	Budget Requested from MOS (US$)			
		Man Months	First Year	Man Months	Second Year
×××	PI**	2.4		2.4	
×××	PI	2.4		2.4	
×××	Lab Engineer	6	8,000	8	10,400
×××	Research students	4	5,400	6	8,000
Total Salary Budget Requested			13,400		18,400

* Do not include professional advancement and sabbatical fund payments.

** Indicate if sabbatical leave is planned.

2. Durable Equipment (see instructions)

Equipment Description	Total Cost (100%)	Budget requested from MOS (US$)	
		First Year	Second Year
Computer and peripherals	100%	5,000	0
Total Equipment Budget Requested	100%	5,000	0

3. Consumable Supplies and Materials

Consumable Supplies and Materials	Budget Requested from MOS (US $)	
	First Year	Second Year
Lab. supplies	2,000	2,000
Total Budget Requested	2,000	2,000

4. Other Expenses

Expense Description	Budget Requested from MOS (US $)	
	First Year	Second Year
Overhead	4,560	4,560
Mutual visits (airfare to China; costs of hosting Chinese co-researchers—see Call for Proposals, par. E)	10,000	10,000
Total Budget Requested	14,560	14,560

Instructions:

1. Travel expenses must be indicated in the table. Details should be given regarding the calculation of travel expenses (number of trips, airfares, and days of car rental, etc.) in the Budget Justification (see Section 6 below).

2. When the services of sub-contractors or consultants are budgeted, please specify the nature of the work to be performed and detail the cost calculation in the Budget Justification (Section 6).

5. Budget Summary (US $)

	First year	Second year	TOTAL
Labor Costs	13,400	18,400	31,800
Equipment	5,000	0	5,000
Materials and Supplies	2,000	2,000	4,000
Other Expenditures	14,560	14,560	29,120
TOTAL	34,960	34,960	69,920

6. Budget Justification

On a separate sheet, please explain in details and justify, in relation to the work plan, the major budget paragraphs and special items, such as travel and consultancy and sub-contractor services.

7. Other Sources of Support—Israeli Team

Please add sheets as needed. For renewal requests, please indicate changes which have occurred in financial support, since the original application was submitted.

1. Has this research project been submitted to other funding sources?
   Yes _____ No __√__

   Funding source:_____ Sum requested:_____

   Has the request been approved? Yes _____ No _____.

   Funding source:_____ Sum requested:_____

   Has the request been approved? Yes _____ No _____.

2. If this project has received support from other sources in the past or is currently receiving support, please name the funding sources, the period of support, and the amount of support. Rights or obligations with relation to the funding source should be indicated, if in effect. Should it be considered necessary, the Ministry of Science, Culture, and Sport (Israel) may request presentation of the relevant contracts and information regarding previous stages of the research.

   _____

3. If patent applications have been presented, or patents have been registered, which relate to the research project, please provide the following details: country in which the patent was registered/requested; patent/request number; names of the inventors; etc.).

   _____

4. If researchers taking part in the project have received research grants or scholarships from the Ministry of Science, Culture, and Sport (Israel) in the last 5 years, please cite the names and the dates of the research projects/scholarships.

   2006—2010—Israel Ministry of Science, Slovenian-Israeli Research Cooperation in

Biotechnology, Robotics, Advanced Materials, BGU: Yael Edan, Ohad Ben-Shachar, **Amir Shapiro**. Slovenia: Marko Hoevar, Brane irok, Matevz Dular, Tom Bajcar, Niko Herakovic, Dragica Noe, Viktor Jejcic, Tone Godea, Toma Poje, Denis Stajnko, Miran Lakota, "Development of a robotic system for targeted spraying in orchards and vineyards," $40,940.

2006—2007—Israel Ministry of Science the Third Call of the Joint Dutch-Israeli Agricultural Science and Technology Program—Workshop Proposal, Israel: Yael Edan, **Amir Shapiro**, Ohad Ben Shahar, Avital Bechar, Dutch: Jochen Hemming, Eldert van Henten. "A new approach to future farming: small and light-weight agrobots," $17,400.

5. Please describe all research projects in which the Principal Investigators are currently active, their budgets and funding sources:

CPI's Name	Project Name	Funding Institute	% work time on project	Project Budget (US $)	Starting Date	Expected Completion Date
×××	Simulation of Size Reduction in Jet-Mills	GSK	10	381,250	12/2007	11/2009
×××	A study of coupled heat and mass transfer of droplets containing micro-andnonoparticles	GIF	10	225,255	01/2009	12/2011
×××	Increase efficiency and reduce human labor in vineyards	Ministry of Agriculture	10	81,018	11/2008	11/2010
×××	Development of a Mule-Like Quadruped Robot	Ministry of Defense	15	55,000	11/2008	9/2009
×××	An Autonomous Climbing Device for Counter-Terrorism Duty	The Institute for Future Defense Te×××	10	27,440	1/2008	1/2010
×××	Technology for Harvesting Energy from Human Motion	Ministry of Defense	10	79,500	3/2008	3/2011
×××	A Robotic Apparatus for Spraying and Pollinating Date Palm Trees	Ministry of Agriculture	15	88,235	1/2008	12/2010

Ⅳ (B). Budget Details in US Dollars—Chinese Team

1. Salaries *

Total time devoted by each researcher, including those whose salaries are not included in the project budgets, must be indicated by man months they invest in the project.

Full Name & Title	Position in the Project	Budget Requested from MOS (US $)			
		Man Months	First Year	Man Months	Second Year
×××	PI**	3.6	0	3.6	0
×××	Literature review	2.4	0	2.4	0
×××	Principle analyses of DDVC electro-hydraulic servo system and structural design of fan impeller locking device for winder power	8.5	6,000	8.5	6,000
×××	Revising the whole system and setting up its final designing plan	6.5	3,200	8.5	4,000
×××	Producing prototype product	6.5	3,200	8.5	4,000
Total Salary Budget Requested			12,400		14,000

* Do not include sabbatical fund payments.
** Indicate if sabbatical leave is planned.

2. Durable Equipment (see instructions on page 8)

Equipment Description	Total Cost (100%)	Budget requested from MOS (US $)	
		First Year	Second Year
Equipments bought (including AC servo motor & driver, dual direction quantitative pump, valve elements, etc.)	100%	5,000	10,000
Accessories (including integrated valve body, closed press oil tank, hydraulic cylinder, etc.)	100%	600	2,000
Total Equipment Budget Requested	100%	5,600	12,000

3. Consumable Supplies and Materials

Consumable Supplies and Materials	Budget Requested (US $)	
	First Year	Second Year
Fuels and power	0	2,500
Extra cooperation for trial test and machine	0	2,500
Total Budget Requested	0	5,000

4. Other Expenses

Expense Description	Budget Requested from MOS (US $)	
	First Year	Second Year
On using equipments available	500	2,000
Housing	500	1,000
Overhead	1,000	1,000
Mutual visits (airfare to China; costs of hosting Chinese co-researchers—see Call for Proposals, par. E)	15,000	0
Total Budget Requested	17,000	4,000

Instructions:

1. Travel expenses must be indicated in the table. Details should be given regarding the calculation of travel expenses (number of trips, airfares, days of car rental, etc.) in the Budget Justification (see Section 6 below).

2. When the services of sub-contractors or consultants are budgeted, please specify the nature of the work to be performed and detail the cost calculation in the Budget Justification (Section 6).

5. Budget Summary (US $)

	First year	Second year	TOTAL
Labor Costs	12,400	14,000	26,400
Equipment	5,600	12,000	17,600
Materials and Supplies	0	5,000	5,000
Other Expenditures	17,000	4,000	21,000
TOTAL	35,000	35,000	70,000

6. Budget Justification

On separate sheets, please explain in details and justify, in relation to the work plan, the major budget paragraphs, and special items, such as travel and consultancy and sub-contractor services.

7. Other Sources of Support—Chinese Team

Please add sheets as needed. For renewal requests, please indicate changes which have occurred in financial support, since the original application was submitted.

1. Has this research project been submitted to other funding sources?

Yes _____ No __√__

Funding source: _____ Sum requested: _____

Has the request been approved? Yes _____ No _____.

Funding source: _____ Sum requested: _____

Has the request been approved? Yes _____ No _____.

2. If this project has received support from other sources in the past or is currently receiving support, please name the funding sources, the period of support, and the amount of support. Rights or obligations with relation to the funding source should be indicated, if in effect. Should it be considered necessary, the Ministry of Science and Education (China) may request presentation of the relevant contracts and information regarding previous stages of the research.

_____

3. If patent applications have been presented, or patents have been registered, which relate to the research project, please provide the following details: country in which the patent was registered/requested; patent/request number; names of the inventors; etc.).

China, Patent No. : 200810137593.0

Patent Name: Direct drive oil executor based on direct drive electro-hydraulic servo power source

Date applied: 2008.11.21

Paten applicant: Jiang Jihai, Chen Jianhua, Shu Wenhai, Wan Baozhong, Chang Hong, He Liao, Liu Qinghe

4. If researchers taking part in the project have received research grants from the Ministry of Science and Technology (China) in the last 5 years, please cite the names and the dates of the research projects.

---

5. Please describe all research projects in which the Principal Investigators are currently active, their budgets and funding sources:

CPI's Name	Project Name	Funding Institute	% work time on project	Project Budget (US $)	Starting Date	Expected Completion Date
×××	Theoretical basis and relevant technique for energy saving hybrid system of hydrostatic transmission	National Natural Science Foundation of China	15	48,000	2009.01	2011.12
×××	Theoretical study and design of mechanical-hydraulic walking device	Ningbo zhenhai Yongli Hydraulic Co. Ltd	10	190,000	2008.06	2009.05

PART Ⅴ. Personal Background Information (new applications only)

Resume

This section should be filled by the two Co-Principal Investigators, both Chinese and Israeli, as listed above

Name of Co-Principal Investigator: <u>×××, ×××, ×××</u>

Institution: **<u>Harbin Institute of Technology, Ben-Gurion University of the Negev</u>**

Please describe the relevance of the researcher's professional background to the proposedresearch (in English).

×××

×××, Doctor of Engineering, Professor of Fluid Transmission and Control, mainly researches on fluid power transmission and control, especially on hydraulic transmission basic theory and application, key technique of hydraulic energy storage and transform, hydraulic hybrid drive theory and application, new type hydraulic element and equipment, etc. He has over 130 articles and 7 books published, and 16 invention patents applied. He is a senior member of Chinese Mechanic Engineering Society (CMES) of China; committeeman of Chinese Hydraulics and Pneumatics Standardization Technology Committee; deputy director of Fluid Control Engineering Institution in the Chinese Society of Theoretical and Applied Mechanics (CSTAM); committeeman of Fluid Transmission and Control Institution of CMES; committeeman of National Key Laboratory in Vehicle Transmission Academy Committee; committeeman of Yu Ci Hydraulic Ltd. Technique Center Committee of experts; hydraulic Machine Journal Editorial Board Member.

×××

Prof. ××× studied Mechanical Engineering at Ben-Gurion University of the Negev, ISRAEL. He got his Ph.D. in 1995 from the same university. He worked as a research scholar in the above university until 1995 and as a research fellow at Glasgow Caledonian University in the Center for Industrial Bulk Solids Handling until 1997. Then he joined to the department of Mechanical Engineering at Ben-Gurion University of the Negev, ISRAEL. In 2005, Prof. Avi Levy was a visiting professor at the Canadian Hydraulics Centre, National Research Centre Canada, Ottawa, ON, Canada. Prof. Levy is the head of the Energy laboratory of the Mechanical Engineering department at Ben-Gurion University of the Negev. The program of the Energy Laboratory is directed at solving problems in energy-related fields that require expertise in overlapping scientific disciplines, such as thermodynamics, heat and mass transfer, fluid dynamics and exploration of new concepts for low thermal heat utilization and development of advanced thermodynamic cycles

Shapiro Amir

Dr. ××× received the B.Sc., M.Sc., and Ph.D. degrees in Mechanical Engineering from the Technion, Israel Institute of Technology, Haifa, in 1997, 2000, and 2004, respectively. Currently, he is a lecturer with the Department of Mechanical Engineering at Ben-Gurion University of the Negev, Beer-Sheva, Israel. On 2005—2006 he was a post doctoral fellow at the Robotics Institute of Carnegie Mellon University, Pittsburgh, PA. His interests include locomotion of multi-limbed mechanisms in unstructured complex environments, navigation algorithms for multi-limbed robots, robot grasping design, control, and stability analysis, climbing robots, snake like robots, and multi-robot on-line motion planning.

In addition, the researcher's curriculum vitae, detailing the following items, should be attached:

1. Academic and professional training, including names of institutions, years of study, degrees and diplomas.

2. Academic and professional experience, including names of institutions and/or companies, position held and period.

3. Research experience (areas of research in which the researcher has been active).

4. Publications and patents (last 5 years only).

5. Any additional detail which may assist in evaluating the professional background of the researcher.

Professor, Dr. Ing ×××

Education career:

August, 1985. Graduated from School of Mechanic, Harbin Institute of Technology, Master of Engineering, majoring in fluid transmission and control;

March, 1999. Graduated from School of Mechanic, Harbin Institute of Technology, Doctor of Engineering, majoring in mechatronics.

Society career:

Senior member of Mechanic Engineering Society (CMES) of China,

Committeeman of Chinese Hydraulics and Pneumatics Standardization Technology Committee,

Deputy director of Fluid Control Engineering Institution in the Chinese Society of Theoretical and Applied Mechanics (CSTAM),

Committeeman of Fluid Transmission and Control Institution of CMES,

Committeeman of Key Labortary in Vehicle Transmission Academy Committee,

Committeeman of Yu Ci Hydraulic Ltd. Technique Center Committee of experts,

Member of China Machinery Industry Education Association Colleges and Universities of Machinery and Electronic Education Committee,

Hydraulic Machine Journal Editorial Board Member.

Research work:

Mainly research on fluid power transmission and control, especially on hydraulic transmission basic theory and application, key technique of hydraulic energy storage and transform, hydraulic hybrid drive theory and application, new type hydraulic element and equipment, etc. Prof. Jiang has over 130 articles and 7 books published, and 16 invention patents applied.

出版教材及著作：

1. ×××，×××，×××. 液压与气压传动[M]. 北京：高等教育出版社，2009年.（国家十一五重点规划教材）

2. ×××. 液压传动[M]. 哈尔滨:哈尔滨工业大学出版社(第4版),2007年.

3. ×××,×××. 液压与气压传动CAI课件[M]. 北京:高等教育出版社,高等教育电子音像出版社,2007年

4. ×××. 液压传动电子教案[M]. 哈尔滨:哈尔滨工业大学出版社,2007年.

5. ×××,×××,×××. 液压与气压传动网络课程[M]. 北京:高等教育出版社,高等教育电子音像出版社,2006年.

6. ×××. 液体变黏度缝隙流动理论与解析[M]. 北京:国防工业出版社,2005年.

7. ×××主编. 袖珍液压气动手册[M]. 北京:械工业出版社. 2004年.(参编15万字).

发表科研文章：

2008年

1. ×××,×××,×××. 基于GFRF的二次调节流量耦联系统的频域非线性H_∞控制[J]. 控制理论与应用,第25卷第1期,2008,2,p.91-94,99. EI检索号:081611206279.

2. ×××,×××,×××. Development of hydraulic power unit and accumulator charging circuit for electricity generation, storage and distribution. Journal of Harbin Institute of Technology, Vol. 15, No. 1, 2008, p.60-64. EI检索号:081211164315.

2007年

1. ×××,×××. 基于液压滑环配油的动力卡盘[J]. 机床与液压. 2007年8月第35卷总第230期 pp.97-100.

2. ×××,×××. 液压滑环端面油膜密封的摩擦转矩研究[R]. 同济大学2007全国博士论坛.

申请专利：

1. 发明专利名称:常规游梁式抽油机的二次调节液压节能系统/发明专利申请号:200710072384.8/发明专利申请日期:2007年6月22日/发明专利人:×××,×××

2. 发明专利名称:双桥液驱混合动力汽车传动系统/发明专利申请号:200710072383.3/发明专利申请日期:2007.06.22/发明专利人:×××,×××

3. 发明专利名称:二次调节流量耦联液压蓄能器储能静液传动装置/发明专利申请号:200710072398.X/发明专利申请日期:2007.06.25/发明专利人:×××,×××

4. 发明专利名称:无源液压制动系统/发明专利申请号:200810063889.2/发明专利申请日期:2008年1月21日/发明专利人:×××,×××

5. 发明专利名称:一种应用水作液压介质的齿轮泵/发明专利申请号:200810064005.5/发明专利申请日期:2008年2月18日/发明专利人:×××,×××

Prof. ××× – Curriculum Vitae and List of Publications

Education
B. Sc. 1986—1990　Mechanical Engineering Department, Ben-Gurion
　　　　　　　　　University of the Negev, Beer-Sheva, Israel.
　　　　　　　　　Graduated Cum Laude

Ph. D. 1990—1995　Mechanical Engineering Department, Ben-Gurion
　　　　　　　　　University of the Negev, Beer-Sheva, Israel.
　　　　　　　　　Name of advisors: Prof. Gabi Ben-Dor & Dr. Shaul Sorek
　　　　　　　　　Title of Thesis: Wave Propagation in a Saturated Porous Medium
　　　　　　　　　Graduated Summa Cum Laude

Employment History
2008—Present Associate Professor—Department of Mechanical Engineering, Deputy Head
　　　　　　Ben-Gurion University of the Negev, Eilat, Israel.
2006—Present Associate Professor—Engineering 1st year Program, Head
　　　　　　Ben-Gurion University of the Negev, Eilat, Israel.

Research Grants
1998—2002　　Ministry of Defense-G. Ben-Dor, M. Perl, O. Igra and **A. Levy** "Structures Shielding and Fortification" (US $ 199,000)

1999—2003　　Israeli Atomic Commission & Planning and Budgeting Committee-**A. Levy**, "Cracks Propagation in Brittle Materials" (US $ 60,000)

2000—2002　　Ministry of Science-BMBF-Joint Israel-Germany Project-I. Borde and **A. Levy** "Development of an Energy-Efficient Absorption Cooling Unit", Grant no. -1718 (US $ 97,500).

Scientific Publications (Last 5 years)
Chapters in Collective Volumes

(1) ×××., ××× D. and ×××.," Two-dimensional effects of the head on interaction between planar shock wave with low density foam", Ed. Z. Jiang, Proceedings of the 24th International Symposium on Shock Waves, Beijing, China, Vol. 2, pp. 1048–1054, 2004.

(2) ×××, I. and ×××., "Pneumatic and Flash Drying", Handbook of Industrial Drying, Third Edition, Ed. A. S. Mujumdar, CRC Press, UK, 2006.

Refereed Articles and Refereed Letters in Scientific Journals

(1) ×××., ×××, M.,×××, I. & ××× F., "Performance of an advanced absorption cycle with R125 and different absorbents", Energy, 29, pp. 2501–2515, 2004

(2) ××× I. and ××× A., "Finite Volume Approach for Solving Multiphase Flows in Vertical Pneumatic Dryers", The International Journal of Numerical Methods for Heat & Fluid Flow, Vol. 14, No. 8 , pp. 980–1001,2004.

(3) ×××, I., ××× A. and ××× I., "Two-Dimensional Numerical Simulations of the Pneumatic Drying in Vertical Pipes", Chemical Engineering and Processing Vol. 44, No. 2, pp. 187–192, 2005.

Presentation of Papers at Conferences/meetings

(1) ×××., ××× D. and ×××., "Two-dimensional effects of the head on interaction between planar shock wave with low density foam", 24th International Symposium on Shock Waves, Beijing, China, 2004.

(2) ××× A., ××× M., ××× A. and ××× I., "The Influence of the Tube Diameter on Bubble Pump Performance", HPC 2004 Conference, Larnaca, Cyprus, 2004.

6.6 基金申请案例实例(中文版)

中华人民共和国　　　　　　　　　　　　以色列
科学技术部　　　　　　　　　　　　　　科学、文化与体育部

2009—2011 年中国-以色列联合研究项目
建议征集书

申请表包括以下内容：
第一部分：基本信息
第二部分：摘要（正在进行的项目-进度报告即可）
第三部分：a. 研究项目说明
　　　　　　b. 时间安排和工作计划
第四部分：预算明细

说明：
1. 以方研究员必须向以色列科技、文化、体育部提交 10 份英文项目建议书，其中原件一份。中方研究员向中国科技部提交 1 份英文建议书和 10 份中文建议书。
2. 建议书应由研究负责人和研究机构分别签署（根据延期要求只需两个副本）。
3. （请详细填写表格中的各个部分），以便及时评估。
4. 申请人可附加其他相关文件以支持其申请。
5. 申请表第二部分必须包括下列资料：
　a. 新提案——研究目标、研究方法和预期成果分析。
　b. 延期请求——研究进展的总结报告。
6. 新提案和延期请求均需提交申请表第三部分（见说明）。
7. 如果可行，申请表后需附以下授权：
　a. 赫尔辛基委员会授权-研究计划涉及人体临床实验。
　b. 由动物实验监督委员会提交申请表并签发授权书-研究计划涉及动物实验。
　c. 教育部授权-研究计划涉及在学校开展实验、调查或其他活动。
8. 申请书应送交下列地址：

以色列	中国
×××	×××
科学、文化和体育部计控处副处长	科学技术部国际合作司亚非处处长
信箱 49100	北京市复兴路乙 15 号
91490 耶路撒冷,以色列	100862
电话:972-2-5411170/3	电话:86-10-58881346
传真:972-2-5823030	传真:86-10-58881344
电子邮箱:avi@ most. gov. il	电子邮箱:hzs_yfc@ most. cn

申请表和附带材料("pdf"或"doc"格式)刻入同一张光盘提交。

中以联合研究资助经费申请表

第一部分　基本信息

标题(中文):风力发电机叶轮锁紧液压装置研究
标题(本国语言)(必须添加):风力发电机叶轮锁紧液压装置研究
研究主题(引用建议征集文件中的节编号):直驱式容积控制电液伺服系统

应用类型: 新:风力发电领域 延期:_____	预算要求: 总计:　$139,920 第一年:$ 69,960 第二年:$ 69,960	研究领域 (根据建议征集文件中的分类)	可再生能源

联合研究负责人的姓名、隶属单位和联系方式

姓名: 姓,名+学位	职务	部,系,所	电话	传真	电子邮件
以方联合研究负责人					
×××+博士	副教授	本.古里安大学工程科学学院机械工程系	+972-8-6477092	+972-8-6477090	avi@bgu.ac.il
中方联合研究负责人					
×××+博士	教授	哈尔滨工业大学机电工程学院流体控制及自动化系	+86-451-86415272	+86-451-86402724	jjh@hit.edu.cn

提交机构地址

ISRAELI institution
Ben-Gurion University, Beer Sheva, Israel
中国机构
科学技术部国际合作司亚非处,中国北京市复兴路乙15号

授权机构

中国和以色列研究负责人签字：			
姓名（中国）：××	签字：		日期：2009.2.1
姓名（以色列）：×××	签字：		日期：Feb. 14th , 2009

中国和以色列授权机构签字			
姓名（中国）：	职位：	签字：	日期：
姓名（以色列）：	职位：	签字：	日期：

中国联合研究负责人的背景资料

姓：	×		
名：	××		
护照：	G28845965		
出生日期：	1957.02.03	性别：	男
头衔：	工学教授 工学博士	其他：	教授 工学博士
学衔（讲师,等）：	主讲教授		
1. 主要机构（名称）：	哈尔滨工业大学		
系：	（机电工程学院）流体控制及自动化系		
部门：	液压与气动研究室		
街号：	中国黑龙江省哈尔滨市南岗区一匡街2号，哈工大科学园		
信箱：	3040 信箱	邮编：	150080
2. 其他 从属机构：			
系：			
部门：			

街号:			
信箱:		邮编:	
办公室电话:	+86-451-86415272		
传真号:	+86-451-86402724		
电子邮件:	jjh@hit.edu.cn		
网站:	yyqq@hit.edu.cn		
家庭地址:	中国黑龙江省哈尔滨市南岗区	街号:	校外街11号,802室
信箱:		邮编:	150001
电话号码:	+86-451-86415272		
专业领域(关键词):	流体传动及控制,机械电子工程,液压传动技术,液压控制技术		

第二部分　摘要

> **说明**
> 以第三人称写一个 20 行的摘要并说明中国和以色列研究小组的工作计划以及他们的工作是如何被整合。
>
> 新申请书摘要应当包括：
> 1. 目标
> 2. 方法
> 3. 研究潜在的科学贡献
> 4. 合作方式
> 5. 研究潜在的社会和经济贡献
>
> **包括项目进度说明的最新摘要必须同延期请求一起提交**

摘要（用中文）：

　　自 20 世纪 70 年代末以来，随着经济的发展以及世界各国对环境保护、能源短缺和节能等问题的日益关注，风能作为一清洁干净、储量极为丰富的可再生能源得到了极大的重视。目前，全球风电都呈现了规模化发展态势。中国的风电在最近两年有了突破性的发展，连续两年的增长速度超过 100%。在这样的情况下，将直驱式容积控制电液伺服系统应用于风电行业，可以促进了交流伺服技术和液压技术的发展，同时也推动了风电行业进步，缓解和解决能源短缺问题，对能源的开发和利用起到了积极作用，对社会和经济的发展也起到了很大的推动作用。

　　本项目属于"可再生能源"领域，它的研究目标是将直驱式容积控制电液伺服系统应用于风力发电机叶轮锁紧液压装置，使其具有控制精度高、调节方便、节约能源、结构紧凑、占用空间小等优点，使液压技术和风能更好地服务于人类。

　　本项目的研究方法是采用调查研究、理论研究、仿真研究和试验研究相结合，理论和实际相结合，用理论研究来指导实践工作，用试验研究验证理论的正确性的符合认知规律方式进行研究。

　　目前现有的风力发电机叶轮锁紧液压装置均采用电液伺服阀控制的电液伺服系统，由于电液伺服阀加工精度要求高、价格昂贵，从而整个系统的成本高，同时由于油质的污染，将会引起电液伺服阀卡涩等故障，因而这类系统对油质的要求也相当高，对温度变化比较敏感，能量损耗严重，节流控制发热大，因此必须设置完善的冷却系统，同时还需要一套泵站提供恒压油源，增大了系统的体积和复杂程度。本项目的研究要在风力发电机中采用直驱式容积控制叶轮锁紧液压装置替代传统的电液伺服液压锁紧装置，来提高叶轮锁紧系统的能量利用率，提高这种系统的可靠性，减少系统发生停机事件的概率。

　　在此项目合作中，双方科研人员共同使用研究设施、材料、设备并进行协作研究，将现有的的材料和研究得到结果以及研究成果共同分享、交流；双方共同确定系统的总体研究方案；分别进行项目子课题的研究，在中方进行直驱式容积控制电液伺服系统原理研究、直驱式容积控制电液伺服系统结构设计、产品的生产和调试（样机的加工生产和工艺文件的编制、量产图纸的设计在中方的合作方上海汇益液压控制系统工程有限公司进行），在以方进行产品参数计算和论证，系统减噪和消除液压冲击的研究，并对直驱式容积控制电液伺服系统进行建模及对其动态特性进行仿真分析；双方共同评估研究成果，共同分享研究成果，并在中以双方进行推广应用。

第三部分 研究主题和工作计划

1. 联合项目的详细说明

项目的说明应当以单独页提交。
新申请项目的说明应当包括：
  研究主题的详细说明。
  项目各组成部分的科技背景探讨。
  根据征集建议文件的要求,详细给出项目同前期研究领域和研究类型的一致性说明。
  项目预期的科学、社会和经济贡献。
  详细的研究计划,包括具体的目标,方法和工作计划。需强调关键的科学问题,并表明中以双方成员在实施研究计划过程中的职能分配以及工作团队的合作模式。
  综述该领域科学研究的发展动态,以及相应研究团队的大致数量,并给出以中研究团队的独到优势。
  报告同提案相关的初步结果(尚未出版)。
  详细说明现有的研究资源,包括研究小组成员情况及相关的设备清单。
  相关文献书目。

注意：
- 请根据以上目录对项目说明的各部分进行编号。
- 各部分总计不得超过 10 页。

项目延期申请必须包括：
  摘要(如上第二部分所述)。
  进度总结报告,需包括截止到申请日期的结果数据。
  未来工作计划:根据已经取得的进展,利用时间表(见第 6 页)并参照原有项目的目标,详细描述未来一年工作计划的不同步骤。

2. 时间安排和工作计划

中以团队在风力发电机叶轮锁紧液压装置项目研究活动期间,双方科研人员协作工作,共享研究所用设施、材料、设备和服务,将现有的调研材料和研究成果分享、交流;双方共同确定系统的总体方案;分别进行项目子课题的研究,在中方进行直驱式容积控制电液伺服系统原理分析、主体结构设计、产品的生产和调试、以方进行产品参数计算和论证,对直驱式容积控制电液伺服系统建立数学模型并对其动态特性进行仿真分析;双方共同完成整个系统的调试。

序号	阶段	月				
		0	6	12	18	24
1	调查研究,双方完成系统的总体方案	1—6				
2	以色列研究团队完成系统参数设计及参数论证,完成液压系统降噪及减少液压冲击的研究	1—6				
3	中方研究团队完成直驱式容积控制电液伺服系统的原理分析及风力发电机叶轮锁紧液压装置的总体结构设计			7—	—15	
4	以方团队完成对直驱式容积控制电液伺服系统的数学模型建立及对其动态特性进行仿真分析			7—	—15	
5	双方完成整个系统的修改并确定最终方案				13—	—24
6	中方完成样机生产				16—	—21
7	中以团队在中国完成整个系统的调试					22—24

关键:

第一阶段:调查研究,双方完成系统的总体方案。
　　　　成果:报告。

第二阶段:以色列研究团队完成系统参数设计及参数论证,完成液压系统降噪及减少液压冲击的研究。
　　　　成果:系统参数数据报告。

第三阶段:中方研究团队完成直驱式容积控制电液伺服系统的原理分析及风力发电机叶轮锁紧液压装置的总体结构设计。
　　　　成果:分析报告和总体结构设计图纸。

第四阶段:以方团队完成对直驱式容积控制电液伺服系统的数学模型建立及对其动态特性进行仿真分析。
　　　　成果:仿真分析数据报告。

第五阶段:双方完成整个系统的修改并确定最终方案。
　　　　成果:系统最终设计方案报告和设计图纸。
第六阶段:中方完成样机生产。
　　　　成果:样机产品。
第七阶段:中以团队在中国完成整个系统的调试。
　　　　成果:调试报告。

第四部分　资金预算说明

中以团队应当准备各自资金预算。

说明

人力资源（薪金）

列出直接参与该项目的所有工作人员，包括工资未包含在项目预算的主要研究人员。

如果项目组尚未完成对某些工作人员的招聘，需对空缺的指定岗位进行命名，或在为人名预留的空白处给出简短说明。例如："程序员""实验室技师""研究助理"等。

个人工作时间计算如下：在项目合同期内工作的月数乘以分配给研究项目的工作时间百分比。

工资总额由以下几个部分组成：基本工资，生活费用的增加，资历提高，成员递增，学历和"待业"增加，包括社会福利。美元专业发展基金和假期补贴可能不包括在内。

秘书服务，内务操作和其他类似的项目不列入管理费用。

主要研究人员（他/她）若计划延期参与该项目超过三个月（包括休假），必须注明该意向。

研究设备、物料和开销

项目第一年设备购买费用的50%由科学、文化和体育部（以色列）提供。第二年设备购买费用，该部分援助不超过费用的40%。

若所购买设备直接关系到项目的实施，科学、文化和体育部（以色列）将提供50%以上资金援助。

购买费用不超过575美元耐用设备应列于表3，"消耗性物料和原料"。

开销费用不得超过总预算的15%。

其他资金来源

关于持续的项目，如果发生了任何变化，请更新。

第四部分(A)　预算明细(美元)——以色列团队

1. 工资*

每一个研究者投入总时间,包括那些工资不在项目预算内的研究人员,必须指出其投入该项目的工作时间。

姓名及头衔	在项目中的地位	预算要求(美元)			
		参与时间	第一年	参与时间	第二年
×××	PI**	2.4		2.4	
×××	PI	2.4		2.4	
×××	Lab Engineer	6	8 000	8	10 400
×××	Research students	4	5 400	6	8 000
总工资预算要求			13 400		18 400

*不包括晋升和休假基金支付

**标明是否计划休假

2. 耐用设备(见第8页上的说明)

设备说明	总共费用 (100%)	预算要求(美元)	
		第一年	第二年
计算机及其他辅件	100%	5 000	0
设备的总预算	100%	5 000	0

3. 消耗性物料和原料，动物试验

消耗性物料和原料	预算要求（美元）	
	第一年	第二年
实验室的消耗	2 000	2 000
总预算	2 000	2 000

4. 其他费用

费用说明	预算要求（美元）	
	第一年	第二年
科学报告	4 560	4 560
互访	10 000	10 000
总预算	14 560	14 560

说明：

1. 旅行费用应当在表中说明。在财政预算证明中应给予详细的旅行费用计算清单（旅游次数，机票价格，租车天数，等等）（见下面第6段）
2. 若分包商或顾问服务已纳入预算，则应在预算方案里具体说明工作的性质和详细的成本计算（第6段）

5. 预算概要（美元）

	第一年	第二年	总计
工作人员费用	13 400	18 400	31 800
设备	5 000	0	5 000
物料和原料	2 000	2 000	4 000
其他费用	14 560	14 560	29 120
总计	34 960	34 960	69 920

6. 预算证明

> 用单独一张表单详细解释并证明主要的预算内容和特殊项目,如旅行、顾问和分包商的服务,同项目计划相关。

7. 其他方面的支持——以色列团队

有必要的话可以添加表单。因为原先的申请已提交。对于续期请求,请注明财政支持方面发生的变化。

1. 这个研究项目是否已提交给其他资金来源?

是＿＿＿＿＿ 否 √＿＿

资金来源:＿＿＿＿＿＿＿＿＿＿＿＿＿＿需要的资金总额:＿＿＿＿＿

要求是否经过核准? 是＿＿＿＿＿ 否＿＿＿＿＿.

资金来源:＿＿＿＿＿＿＿＿＿＿＿＿＿＿需要的资金总额:＿＿＿＿＿

要求是否经过核准? 是＿＿＿＿＿ 否＿＿＿＿＿.

2. 若该项目已经获取或正在获取资金资助,请写明资金来源、支持时间和资金的数额。同时有必要指出同资金来源相关的有效权利或义务。如果科学、文化和体育部(以色列)认为有必要的话,可能要求提交相关合同和前期研究阶段信息。

＿＿＿＿＿＿＿＿＿＿＿＿＿＿＿＿＿＿＿＿＿＿＿＿＿＿＿＿

3. 如果已经申请或注册了同研究项目相关的专利,请提供以下详细信息:专利注册/申请所在国;专利/申请号码;发明者姓名;等等。

＿＿＿＿＿＿＿＿＿＿＿＿＿＿＿＿＿＿＿＿＿＿＿＿＿＿＿＿

4. 如果参加该研究项目的研究人员在最近 5 年已从科学、文化和体育部(以色列)获得资助或奖学金,请说明研究项目/奖学金的名称和日期。

2006—2010—Israel Ministry of Science, Slovenian-Israeli Research Cooperation in Biotechnology, Robotics, Advanced Materials, BGU:Yael Edan, Ohad Ben-Shachar, **Amir Shapiro**. Slovenia:Marko Hoevar, Brane irok, Matevz Dular, Tom Bajcar, Niko Herakovic,

Dragica Noe, Viktor Jejcic, Tone Godea, Toma Poje, Denis Stajnko, Miran Lakota, "Development of a robotic system for targeted spraying in orchards and vineyards", $40,940.

2006—2007—Israel Ministry of Science the Third Call of the Joint Dutch-Israeli Agricultural Science and Technology Program-Workshop Proposal, Israel: Yael Edan, **Amir Shapiro**, Ohad Ben Shahar, Avital Bechar, Dutch: Jochen Hemming, Eldert van Henten. "A new approach to future farming: small and light-weight agrobots", $17,400.

---

5. 请说明已被调查的所有研究项目目前的情况、资金预算和资金来源：

负责人姓名	项目名称	资助机构	项目从事时间	项目预算（美元）	开始日期	预计完成日期
×××	Jet-Mills尺码缩减的模拟研究	GSK	10	381,250	12/2007	11/2009
×××	微滴耦合热-质转移的研究	GIF	10	225,255	01/2009	12/2011
×××	葡萄园增效减工的研究	农业部	10	$81,018	11/2008	11/2010
×××	四足骡式机器人的研究	国防部	15	$55,000	11/2008	9/2009
×××	实现反恐任务的自动爬壁装置的研究	未来防御技术研究院	10	$27,440	1/2008	1/2010
×××	从生物垃圾中回收能源的技术	国防部	10	$79,500	3/2008	3/2011
×××	用于自动确定棕榈树喷雾和授粉日期装置的研究	农业部	15	$88,235	1/2008	12/2010

第四部分(B) 预算明细(美元)——中国团队

1. 工资*

每一个研究者投入总时间,包括那些工资不在项目预算内的研究人员,必须指出其投入该项目的工作时间。

姓名及头衔	在项目中的地位	预算要求(美元)			
		参与时间(月)	第一年	参与时间(月)	第二年
×××	首席研究员**	3.6	0	3.6	0
×××	研究人员	2.4	0	2.4	0
×××	研究人员	10	6 000	10	6 000
×××	研究人员	8	3 200	10	4 000
×××	研究人员	8	3 200	10	4 000
总工资预算要求			12 400		14 000

* 不包括晋升和休假基金支付

** 标明是否计划休假

2. 耐用设备

设备说明	总共费用(100%)	预算要求(美元)	
		第一年	第二年
购置设备费(包括交流伺服电机和驱动器、双旋向定量泵、阀类元件等)	15 000	5 000	10 000
试制设备费(包括集成阀块、密闭压力油罐、锁紧油缸等)	2 600	600	2 000
设备的总预算	17 600	5 600	12 000

3. 消耗性物料和原料,动物试验

消耗性物料和原料	预算要求(美元)	
	第一年	第二年
燃料及动力费	0	2 500
外协测试化验与加工费	0	2 500
总预算	0	5 000

4. 其他费用

费用说明	预算要求(美元)	
	第一年	第二年
现有仪器设备使用费	500	2 000
房屋占用费	500	1 000
其他管理人员费用	1 000	1 000
旅行费用(3人往返1次)	15 000	0
总预算	17 000	4 000

说明:

1. 旅行费用应当在表中说明。在财政预算证明中应给予详细的旅行费用计算清单(旅游次数,机票价格,租车天数,等等)(见下面第6段)
2. 若分包商或顾问服务已纳入预算,则应在预算方案里具体说明工作的性质和详细的成本计算(第6段)

5. 预算概要(美元)

	第一年	第二年	总　计
工作人员费用	12 400	14 000	26 400
设备	5 600	12 000	17 600
物料和原料	0	5 000	5 000
其他费用	17 000	4 000	21 000
总　　　计	35 000	35 000	70 000

6. 预算证明

　　用单独一张表单详细解释并证明主要的预算内容和特殊项目,如旅行、顾问和分包商的服务,同项目计划相关。

7. 其他方面的支持——中国团队

　　如有必要,可以添加表单,因为原先的申请已提交。对于续期请求,请注明财政支持方面发生的变化。

1. 这个研究项目是否已提交给其他资金来源?
　　　是_____　否__√__

　　资金来源:_____需要的资金总额:_____

　　要求是否经过核准? 是_____　否_____

　　资金来源:_____需要的资金总额:_____

　　要求是否经过核准? 是_____　否_____

2. 若该项目已经获取或正在获取资金资助,请写明资金来源,支持时间和资金的数额。同时有必要指出同资金来源相关的有效权利或义务。如果中国科技部认为有必要的话,可能要求提交相关合同和前期研究阶段信息。

　　_____

　　_____

3. 如果已经申请或注册了同研究项目相关的专利，请提供以下详细信息：专利注册/申请所在国；专利/申请号码；发明者姓名；等等。

  中国 申请号：200810137593.0

发明专利名称：基于直驱式电液伺服动力源的直驱式油动机

专利申请日期：2008.11.21

发明人：×××，×××，×××，×××，×××

4. 如果参加该研究项目的研究人员在最近5年已从中国科技部获得资助或奖学金，请说明研究项目/奖学金的名称和日期。

5. 请说明调查所有研究项目目前的情况，资金预算和资金来源：

负责人姓名	项目名称	资助机构	项目从事时间	项目预算（美元）	开始日期	预计完成日期
×××	节能型静液传动混合动力系统的理论基础及相关技术研究	国家自然科学基金	36个月	4.8万	2009.01	2011.12
×××	机液一体化液压行走装置的理论研究与设计	宁波镇海泰康液压有限公司	12个月	19万	2008.06	2009.05

第五部分 个人背景资料

简历

本部分应由中以合作双方的两位项目负责人填写。

项目负责人姓名:×××,×××,×××

机构:哈尔滨工业大学,本·古里安大学

请说明研究人员的专业背景与项目的相关性(中文)

> ×××多年来一直从事流体传动及控制方面的研究工作,1990年3月—1993年10月在德国克劳斯塔尔工业大学(TU Clausthal)进修,进行流体传动及控制方面的研究工作;2003年11月—2004年2月在德国德累斯顿工业大学(TU Dresden)流体技术研究所做客座教授。1999年在国内获工学博士学位。近年来一直从事流体传动及控制方面的研究工作,先后主持过国家教委留学回国基金项目、国家流体传动及控制国家重点实验室基金项目、黑龙江省青年基金项目和国家自然科学基金项目;到目前为止,已发表论文130余篇。
>
> 1985年9月开始在哈尔滨工业大学流体控制及自动化系从事教学和科研工作,主要从事流体传动及控制方面的研究,尤其是对液压传动基础理论及应用研究、液压流体能量存储与转换关键技术研究、液压混合动力驱动理论及应用研究、新型液压元件及装置研究等。
>
> ×××教授在以色列本·古里安大学从事机械工程研究。1995年以前在现工作的同一所大学获得博士学位;1995年后他作为研究型学者在这所大学工作;到1997年他在Glasgow Caledonian大学的Industrial Bulk Solids Handling研究中心做研究员;之后他进入以色列本·古里安大学的机械工程系,2005年他曾作为客座教授进入加拿大国家液压研究中心工作。Avi Levy教授是本·古里安大学机械工程系里的能源实验室的负责人。他所做的工作旨在解决与能源领域相关的项目以及涉及跨学科领域的研究,包括热动力学、热质转换、流体动力学以及与低热能应用和先进的热动力循环相关新概念的探索等。
>
> ×××博士分别于1997、2000、2004年在以色列的Mechanical Engineering from the Technion, Israel Institute of Technology学院获得理学士、硕士、博士学位。目前,他是本·古里安大学机械工程系的一名讲师。2005—2006年他在Carnegie Mellon大学的机器人研究所作博士后。他的研究工作包括:无结构复杂环境中多臂机械装置与动力、多臂机器人的轨迹规划、机器人抓拿设计、控制和稳定性分析、爬壁机器人、蛇形机器人以及多机器人的非线性运动算法等。

此外,应附上研究人员的简历,详细说明下列事项:

1. 学术和专业培训,包括机构的名称,学习年限、学历和文凭。

2. 学术和专业经验,包括机构和/或公司的名称、职位和期限。

3. 研究经验(研究人员从事的研究领域)。

4. 出版物和专利(最近5年)。

5. 可协助评估研究人员专业背景的任何额外说明。

×××　教授

学习经历:
　　1982年09月—1985年08月:毕业于哈尔滨工业大学流体传动及控制专业获硕士学位
　　1994年10月—1999年03月:毕业于哈尔滨工业大学机械电子工程专业获博士学位

国外经历:
　　1990年03月—1993年10月:联邦德国克劳斯塔尔工业大学(Germany, TU Clausthal)访问学者
　　2003年12月—2004年02月:德国德累斯顿工业大学(Germany, TU Dresden)客座教授

社会兼职:
　　中国机械工程学会高级会员
　　全国液压气动标准化技术委员会委员
　　中国力学学会流体控制工程专业委员会副主任委员
　　中国机械工程学会流体传动及控制分会委员
　　车辆传动科技重点实验室学术委员会委员
　　榆次液压有限公司技术中心专家委员会委员
　　《机床与液压》杂志编委

科学研究:
　　主要从事流体传动及控制方面的科学研究工作。研究方向为:液压传动基础理论及应用研究;液压流体能量存储及转换关键技术研究;液压混合动力驱动及应用研究;新型

液压元件及装置研究。已发表相关科研论文 130 余篇,出版教材及专著 7 部,申报发明专利 16 项。

出版教材及著作：

[1]×××,×××,×××. 液压与气压传动[M]. 北京:高等教育出版社,2009 年.（国家十一五重点规划教材）

[2]×××. 液压传动[M]. 哈尔滨:哈尔滨工业大学出版社(第 4 版),2007 年.

[3]×××,×××. 液压与气压传动 CAI 课件[M]. 北京：高等教育出版社，高等教育电子音像出版社，2007 年.

[4]×××. 液压传动电子教案[M]. 哈尔滨：哈尔滨工业大学出版社,2007 年.

[5]×××,×××,×××. 液压与气压传动网络课程[M]. 北京:高等教育出版社,高等教育电子音像出版社,2006 年.

[6]×××. 液体变粘度缝隙流动理论与解析[M]. 北京：国防工业出版社,2005 年.

[7]×××. 袖珍液压气动手册[M]. 北京：机械工业出版社. 2004 年.（参编 15 万字）.

发表科研文章：

2008 年

[1]×××,×××,Okoye CN. 基于 GFRF 的二次调节流量耦联系统的频域非线性 H_∞ 控制[J]. 控制理论与应用, 第 25 卷第 1 期, 2008, 2, p. 91-94, 99. EI 检索号：081611206279.

[2]×××,×××,×××. Development of hydraulic power unit and accumulator charging circuit for electricity generation, storage and distribution [J]. Journal of Harbin Institute of Technology, Vol. 15, No. 1, 2008, p.60-64. EI 检索号：081211164315.

2007 年

[1]×××,×××. 基于液压滑环配油的动力卡盘[J]. 机床与液压. 2007 年 8 月第 35 卷总第 230 期 pp.97-100.

[2]×××,×××. 液压滑环端面油膜密封的摩擦转矩研究[R]. 同济大学 2007 全国博士论坛.

申请专利：

[1] 发明专利名称:常规游梁式抽油机的二次调节液压节能系统/发明专利申请号：200710072384.8/发明专利申请日期:2007 年 6 月 22 日/发明专利人:×××,×××

[2] 发明专利名称：双桥液驱混合动力汽车传动系统/发明专利申请号：200710072383.3/发明专利申请日期:2007.06.22/发明专利人:×××,×××

[3] 发明专利名称:二次调节流量耦联液压蓄能器储能静液传动装置/发明专利申请号:200710072398.X/发明专利申请日期:2007.06.25/发明专利人:×××,×××

[4] 发明专利名称:无源液压制动系统/发明专利申请号:200810063889.2/发明专利

申请日期:2008年1月21日/发明专利人:×××,×××

[5] 发明专利名称:一种应用水作液压介质的齿轮泵/发明专利申请号:200810064005.5/发明专利申请日期:2008年2月18日/发明专利人:×××,×××

×××教授的个人履历和学术著作

所受教育
理学士 1986—1990 Mechanical Engineering Department, Ben-Gurion
University of the Negev, Beer-Sheva, Israel.
Graduated Cum Laude
博士 1990—1995 Mechanical Engineering Department, Ben-Gurion
University of the Negev, Beer-Sheva, Israel.
指导教授:Gabi Ben-Dor 和 Dr. Shaul Sorek
论文题目: 波在饱和有孔介质中的传播

就业经历
2008—目前　　Associate Professor—Department of Mechanical Engineering, Deputy Head
Ben-Gurion University of the Negev, Eilat, Israel.

2006—目前　　Associate Professor—Engineering 1st year Program, Head
Ben-Gurion University of the Negev, Eilat, Israel.

获得过的科研基金
1998—2002—　Ministry of Defense- G. Ben-Dor, M. Perl, O. Igra and **A. Levy**
"Structures Shielding and Fortification" (US $ 199,000)

1999—2003—　Israeli Atomic Commission & Planning and Budgeting Committee -**A. Levy**, "Cracks Propagation in Brittle Materials" (US $ 60,000)

2000—2002—　Ministry of Science-BMBF - Joint Israel-Germany Project -I. Borde and **A. Levy** "Development of an Energy-Efficient Absorption Cooling Unit", Grant No. -1718 (US $ 97,500).

近五年的学术出版物
书卷中的部分章节
[1]×××., ×××. and ×××.,"Two-dimensional effects of the head on interaction between planar shock wave with low density foam", Ed. Z. Jiang, Proceedings of the 24th International Symposium on Shock Waves, Beijing, China, Vol. 2, pp. 1048-1054, 2004.

[2]×××. and ×××., "Pneumatic and Flash Drying", Handbook of Industrial Drying, Third Edition, Ed. A. S. Mujumdar, CRC Press, UK, 2006.

相关期刊上发表的文章

[1] ×××., ×××., ×××. & ×××., "Performance of an advanced absorption cycle with R125 and different absorbents", Energy, 29, pp. 2501-2515, 2004

[2] ×××. and ×××., "Finite Volume Approach for Solving Multiphase Flows in Vertical Pneumatic Dryers", The International Journal of Numerical Methods for Heat & Fluid Flow, Vol. 14, No. 8, pp. 980-1001, 2004.

[3] ×××., ×××. and ×××., "Two-Dimensional Numerical Simulations of the Pneumatic Drying in Vertical Pipes", Chemical Engineering and Processing Vol. 44, No. 2, pp. 187-192, 2005.

会议宣读的论文

[1] ×××., ××× D. and ×××., "Two-dimensional effects of the head on interaction between planar shock wave with low density foam", 24th International Symposium on Shock Waves, Beijing, China, 2004.

[2] ×××., ×××., ×××. and ×××., "The Influence of the Tube Diameter on Bubble Pump Performance", HPC 2004 Conference, Larnaca, Cyprus, 2004.

附录 I 表和图的形式

统计分析之后,你就要向读者提供你对数据和结果的概述。

对数据和结果的概述主要采用下面的三种形式:文本、表和图。

文本:同你以往听说的可能不一样,并非所有分析和结果都一定要有表或图。有些简单的结果最好是用一个简单句来陈述,而把对数据的概述放在括号里,如:

Seed production was higher for plants in the ful-sun treatment (52.3 +/−6.8 seeds) than for those receiving filtered light (14.7+/− 3.2 seeds, $t=11.8$, $df=55$, $p<0.001$.)

表:表是用专栏的形式把数字列表或用专栏的形式再现文本,每一专栏都应有一个标题或标注。当你想要表达的是数值间的趋势或关系式的时候,最好不用表来表示,而是用图来表示。比如,如果你要表达的是所研究的有机体在一些场所的群体大小,你会选用表,这样有助于体现不同栖息地之间的差别;然而,如果你要表明的是性别比例同人口多少的关系时,你就会需要一个图。

图:图是用形象化的方式来表达研究结果的一种方式,包括曲线图、图示、照片、制图、地图等。图中最常见的是曲线图,因此我们会对它进行详细讨论。本部分在结束前也会给出其他类型的图。曲线图能表明趋势或相互之间的关系式。

表达要有条理、系统:一旦结束了分析并开始考虑如何表达,就要首先想一想你该如何整理、布局。你的分析要像讲"故事"一样,引导读者一步一步、合理地接近你在引言部分提出的问题。你用什么顺序给出研究结果就如同你在文本中考虑如何阐述使其更具说服力一样是十分重要的。

如何涉及文本中的表和图:文章中包含的每一个图和表都必须与文本的内容相关。文字的表述目的是把读者的注意力吸引到你想要读者关注的、你要突出的相互关系或趋势上。

应把有关图或表的内容放在括号里,如:

实例1

  Germination rates were significantly higher after 24 h in running water than in controls (Fig. 4).

实例2

  DNA sequence homologies for the *purple* gene from the four congeners (Table 1) show high similarity, differing by at most 4 base pairs.

避免写出那些没有任何新意、只是用来提醒读者这是图或表的句子,例如:

  Table 1 shows the summary results for male and female heights at Bates College.

缩写"Figure"(图)这个词:如果在文本中需要提及图,要把图"Figure"这个词缩写成Fig.;表"Table"不能缩写。这两个词在插图说明中都要全拼,不能缩写。

如何给表和图编号码:表和图都是单独编号码,按照你在文本中提及的顺序,从表1和图1开始。如果你在修改时改变了图、表的顺序,一定要重新编号,按照新的编号排序。

图和表在文章中的位置:在写论文的初期(如草稿阶段),表和图可能同文本材料相分离。你应从读者的角度出发,尽量把表和图置于第一次在文本中提到它的位置。可以把说明性的材料放在结果部分的最后,以便不破坏文本的流畅。也可把表和图嵌入在文本中,但要避免把文本分割得支离破碎、互不相连。为了保证文本的完整,也可以把表和图单独列出。

检验表和图是否有效的方法:提供的所有的表或图都必须十分有条理,标注好表、图的标题(即表注和图注),以便使读者在不阅读结果部分的情况下通过插图说明就能很好地了解表或图的内容。也就是说,表或图本身就要能说明问题。过分复杂的表或图在有上下文和无上下文的情况下都会使读者产生理解上的困难,因此,应尽可能地使其简单明了。如果你自己无法把握你的表或图是否符合这些标准,可以把表或图交给你的同行,看看他们是否能以此解释你的结果。

描述性的插图说明或表、图说明/标题的用法:通过上述的"严格检验",加上一个既清晰、又完整的插图说明(有时被叫作表标题或图标题)也是十分重要的。像文章的标题一样,每一个表或图的说明都应该尽量向读者传达有关表或图的信息,包括:

- 曲线图中给出了有关结果的何种信息,包括绘制的统计简表;
- 实验研究的有机体(如果是可应用的);
- 产生特定结果的背景:使用的处理方法或显示的相互关系等;
- 方位(如果是野外实验);
- 用以解释说明表中展现结果的具体信息(常用脚注的形式出现);
- 如果是可应用的,给出培养参数或条件(温度、培养基等);

- 试样量和它们应用的统计试验总结；
- 不能单纯地在轴线标示之间用 versus 一词来重述轴标。

例如：

> Fig. 1. Height frequency (%) of White Pines (*Pinus strobus*) in the Thorncrag Bird Sanctuary, Lewiston, Maine, before and after the Ice Storm of '98. Before, $n = 137$, after, $n = 133$. Four trees fell during the storm and were excluded from the post-storm survey.

下面这些例子中给出的表或图的标题都是完整的。你要是对制表不是十分熟悉，可模仿下面的例子来写你自己的表或图的标题（或者用已发表的论文做范例来模仿）。

注：常有人询问在表、图这类标题中该包含多少有关方法和结果的信息。对于实验报告，不仅要有可应用的表或图，而且要把表或图给出的具体的结果用文字的形式表述出来。

事实：在具体的刊物中该写出多少有关方法的内容呢？就美国发行的《科学》和《自然》两刊物而言，由于对文本的主体部分有严格要求，因此有关方法的内容都要在表、图标题或脚注中体现出来；大部分的结果也要在表或图的标题或脚注中体现出来。

表、图的标题的位置：
- **表的标题**放在表之上，左对齐；读的顺序是从上到下。
- **图的标题**放在图之下，曲线图和其他类型的图通常是从下向上读。

解析表

实例 1 中的表是一个由横线分割的、三部分构成的典型的表（三线表），用文字处理器的表列函数或表处理软件就能轻松地绘制。

实例 1： Courtesy of Shelley Ball

Table 4 Population variation in hatch success (mean percent) of unfertilized eggs for females from populations sampled in 1997   N=number of females tested   <--Table legend

Population	Mean(%)	Standard deviation	Range	N
Beaver Creek[T]	7.31	13.95	0—53.16	15
Honey Creek[T]	4.33	7.83	0—25.47	11
Rock Bridge Gans Creek[T]	5.66	13.93	0—77.86	38
Cedar Creek[P]	6.56	9.64	0—46.52	64
Grindstone Creek[P]	8.56	14.77	0—57.32	19
Jacks Fork River[P]	5.28	8.28	0—30.96	28
Meramec River[P]	5.49	10.25	0—45.76	45
Little Dixie Lake[L]	7.96	14.54	0—67.66	71
Little Prairie Lake[L]	6.86	7.84	0—32.40	36
Rocky Forks Lake[L]	3.31	4.12	0—16.14	43
Winegar Lake[L]	10.73	17.58	0—41.64	5
Whetstone Lake[L]	7.36	12.93	0—63.38	57

<--Column titles

<--Table body (data)

[T]=temporary stream, [P]=permanent streams, [L]=lakes   <--footnotes

<--Lines demarcating the different parts of the table

实例 2：Courtesy of Shelley Ball

Table 2 Log-likelihood tests of deviation from 1:1 sex ratios for nymphs collected from each population in 1997 and 1998. Values are ratios of females:males : sample sizes are in parentheses. Bonferroni corrected probabilities are shown with an asterisks.

Population	Year	
	1997	1998
Beaver Creek[T]	9.00:1(20)***	2.67:1(22)*
Honey Creek[T]	9.00:1(56)***	2.27:1(98)***
Rock Bridge Gans Creek[T]	3.33:1(26)**	2.09:1(68)**
Cedar Creek[P]	2.05:1(119)***	1.87:1(198)***
Grindstone Creek[P]	—	2.26:1(140)***
Jacks Fork River[P]	2.89:1(35)**	5.17:1(37)***
Meramec River[P]	2.80:1(38)**	2.41:1(58)**
Little Dixie Lake[L]	2.45:1(494)***	2.46:1(384)***
Little Prairie Lake[L]	2.38:1(71)***	2.08:1(157)***
Rocky Forks Lake[L]	2.55:1(213)***	2.93:1(299)***
Winegar Lake[L]	3.41:1(207)***	2.34:1(204)***
Whetstone Lake[L]	2.69:1(381)***	2.01:1(268)***

*significant at $p<0.05$, **significant at $p<0.005$, ***significant at $p<0.001$
[T]=temporary stream, [P]=permanent streams, [L]=lakes

实例 3：Courtesy of Greg Anderson

Table 2 Planting date, mean planting density, and total number of seed clams planted in plots at Filucy Bay and Wescott Bay in 1979

Location	Plot code	Planting date	Mean planting density in no. Clams/m^2±1 St. Dev. (N)	Total no. Clams planted
Filucy Bay	F10×30	5-16-79	994±39(5)	298200
	F3×10	5-24-79	994±39(5)	29820
Wescott Bay	W10×25	5-16-79	994±39(5)	248500
	W3×10	6-2-79	895±35(5)[a]	26850

[a] Calculated after clams were planted based on estimated 11% morality of seed clams between 5-24 and 6-2-79

在这些实例中要注意以下几点：

- "Table #"之后要有句号；
- 表的标题在表之上；
- 如有可能，专栏标题中的单位要具体化；
- 用线条把标题、页眉、日期和脚注之间隔开；
- 脚注用于说明表中的要点，或重复表达有关条目的信息；
- 也可用脚注表示数据组之间的统计差分。

解析图

下面分别介绍何时以及如何使用常用的四种图（条形图、频率直方图、XY 分布图/曲线图、XY 线图);最后给出几种不太常用的其他类型图的实例。

图的组成:下面是由不同部分组成的图的实例(典型的曲线图和条形图)。如果你在阅读以下部分时遇到不熟悉的术语,可以回来查找和参考这些实例。

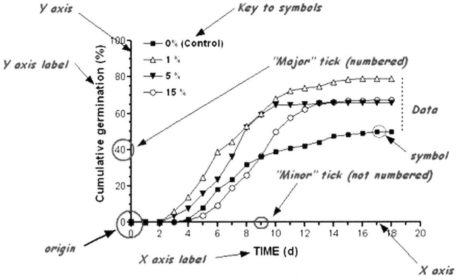

附录Ⅰ-图1　XY 曲线图

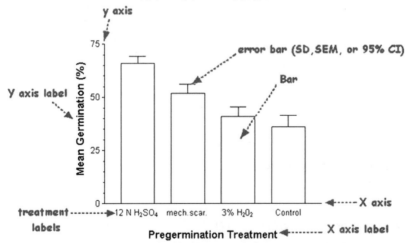

附录Ⅰ-图2　条形图

有关图的注意事项：

·是大还是小？经验告诉我们，图的大小以不超过大约半页纸为宜，但也不宜太小，这样读者就不必拿着放大镜才能辨认出细节了。

·着不着色？通常采用黑白色，理由是如果你要影印或电传文章的话，颜色的区别就会失去作用。但如果是采用张贴或投影仪展示的方式，颜色有助于区分不同的数据组。图的每一部分都该是传递一定信息的，色彩的选用不应仅仅是为了好看。

·有没有标题？不要在文章中单独再为图设标题，图中说明已足以表达所有该有的信息，单独再设标题浪费空间。但对于张贴和利用投影仪形式的图，由于读者不易辨别太小字的图的说明，用大字体打出一个标题还是非常有用的。

·用不用 Error bars？在绘制平均值图时，一定要有误差条形图（SD 或 SEM），有时可能要求你绘制与平均值相关的图，如可靠区间的其他测度的图。

组合图

组合图是把几个图合为一个图，共用一个图标题/说明；其中的图分为 A、B、C 等。当提到文本中的具体图时，要和属于同一图的其他图的标识是一致的。组合的图的标题说明也代表其中的每一个图和图的日期，如：

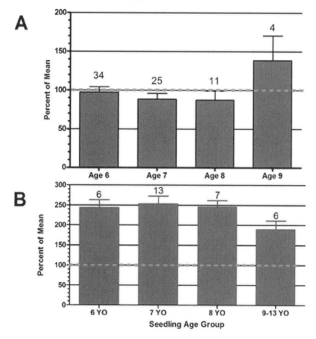

Figure 3　Age-specific primary growth of seedling white pine in the harvest zone in (A) 2006 and (B) 2007, relative to the mean primary growth increments of the three years ('03–'05) prior to the selective harvest. Data shown are the mean (SEM); number over bar is number of seedlings. Dashed line at 100% indicates level where post-harvest growth equals mean pre-harvest growth.

附录Ⅰ-图3

四种常用的图

(1)条形图。

通常条形图的使用是为了在不同的分组中对每一变数值做比较(通常是总值,如平均值),例如,不同土地在用了不同的化肥处理后收获的植物的平均量(注意:尽管条形图可以用来表明两组之间的不同,特别是用于教学法的研究,但很多期刊编辑更倾向于你把这样的信息直接置于文本中,以便节省空间)。

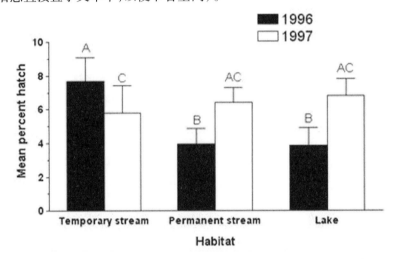

Figure 3 Effects of habitat and year on tychoparthenogenetic capacity (mean % hatching success ±1 SD of unfertilized eggs) in mayflies. Means with different letters are significantly different (Tukey's HSD, $p<0.05$).

附录Ⅰ-图4

在上述这个实例中要注意:

● 条形图的标题在条形图的下方;

● 在"Figure X"和条形图标题说明的结尾都要有句号(见上下例子);

● 把测得的变量在 Y 轴上用标签标出,通常在此也要给出单位;

● 习惯上把分类变数标在 X 轴上,确定每一类别;

● 栖息地中的第二分类变量(年)由条状图形表明,而且要在图形中的某个合适的地方解释说明一下;

● 包括误差图,使+1 SD 或 SEM 超过平均值;

● 统计差可用几个字母标在条形图的上方,在标题中注明使用的测试方法和显著差异。

注意:

● 图表说明要完整,上面的实例中用以描述使用的处理方式和测得的变量的图说明超过了三行;

● 给轴做标注,要标上单位;

● 明确地把处理的不同批次的(pH)值标在轴上;

● 每个条形图都伴有误差图和批次式样量;而且每个图表都有标题说明;

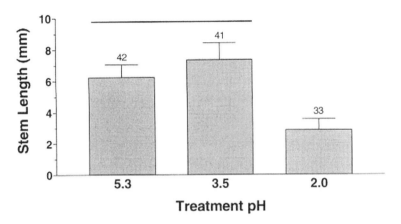

Figure 1　Mean stem length (±1 SD) of seedling clover watered to soil saturation daily for 2.5 weeks with simulated acid rain of varying pH. The control (pH 5.3) was normal city tapwater. The pH 3.5 and 2.0 water was acidified with 2M sulfuric/1M nitric acid solution. Line over bars indicates groups which were not significantly different (Kruskal-Wallis Test and Dunn's Multiple Comparison's Tests). Number over bar indicates sample size.

附录Ⅰ-图5

- 这时的误差用条形图上方划出的线来表示,统计测试和显著差异体现在标题中。

(2)频率直方图。

频率直方图(也叫频率分布图)属于条形图,用于表明每个测得的变量是如何沿着被测得变量轴分布的。频率(Y轴)可以是绝对的(也就是计算数)或相对的(也就是百分比或取样比例)。常见的例子有表明取得相同分数的学生数的考试分数直方图。频率直方图非常适用于描述人口的数量和年龄的分布。

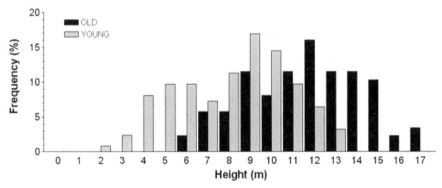

Figure 4　Height distribution in two recruitment cohorts of eastern white pine (Pinus strobus) near the eastern shore of Lake Auburn, Maine, in January 2001. N= 88 OLD and 123 YOUNG trees.

附录Ⅰ-图6

要注意:

- Y轴明确表明使用的相关频率("%")(绝对频率的例子有"Number of stems",

"Number of birds observed");

- 测得的变量(X轴)被分成宽度适当的类目("仓")以便显现人口的分布,0.2 cm 的仓把人口分成7个高度不等的柱体。把仓划定在0.5 cm,就只会有3个柱体,形成的图案不易辨别;相反,要是把仓分为0.05 cm 的,就会产生非常小的柱体沿着一条长轴分散着,同样也会给图案的识别造成困难;
- X轴上标出的值是仓的中心;
- 要明确标出试样的大小,或者是长度的,或者像这个图中标出的那样;
- Y轴包括被编号的小记号,以方便确定条形图值。

(3) X、Y 散布图。

X、Y坐标图可表示在两个变数上的每个采样的分数。用这种方法绘制数据图的目的是想要知道是否两个变数存在一种"关系",也就是说它们的值是否始终一起发生变化?

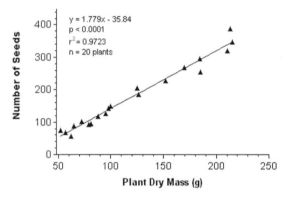

Figure 3　Seed production as a function of plant biomass in waterlilies (*Nuphar luteum*) harvested from Great Works Pond in Northern Maine in August, 2001.

附录Ⅰ-图7

要注意:
- 每个轴都要标上单位、编号,以便于识别绘制出的点的数值;
- 图和图的标题中要包括试样尺寸;
- 如果用统计方式分析数据后变数之间存在着一种关系,这个关系可在图上以回归线的方式来表明,也可以由回归方程式来表示,或用它在图标题或图中的统计显著性来表示;
- 每个轴程的选择都要小心,目的是要最大限度地体现点的分布和尽量少地浪费没有点的空间,如X轴要缩短在50 g以下,因为没有测得到小于52 g的植物。轴程选择后,还要有表示的记号,便于理解(50、100、150等,但不要写为48、96、144等)。

X轴上是什么变数? 当一个变数依赖于另一个变数时(如高度取决于年龄,但很难想象得出年龄取决于高度),通常的做法是把**因变量绘在Y轴上,自变量绘在X轴上**。有时不能明显地看出哪个是自变量(如树叶的长度与宽度,是长度取决于宽度,还是宽度取决于长度),在这种情况下,无法区别哪个变量在哪个轴上,变量之间是相互依存的关系,X、Y图表明的是它们之间的相互关系(而不是谁对谁的影响)。

在上述给出的图例中,我们能够想象得出种子的生产可能取决于植物的生物量,但很难理解为什么生物量可能直接取决于种子的生产,因此我们选择了生物量为 X 轴;关系也可能不是直接的:种子的生产和植物的生物量可能同时依赖于其他没有测出来的变量。以这种对轴的选择可表明相关性的方法不一定意味着必然存在某种因果关系。

(4) X、Y 曲线图。

曲线图给出的是能够描述 Y 轴变化的一系列相关数值(作为 X 轴的函数)。常见的两个例子有用以表明个体变化的生长曲线和能反映药物剂量增加的影响的药物-反映曲线图。

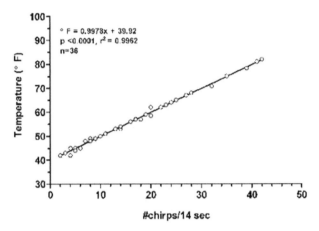

Figure 7　Temperature-dependence of cricket chirp frequency in south central Maine. Temperature (F) = #chirps in 14 sec +40. n = 36 cricket chirp bouts.

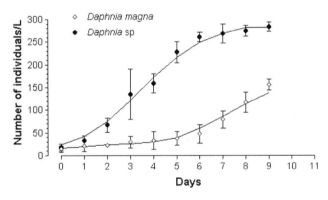

Figure 2　Mean population density (±1 standard deviation) of two species of *Daphnia* following artificial eutrophication of a small farm pond by application of organic fertilizer. Six replicate 1 L water samples were drawn from 50 cm depth at 1100 hr each day.

附录 I -图 8

何时连接这些点? 如果一系列的点都源于同一出处,而且隶属于前面的数值,那么应该用线把各点连接起来。然而如果这些点体现的是某一变数的独立的测量数,用以表明某种趋势(如计算机存储器在一段时间内的平均价格;光学密度的标准曲线与溶质浓度之比较等),那么可通过计算线段或曲线进而建立模型的方式来表明应有的趋势或关系。如果量得的数量之间没有联系,就不要把这些点连接起来。

在上述的图 Figure 2 中要注意:
- 每组(种类)使用了不同的符号,而且如果有地方的话,把对符号的解答放在图中;符号的大小要以能否在最后确定的图中识别为标准;
- 每一个点代表一个平均值,这在图的标题中已阐明,因此也要给每个点绘制误差条形图,并且要在标题中加以说明;
- 因为量得的数量是属于每一种类的独立群体,因此这些点不属于相连接的点;相反,曲线更适合用于这类数据来表明趋势。

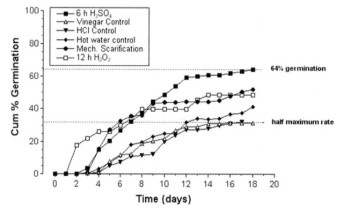

Figure 2　Cumulative germination of gourd seeds following various pregermination treatments. n = 100 seeds per trial.

附录Ⅰ-图9

在上述图中要注意:
- 在此把所有的点都连接起来了,因为每天都会在同一批种子中测量累积的百分比发芽率,故测得的数量也与前几天的相关;
- 每次处理使用不同的符号,符号的大小要适中,以便在最后的图中能被识别;
- 除了要对图表中符号加以说明,还要给出两种有用的信息:①最终的累积百分比的最高和最低值;②给出虚线(基线)用以表明得到的累积发芽百分比的最低值,这条基线要在标题中加以说明。

(5)其他类型的图表。

照片

在此要注意:
- 照片属于图;
- 任何来自于他处的照片都要在图的标题中标明归属;
- 照片要有足够的清晰度以便能被影印。

Figure 9 Aerial photo of the study site ca. 1949 and in 1998 (inset) showing the regeneration of the forest. Photos courtesy of the USDA Field Office, Auburn, Maine.

附录 I -图 10

彩色透明滤光板

Source: Lawson et. al, 1999. J. Biol. Chem. 274(14): 9871-9980. Used by permission of the authors.

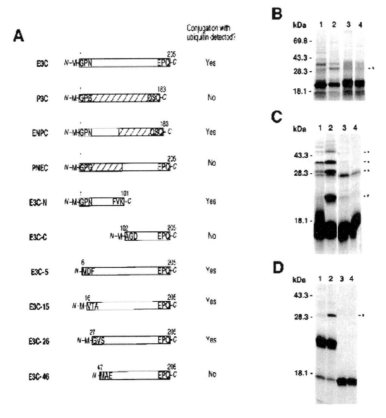

附录 I -图 11 彩色透明滤光板复制件

附录 II 记录原始资料

所有来自于他人原始资料的引证、意译和观点都要在文本中或文章末尾的参考文献中有所体现。文本中的引用必须是读者在文章末尾的参考文献中能够找到的。

本附录提供了能帮助你解决记录原始资料中遇到的问题的手册或指南的名称，你可通过网络或其他渠道获得这些资源，它们会对你的学术写作提供很大的帮助：

APA 格式（American Psychological Association）
- *Publication Manual of the American Psychological Association*
- *APA：Electronic Reference Formats*
- *APA Style Guide（Ohio State Univ.）*

MLA 格式（Modern Language Association）
- *MLA Handbook for Writers of Research Papers*
- *How to：MLA Citation Style（Concordia University Library）*
- *MLA Citation Style Guide（Cornell University Library）*

Chicago 格式
- *Chicago Manual of Style*
- *Chicago Format（Univ. of Wisconsin）*

Turabian 格式
- *A Manual for Writers of Term Papers, Theses, and Dissertations*（by Kate Turabian）
- *Turabian Style Guide（Univ. of Southern Mississippi）*

其他部分科技文体指南

美国化学学会 ACS（American Chemical Society）
- *ACS Style Guide*
- *ACS Guidelines for Documenting Sources（OhioLINK consortium）*

美国物理学会 AIP（American Institute of Physics）
- *AIP Style Manual*
- *AIP Style Manual*

美国数学学会 AMS（American Mathematical Society）
- *Author Packages for Publishing with the AMS*

美国农艺学学会、农作物科学学会、农作物和土壤科学学会 ASA-CSSA-SSSA（American Society of Agronomy, Crop Science Society of America & Soil Science

Society of America)
- ASA-CSSA-SSSA Publications & Style Manual

生物学编者委员会 CBE（Council of Biology Editors）
- *Scientific Style and Format: the CBE Manual for Authors, Editors, and Publishers*
- Using CBE Style to Cite and Document Sources

美国地质学会 GSA（Geological Society of America）
- Author Information for GSA Publications

电气和电子工程师协会 IEEE（Institute of Electrical and Electronics Engineers）
- IEEE Information for Authors

美国石油工程师学会 SPE（Society of Petroleum Engineers）
- SPE Publications Style Guide

从全文数据库中引用
- InfoTrac Databases
- Expanded Academic ASAP, General Reference Center, Informe! etc.
- FirstSearch Databases (Central Michigan Univ.)
- List of all FirstSearch databases

参考文献

[1] BERGE P. Basic college research[M]. 3rd ed. New York: Neal Schuman Publishers, 1987.

[2] BERRY R. How to write a research paper[M]. Second ed. Oxford: Pergamon Press, 1986.

[3] CULLER J. "Bad writing and good philosophy." In just being difficult? academic writing in the public arena[M]. Standford: Standford University Press, 2003.

[4] DAY R A. How to write and publish a scientific paper[M]. Second ed. Philadelphia: ISI Press, 1988.

[5] DEES R. Writing the modern research paper[M]. Second ed. Boston: Allyn & Bacon, 1997.

[6] GIBALDI J. MLA handbook for writers of research papers[M]. Fourth ed. New York: The Modern Language Association of America, 1995.

[7] GIBALDI J. MLA handbook for writers of research papers[M]. Fifth ed. New York: The Modern Language Association of America, 1999.

[8] HACKER D. The bedford handbook[M]. Boston: Bedford/St. Martin's, 1998.

[9] HYLAND K. Disciplinary discourses: social interactions in academic writing[M]. Ann Arbor: University of Michigan Press, 2004.

[10] KREBER C. The university and its disciplines: teaching and learning within and beyond disciplinary boundaries[M]. New York and London: Routledge, 2009.

[11] O'CONNOR M. Writing successfully in science[M]. London: Chapman & Hall, 1995.

[12] PEAT J, ELLIOTT E, BAUR L, et al. Scientific writing—easy when you know how [M]. London: BMJ Books, 2002.

[13] PYNE S Jr. Voice and vision: a guide to writing history and other serious non-fiction [M]. Cambridge, MA: Harvard University Press, 2009.

[14] RAIMES A. Keys for writers: a brief handbook[M]. Boston: Houghton Mifflin, 1999.

[15] STRUNK W Jr., WHITE E B. The elements of style[M]. 4th ed. Needham Heights, MA: Allyn and Bacon, 2000.

[16] SWALES J M. Genre analysis: English in academic and research settings[M]. Cambridge: Cambridge University Press, 1993.

[17] STRUNK W Jr. The elements of style[M]. New York: Penguin, 2005.

[18] The Editorial Staff. The Chicago manual of style, CMS[M]. The University of Chicago: Chicago Press, 2001.

[19] The University of Chicago Press Editorial Staff. The University Manual of Style[M]. Chicago: The University of Chicago Press, 2017.

[20] WILLIAMS J M. Style: The Basics of Clarity and Grace[M]. New York: Longman, 2008.

[21] 蔡基刚. 英汉写作对比研究[M]. 上海: 复旦大学出版社, 2001.

[22] 考夫蔓. 北大英文写作教程[M]. 北京: 北京大学出版社, 2003.

[23] 丁往道, 吴冰, 钟美荪, 等. 英语写作手册[M]. 中文版. 北京: 外语教学与研究出版社, 2010.

[24] 丁往道, 吴冰, 钟美荪, 等. 英语写作手册[M]. 英文版. 北京: 外语教学与研究出版, 2009.

[25] 冯翠华. 英语科研论文写作概要[M]. 上海: 上海外语教育出版社, 2003.

[26] 郝丹. 学术期刊论文写作技巧与实战[M]. 北京: 人民邮电出版社, 2022.

[27] 格拉夫, 比肯施泰因. 高效写作的秘密[M]. 成都: 天地出版社, 2019.

[28] 刘振海. 中英文科技论文写作教程[M]. 北京: 高等教育出版社, 2007.

[29] 熊第霖, 滕弘飞. 英文科技写作[M]. 北京: 国防工业出版社, 2001.

[30] 杨永林. 体验英语写作3:实践手册[M]. 北京: 高等教育出版社, 2011.

[31] 赵纬本. 普通与科技英语写作技巧[M]. 北京: 人民教育出版社, 2000.

[32] 郑福裕. 科技论文英文摘要编写指南[M]. 北京: 清华大学出版社, 2003.